Sphe

For our families

FAMILY COOK

more fabulous food for next to nothing

by Susan Campbell & Caroline Conran

Authors of Poor Cook

First published in Great Britain by Macmillan Ltd, 1972

Published by Sphere Books, 1974

Graphics: Conran Associates
Series Typography: Peter Kindersley
Drawings: Susan Campbell

TRADE MARK

Set in Scotch Roman

Printed in Great Britain by
Hazell Watson & Viney Ltd,
Aylesbury, Bucks

ISBN 0 7221 2197 0

Contents

Diagrams

Introduction

This book is a continuation of our first book ***Poor Cook***, which was written for people whose love of cooking and eating was deeper than their pockets. In other words, it was about cheap food and how to cook it well. It was also about finding cheap food, because a great deal of it, especially meat, has become uneconomic to sell. This is partly because some things, like calves' heads, need a great deal of preparation before they can be offered over the counter, and other things, like lambs' tails and pigs' trotters, are too fiddly to cook and so few people buy them.

Family Cook is intended for the same people but there is a little more emphasis on party food, because everybody who has a family has celebrations of one kind or another. So we have included a few recipes for things like stuffed duck, or game, but there is still no lobster or turbot, as we prefer the idea of spending extra money on wine or cream for cooking, than spending it on disproportionately expensive luxuries. Many people said about ***Poor Cook***, 'That's fine if you have lots of time, but most people don't have all day to spend cooking hog's tail stew.' The point is that these things may take a long time to cook but you don't have to stand over them while they do it. And if you do not have much time you can always choose things that can be prepared beforehand, some of which, like stews and pâtés, are actually improved by being kept overnight. Or if you are making a rather time-consuming dish eat it with something that's simple to get ready, like baked potatoes and green salad.

Another way of saving time is by mental organisation, which is hard work, but much easier if you write everything down, listing what sort of things you may eat over the next few days and itemising what you will have to buy — you don't have to keep to it, but it means you need never stand in the butcher's in a state of total indecision, nor have to go back for things you need all of a sudden.

There is still a strong emphasis on avoiding convenience foods unless they really are cheap, convenient and just as good as the real thing or excellent in their own way. This would apply to tinned tomatoes and sardines but would exclude such things as frozen beans (not as good and more expensive than fresh) or dehydrated mashed potatoes (in our opinion, at least, simply horrible, unnatural and lazy and much more expensive).

Where tinned, dehydrated and frozen foods fall down is in trying to reproduce the original taste and texture of the food being preserved, whereas older methods of preservation transform the food into something else, related but quite different. For example a tinned or frozen strawberry is always disappointingly less good than a fresh one, but strawberry jam is good in its own right. And think of salami or ham (preserved meat) and then of frozen dinners (or any popular frozen foods) which are drearily standardised to offer universal acceptability and are full of Monosodium glutamate which can give you hot flushes if you eat too much of it, so goodness knows what it may be doing to your insides.

Convenience food is big business now, and the selling of food has become less of a service than a way of making lots of money. So combining this with the fact that most people don't have much time for cooking and that you may have to go quite a long way to find the best shops, it is often difficult to buy only food that is good and genuine. But there still are some good shops, especially those run for immigrants, who wisely stick to traditional notions about food. And while the choice is there we must take advantage of it, otherwise even that small amount of leeway will be gone — there simply won't be anything but convenience foods. Dried haricot beans and salt pork will vanish so there will be no question of making baked beans at home, or anything else much, if we don't use some of our precious time, energy and intelligence now on finding and cooking real foods.

Recently, as food prices continued to rise, readers of

the *Sunday Times* were invited to take part in a competition to find really good cheap recipes using only fresh ingredients. The response was enormous, over a thousand entries, from which we chose a few of the best ones to include in this book. Our thanks to all the contributors, whose names appear in the acknowledgments. We have also included a few basic recipes from *Poor Cook* for readers who don't have a copy and who may find them useful, and have added in the Basic Recipes section at the end of the book several more recipes which are invaluable for day-to-day cooking at home.

Acknowledgments

To fishmonger Steve Hatt of Essex Road, N.1. and Inspector G. R. Watkin of Billingsgate for their considerable help with the fish section; to Fred Knock of Simpson's-in-the-Strand for his demonstrations and expert advice on carving; to Lina Stores, Brewer Street, Soho, for information on pasta; to Helen Whitten, Ivy Bright and Carol Amos for practical help and moral support; to Jennifer Beams, Valerie Chapman, Margaret E. Clark, Margaret Ellis, Elizabeth Godwin, Virginia Hawkins, Georgina Ingleby, Teresa Juni, Courtney Jane Ford Moita de Deus, Renata Morgan, Goodney Munce, Frances Neill, Mabel Newgrosh, Margery Pratt, Cynthia Reavell, Fabienne Smith of Edinburgh (compiler of '*Simply Delicious — Deliciously Simple*', a charity cookery book in aid of the Muscular Dystrophy Group of Great Britain), Muriel Stoakes, Esther Wasserman and Isabel Winthrop, whose recipes are included; to all our friends who contributed ideas and recipes and to the *Sunday Times* and *Nova* for allowing the use of recipes written for their readers.

To Conran Associates for their help with the graphic design and to Habitat for the loan of many of the utensils illustrated.

Storecupboard

Cheap **butter** for cooking
A large tin of **olive oil** (cheaper by the gallon)
A large tin of **arachide oil** for deep frying. Keep separate bottles, one for fish and one for other things, and always strain the oil before it goes back in the bottle, or it will not stay fresh
Dripping, lard, margarine and **cooking fat**
Large chunks of **Parmesan** and **Gruyère cheeses**
Streaky bacon in a piece, **Salami, Salt Cod**
Tins and tins of Italian peeled **tomatoes**
Tubes or tins of **tomato purée**
Packets of **pasta** and **semolina**
Pounds of dried **haricot beans, kidney beans, flageolets, lentils, chick peas, dried peas**
Rice: long-grain for curry, Italian for risotto, round for puddings
Large bag of **dried mushrooms,** better than tinned and cheaper
Spices: coriander, cumin, turmeric, cardamom, chilli, paprika, allspice, mixed spice, cloves, cinnamon sticks, mace, nutmeg
Herbs (do not keep them too long) : bay leaves on a branch, rosemary, thyme, oregano, basil, marjoram, sage, tarragon. Keep parsley, chives and mint fresh in polythene bags in the refrigerator
Caraway seeds, fennel seeds, cheap **sherry, brandy, port** and **cooking wine**
Garlic
Stock cubes: chicken and beef. Maggi are best
Tins of **tunny fish, anchovies** in oil, **sardines, pimentoes, capers** in wine vinegar
Dijon **mustard, mustard powder**
Sea salt, peppercorns
Olives: buy them loose and keep them in a jar of oil
Plain flour and **baking powder,** so you do not have to worry about self-raising flour
Porridge oats and **wheatgerm** for muesli
Gelatine
Home-made **pastry-mix** (margarine or cooking fat rubbed into twice its weight of flour)
Dried yeast, or fresh yeast from the baker which keeps for up to a week in the refrigerator
Demerara, granulated, soft brown, caster and icing **sugar**
Golden Syrup, honey
Cooking chocolate, cocoa powder
Vanilla sugar: keep a pod of vanilla in a jar of caster sugar, and top it up as you need to
Wine vinegar
Dried fruit, whole **almonds**
Saffron, pine nuts, pistachio nuts, juniper berries and **truffles** are all cheaper bought abroad

Temperatures

		Degrees	
Electricity and Solid Fuel	**Gas**	**Fahrenheit**	**Centigrade**
Cool	$\frac{1}{4}$–$\frac{1}{2}$	250	121
Very Slow	1	275	135
Slow	2	300	149
	3	325	163
Moderate	4	350	177
	5	375	190
Moderately hot	6	400	204
Hot	7	425	218
Very hot	8	450	232
	9	475	246

Meat Roasting Table

Meat	Quick Roast	Slow Roast
	For good quality meat. Sear at Reg 8/450° for 15 minutes. Reduce to Reg 5/375° for the remainder of the cooking time.	Best for poor quality joints. It helps make them tender. Roast at Reg 3/325°.
Beef	15 minutes per lb plus 15 minutes for rare roasting. 20 minutes per lb plus 20 minutes for meat well done.	40 minutes per lb plus 45 minutes.
Lamb	25 minutes per lb plus 25 minutes.	45 minutes per lb plus 45 minutes.
Pork	35 minutes per lb plus 35 minutes.	60 minutes per lb
Veal	30 minutes per lb plus 30 minutes.	50 minutes per lb plus 50 minutes.
Chicken	20 minutes per lb plus 20 minutes.	Over 4lb 25 minutes per lb plus 25 minutes.
Turkey	8–10 lb bird 2–2½ hours. 10–14 lb bird 2–3½ hours. 14–20 lb bird 3–4½ hours.	8–10 lb bird 3½–3 hours 10–14 lb bird 3½–4 hours 14–20 lb bird 4½–5 hours

N.B. Bone is a good conductor of heat, so meat with the bone in does not need the extra minutes over. Stuffing on the other hand is a poor conductor of heat, so joints that are stuffed need perhaps fifteen minutes extra, depending on the thickness of the stuffing. You should always judge by the shape of the joint that is to be cooked. If it is a long thin piece of meat it will obviously need less cooking than a compact thick piece. So use the chart as a general guide, supported by your own judgment.

The Metric System

Conversion tables for measurements and temperatures.

Weight

1 oz	28·35 g
2 oz	56·7 g
4 oz	113·4 g
8 oz	226·8 g
12 oz	340·2 g
16 oz	453·6 g

1 kilogramme — 1000 g	2 lb 3 oz	approx
500 g	1 lb 1½ oz	,,
250 g	9 oz	,,
125 g	4¼ oz	,,
100 g	3½ oz	,,
25 g	1 oz	,,

Liquids

¼ pt (1 gill)	142 ml
½ pt	284 ml
1 pt	568 ml

1 litre	1000 g	1¾ pt — 35 fl oz	approx
½ litre	500 g	¾ pt plus 4½ tablespoons	,,
¼ litre	250 g	½ pt less 2 tablespoons	,,
1 decilitre	100 g	6 tablespoons	,,
1 centilitre	10 g	1 dessertspoon	,,
1 millilitre	1 g	a few drops	,,
5 millilitres	5 g	pharmaceutical teaspoon	

Soups

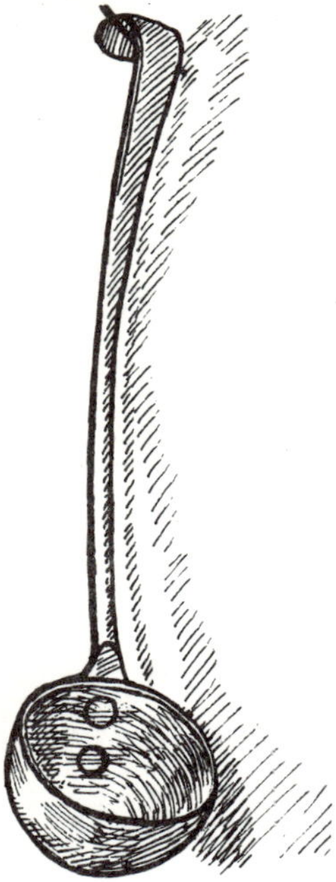

Soups

Beautifully made soup is one of the most sane and stabilising things you can cook; like hot toddy it has a soothing effect, it is almost impossible to be agitated and difficult over a bowl of hot soup, and if you are exhausted by your day it will revive you. And should you need to fill people up then you can do that with soup too; by adding noodles or some other small pasta, rice, dumplings, pieces of toasted French bread, poached eggs or croûtons.

Soup at home is the best soup, apart from soup in Chinese restaurants, because at home you have the means for making it, however plain, into a treat. If for example the carrots in the carrot soup have less flavour than the greengrocer would have you believe, then at home sugar can be added, lightly caramelised in a spoon, and a lump of butter, a sprinkling of parsley or some cream and plenty of freshly ground pepper, which will make all the difference.

If a clear soup is a bit insipid it can be reduced quite a bit by boiling, and given an effective lift with sherry if you have it and a dash of Worcester sauce. Grated Parmesan improves vegetable soups, especially if they have garlic in them. A sprinkled handful of very finely chopped garlic with a herb such as basil or a dollop of sour cream and some chives can be added to un-sieved and puréed vegetable soups respectively.

Although the flavour of soup made at home always has a great deal of character, the liquidiser can be relied on to rob it of most of its individuality of texture and will consistently turn it into emulsion paint. It is obviously invaluable where time is short, but a better result is given by the Moulin-légumes or by means of an electric purée maker which fits onto a mixer. This is a sieve with a paddle, it is noisy and takes as long as you do to purée a bowl of cauliflower soup, but at least you can be getting on with something else while it does it. If you do use a liquidiser, use it on a low speed and for the shortest possible time, so that you do not incorporate too much air. Take care not to put the soup in boiling hot, when it may either crack the container, or build up a head of steam and blow the top off. Also be careful not to fill the container too full or the same thing may happen and you will be sprayed across the chest with scalding hot soup. If you have time, let the soup stand for a while before you return it to the heat, to allow it to settle down again.

Ideally, soup should always be served with delicious fresh chunks of bread.

Red Bean Soup

½ lb red haricot beans (soaked overnight)
3 medium onions
¼ lb streaky bacon in a piece
2–3 pints stock
salt, pepper
butter
parsley

Cook the soaked beans with the quartered onions and bacon in a light, but not salty, stock until they are tender. Sieve, removing the bacon first, add enough stock or water to make the soup the consistency you prefer. Heat without reboiling, season with salt and pepper, and add a large knob of butter. Stir it in and serve with chopped parsley.

□ *Delicious, and a very pretty pinky-beige. It can also be made with other beans, for instance white haricots, flageolets, kidney beans or any other dry beans.*

For 6

Clear Beetroot Soup

3 pints home-made consommé or very good clear stock (duck or beef stock are excellent for this soup)
juice of ½ lemon
2 lumps sugar
2 raw beetroots
sour cream
salt, pepper

Heat the stock. Peel the beetroots and grate them into a bowl. Pour the hot stock over them, return them to the pan together with the sugar and lemon juice and bring to the boil. Skim if necessary and simmer for 20 minutes. By this time the soup will be a beautiful clear garnet colour and the beetroot will be lightly cooked. Season and serve either with the beetroot in or strained and with a dollop of sour cream in each bowl.

For 6

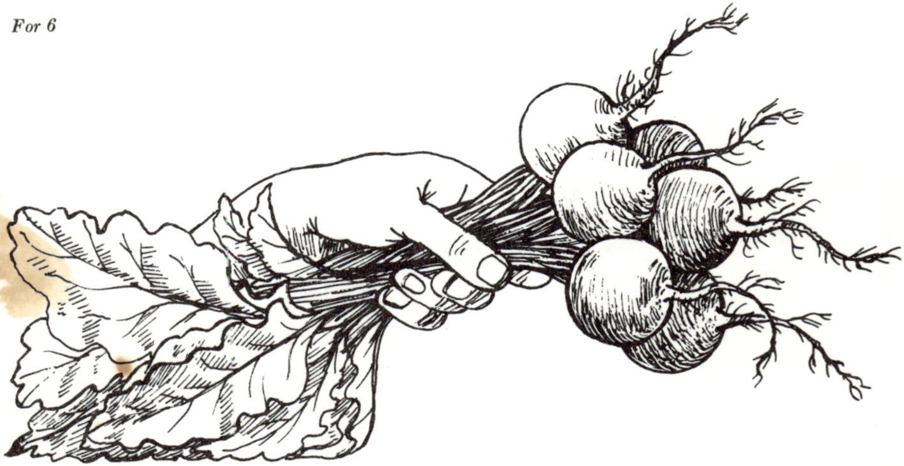

Crab Bisque

1 shell and legs of a large cooked crab
1 small cooked crab
1 halibut or cod's head
1 glass white wine (or less)
1 onion
2 carrots
peppercorns, salt
a few twigs of fennel
4–5 tomatoes
⅛–¼ pint cream
a small glass sherry

Remove the meat from the small crab and keep it on one side. Put the well-washed and crushed crab-shells, fish-head, white wine, onion, carrots, peppercorns, salt and fennel into two pints of water. Simmer for one hour. Add the roughly chopped tomatoes and cook a further 20 minutes. Strain, taste for salt and pepper, add sherry and reduce a little. (At this stage it might look a rather gloomy colour, in which case a little tomato purée will improve it.) Add the crab-meat from the small crab and all but a couple of spoonsfull of the cream. Serve as soon as it is thoroughly heated through, with a dollop of cream in each bowl.

☐*You eat the meat of the large crab at another meal with brown bread and butter and mayonnaise, or just quartered lemons. This soup is on the costly side, but a hundred times nicer and cheaper than tinned. You could make it for a treat, rather than every day, and the amount of crab-meat could be quite small leaving more for salad. The fish-head is included to give the soup more body as well as to help the flavour.*

For 4

Carrot Soup

1 lb nice tasty carrots, preferably young or middle-aged
1 very small turnip (or ¼ large one)
1 onion
1 leek
1½ oz butter
1 lump sugar
salt, fresh-ground white pepper
2–3 pints chicken stock, or cube stock

Clean the vegetables and cut them into small pieces. Melt the butter in a heavy pan. Add the vegetables and sugar, stir to coat them in butter, cover the pan tightly and turn the heat very low. Allow the vegetables to soften slowly for ¾ hour to an hour. If you use a thick enough pan you can stew them in butter for ages without burning.

When they are soft, but not brown, sieve or liquidise them with the stock. Season with plenty of salt and pepper and return to the stove. Serve very hot but don't allow the soup to boil. Chopped parsley and a knob of butter or croûtons fried in butter are served with this.

☐*This soup bears no resemblance to the dreary 'Potage Crecy' often found on hotel menus.*

For 6–8

Gaspacho

1 pint tomato juice (unseasoned tinned or made with fresh tomatoes)
1 pint water (iced)
2–3 slices bread (crusts off)
salt, pepper (white if possible)
4 tablespoons olive oil
1 tablespoon wine vinegar
1–2 cloves garlic
For the garnish:
2 or 3 tomatoes, ½ cucumber, 1 green pepper, 1 hardboiled egg
1 onion, croûtons

This is very easy to make if you have a liquidiser. Pound the peeled garlic in a mortar. Soak the bread in iced water. Put tomato juice, salt, pepper, garlic, bread, water and vinegar into the liquidiser and whizz till smooth. Add the oil drip by drip, and put the resulting soup-base into the refrigerator until ready to serve. (If you have no liquidiser, pound the bread with the garlic, add the oil drop by drop and then dilute slowly with the tomato juice, vinegar and water.) Peel and slice the onion and soak the slices in water while you prepare the other garnishes. Peel and chop the tomatoes, removing the seeds if you like, peel the cucumber and chop it finely. Remove the seeds from the green pepper and chop it finely. Peel and chop the egg. Add iced water to the soup if it is too thick. Just before serving drain the onion and chop it finely. Serve each item of garnish in a separate little dish on a bed of crushed ice if possible. Serve soup in bowls, each guest helps himself to garnish.

☐*This is an iced soup, very refreshing and nourishing for summer.*

For 6

Leek and Green Pea Soup

4–5 leeks
1 medium Spanish onion
1 oz butter
2 handfuls of shelled green peas, or frozen peas
1 bay leaf
¼ pint milk
salt, white pepper
a squeeze of lemon juice
a knob of butter to finish the soup

Chop the leeks and onions finely and sweat them in the butter, without browning, for several minutes until they are soft. Add the peas and pour on enough boiling water to float everything. Add the salt, pepper and bay leaf and simmer until it is just cooked — 20–30 minutes — adding a little more water if necessary. Remove the bay leaf. Sieve three quarters of the soup (or liquidise it) keeping the remainder unsieved so that there are still a few whole peas and pieces of leek in the finished soup. Add the milk and lemon juice, check seasoning, heat through, stirring, and add the lump of butter at the last moment.

☐*Delicate, fresh, a good consistency and a pretty pale green. In France this is called Potage St Quentin.*

For 3–4

Lentil Soup with Salt Pork

½ lb brown lentils
¼ lb piece salt pork or bacon
1 large onion, chopped
2–3 sticks celery, cut up into 1 inch pieces
3 cloves garlic
a handful of Italian dried mushrooms (cèpes)
salt, pepper, parsley, olive oil

Soak the lentils overnight and the salt pork if necessary (the butcher will tell you). Also soak the dried mushrooms for about an hour, keeping the water they have soaked in. Put the lentils, pork, mushrooms with their water, garlic cloves, onion and celery in a pan and cover with about 2 pints cold water. Bring slowly to the boil, skim and simmer until the lentils are tender (up to 1½ hours). Add more water if necessary and a glass of red wine if you like. Taste for seasoning and serve just as it is, with a slice of the pork in each bowl if you like it. Sprinkle each soup bowl with chopped parsley and pour in a teaspoonful of olive oil or add a knob of butter.

For 5–6

Lentil Soup with Pasta

Make the soup as described above and about 10 minutes before the end throw in 3 ounces of small soup pasta and cook on until the pasta is done. Add more boiling water if more liquid is needed. Taste for seasoning and serve with a spoonful of olive oil in each plate and grated Parmesan.

☐*An exceedingly filling and soothing winter soup.*

Minestrone

2–4 oz haricot beans (previously soaked)
1 small turnip, 2 onions
2 medium potatoes, 1 leek
1–2 carrots, ½ small cabbage
3–4 large tomatoes
3 cloves garlic
5–6 pints water or water and stock
2 oz short macaroni
1 tablespoon tomato purée
a bunch of thyme and parsley
oil, salt, pepper
grated Parmesan cheese

Heat enough oil to cover the bottom of a large pan. Soften the chopped onions for a few minutes. While they cook, put the beans in another pan with 1 pint of water and bring slowly to the boil. Then pour the beans over the onions, add the rest of the water and simmer for 1 hour. Add the chopped carrots, turnip, leeks, garlic, potatoes and cabbage, herbs, salt and pepper and simmer for 30 minutes, then add the tomatoes, skinned and chopped, the pasta and the tomato purée.

Cook until pasta is done and serve, having removed the herbs, with grated Parmesan cheese to hand round.

☐*You can vary the ingredients tremendously, using any vegetables in season. The thing to aim at is a soothing mixture of starchy things — beans, potatoes, pasta — with vegetables. The soup should be thickish and a rich brown. If you leave this soup overnight it improves surprisingly.*

For 6–8

Mushroom Soup

½ lb very fresh white button mushrooms
butter
1 onion
½ oz flour
1 pint milk
1½ pints chicken stock
¼ pint cream
salt, pepper and nutmeg

Chop the onions and melt them in a little butter. Add all the mushroom stalks and half the mushrooms, chopped, and allow to soften over a low heat.

In a separate pan soften the remaining mushrooms, finely sliced, in more butter.

When the onions are cooked through but not brown add the stock and simmer for 20 minutes. Sieve or put through the fine blade of a Moulin-Lègumes.

Stir the flour into the sliced mushrooms, season them with salt, pepper and nutmeg and stir until the flour thickens and absorbs the butter, then gradually add the sieved mushroom soup, stirring all the time to keep the texture smooth. Add up to a pint of milk — the less you add the richer the soup will be — and heat through. Simmer a few minutes, taste for seasoning, stir in the cream and serve.

For 6

Pappa di Pomodori

2 tablespoons olive oil
1 small onion
1 small clove garlic
1 lb tomatoes
2 inch thick slices country-type bread (coarse and not too white)
Salt, pepper, sugar, basil

Soften the chopped onions and garlic in the oil until transparent and tender. Put in the skinned chopped tomatoes and simmer until you have a thickish sauce. Crumble in the bread and mash it with a wooden fork or spoon until you have a complete mush. Season with the salt, pepper and sugar and pour on 1 pint of cold water. Bring to the boil, simmer a few minutes, add chopped basil, and serve.

□ *This can be made with other vegetables, tomato and courgettes, tomato and celery and beans, or tomato and leeks. It is a Florentine speciality, and is thick, almost like porridge.*

For 3–4

Onion Soup

For each Person you will need
1 large Spanish onion, or 2 medium-sized ones, sliced in rings
½ oz butter
pinch sugar, pinch salt
½ pint beef stock or water
1 dessertspoon brandy (if you are feeling rich)
1–2 slices French bread dried in the oven, or ordinary toast
Emmenthal or Cheddar cheese, grated

Slice the onions rather finely. Melt the butter in a large heavy saucepan, and cook the onions gently, stirring them round from time to time, until they are tender and just starting to brown. Sprinkle with the sugar and salt. If you like you can caramelise the sugar by holding it over the heat in a spoon until it is a dark brown before adding it to the soup. This gives the soup a richer colour. Bring the stock or water to the boil and pour it over the onions. Cover and simmer for half an hour, add the brandy (if any) and simmer 5 minutes more, then serve with the toasted bread floating in each bowl, and grated Emmenthal to sprinkle on top. Traditionally each bowl is placed under a hot grill for a few minutes to melt and brown the cheese.

☐*We don't recommend stock cubes for this soup as they taste rather dominant.*

Portuguese Tomato and Onion Soup

3 large onions
1 lb tomatoes, peeled
3 thick slices white bread, crusts removed
1 egg for each person
olive oil, a little sugar, salt, pepper
2 pints chicken stock (or cube stock)

Slice the onions and sauté in oil for 5 minutes (gently, with a lid on), add peeled sliced tomatoes, 2 pints stock, or water and chicken stock cube, a little sugar to taste, salt and pepper. Cook gently for half an hour. Before serving add bread cut into pieces, and poach eggs in the soup. Serve in soup bowls, giving every person an egg.

The eggs may sink below the bread cubes, so be careful how you fish them out, and don't overcook them. If you make the soup in a rather shallow pan, it makes it all much easier.

☐*A winter dish, very filling.*

For 4–5

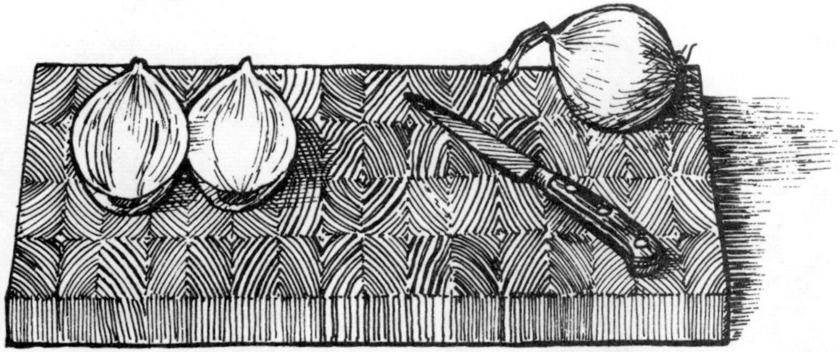

Bouillabaisse of Vegetables

4 tablespoons olive oil
2 medium onions, chopped finely
2 small potatoes, peeled and diced
1 lb tomatoes, skinned and roughly chopped
choice of whatever vegetables you have FRESH, (but not cabbage or roots or celery) for instance:
1 lb spinach, washed and chopped
3–4 cubed courgettes
a cupful of shelled peas or broad beans,
or a handful of french beans, cut into short lengths or watercress
Pinch saffron (if you have it)
2–3 cloves garlic, finely sliced
salt, pepper
bouquet of herbs (try to use fennel)
2–3 tablespoons Parmesan, grated, per person
1 egg per person
for croûtons:
1 slice bread, cut into cubes
butter

If possible cook this soup in a large earthenware casserole (you can do this on an electric or gas cooker if you put an asbestos mat between the hob and the pot, and keep it on a low heat throughout).

Heat the oil in the casserole, and let the onion cook gently in it until transparent; add the potatoes, and whatever vegetables you have available. Stir them about a bit before adding the tomatoes, herbs, saffron, and garlic. Season and add 2 pints of hot water. Cover and simmer until the vegetables are just tender, remove herbs and break an egg for each person into the soup. Make croûtons. Put the croûtons into each soup bowl, and when the eggs are done, ladle each one carefully into the bowls with some of the soup and vegetables.

□ *This is very good for home gardeners. Courgettes, beans or peas give the best results.*

For 4 as a main dish rather than as a 'soup' on its own

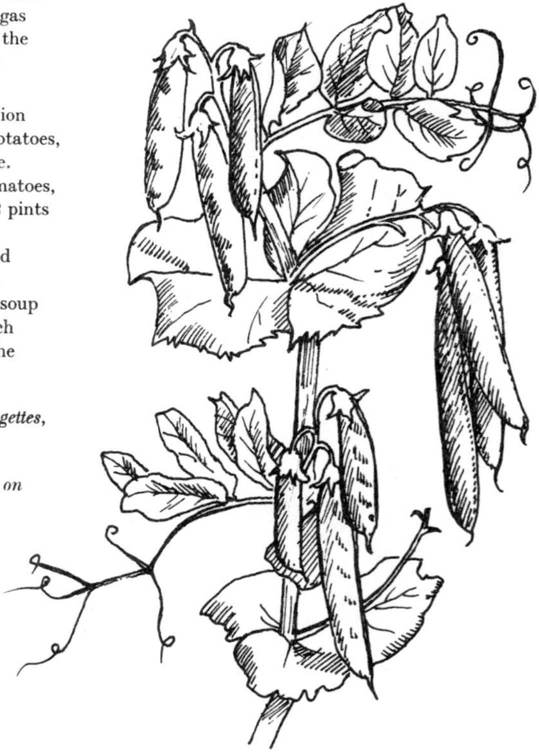

Soupe au Pistou

½ lb white haricot beans
¾ lb salt pork in a piece (lean end of belly)
½ lb green beans
2 carrots, 3 potatoes
2 tomatoes
3 oz soup pasta (shells or small macaroni)
salt, pepper
For the sauce:
3 oz grated Gruyère
15 leaves basil, fresh (or 1 teaspoon dried)
2 cloves garlic, olive oil

Soak the beans and the salt pork. Peel the potatoes and carrots and cut them into squares. Prepare the green beans and cut them into 1-inch lengths.

Put the salt pork and beans in a large pan with 6 pints of water. Bring to the boil and throw in the carrots. Cover and simmer 45 minutes. Now add the potatoes, green beans, chopped peeled tomatoes, and some pepper and salt if you need it, depending on how salty the pork is. Cook a further half-hour. Add the soup pasta and cook 10 minutes more.

In a pestle and mortar pound the garlic and basil. Stir this mixture, gradually adding grated cheese and oil alternately. Ladle the mixture into the soup tureen, pour on the soup, stirring, and allow to infuse 5 minutes.

☐*You can serve the salt pork hot afterwards, or cold later.*

For 8–10

Puchara (Chick pea Soup)

½ lb chick peas, soaked overnight
½ lb piece belly of pork
1–2 cloves garlic
2 onions
3 potatoes
3 tomatoes
½ teaspoon ground hot pimento
3 tablespoons olive oil
salt
a couple of handfuls of green beans (optional)

Put the soaked chick peas in a large lidded saucepan with the belly of pork, peeled whole cloves of garlic, and about 4 pints of cold water. Bring to the boil and simmer until the chick peas are almost tender, about 1½ hours.

Chop the onions and fry them in the oil. When they are tender and starting to sizzle cut the tomatoes in half and grate them into the pan on the coarse side of the grater leaving out the skins. Add a large pinch of hot pimento or cayenne and let this mixture fry until all the liquid has evaporated. Then add it and the potatoes cut in cubes to the soup, season and simmer until the potatoes are half done. Finally add the beans and cook on until all the vegetables are tender and you are ready to eat the soup, which is practically a stew and very filling.

☐*In Spain this is often served with small dumplings floating in it.*

For 8

Watercress and Cucumber Soup

½ cucumber
2 medium potatoes, or 1 large
1 small onion
sprig of parsley
1 pint chicken stock
½ pint milk
1 bunch watercress
salt
3–4 tablespoons sour cream, or fresh cream and lemon

Simmer the peeled and chopped cucumber, potatoes, onion and the parsley in the stock for 30 to 35 minutes, until completely tender. Put everything through the Moulin-Légumes, sieve or liquidise, add enough milk to make the soup smooth and not too thick. Season and add the watercress, preferably chopped finely by hand, or only whirred for a couple of seconds in the liquidiser. Heat to boiling point, take off the heat, stir in the sour cream, or fresh cream and lemon. Serve hot, or chill and serve with a sprig of watercress floating in each plate.

For 4

How to make Croûtons for Soups, etc.

1 slice stale white bread per person
1 tablespoon olive oil per slice
½ oz butter per slice

Trim the crusts from the bread and cut it into cubes, fingers or triangles. Cubes are usual for soup, fingers and triangles for 'sippets'. Take a thick heavy pan with a wide base and a lid. Heat the oil and butter, and when a crumb dropped into it sizzles, add the bread, so that the bottom of the pan is filled, but not so that the pieces are overlapping. Turn down the heat a little, cover the pan, and after a few minutes shake the whole thing, holding the lid down, so that all the pieces of bread get turned about. When they sound crisp they are ready. Drain them on kitchen paper, and keep them hot. Drop them into the soup as you serve each helping. They should be just golden, not black or brown.

☐*This method of cooking is less likely to burn the croûtons, and it is also supposed to make them more digestible.*

Eggs
Cheese Rice Pasta

Eggs, Cheese, Rice and Pasta

Eggs should never be cooked too long, overcooked eggs lose all their charm, and most people would be keenly disappointed if their poached, baked, fried or jellied egg did not have a soft yolk, nor their scrambled eggs, soufflé or omelette an unctuous texture. Once you have mastered their peculiar chemistry — heating them slowly makes them absorb liquid, heating them fast may make them exude it, you can improvise endlessly with eggs and never get tired of them. White eggs or brown makes no difference at all except perhaps psychologically — brown eggs do look healthier — the difference in quality, deep golden tasty yolks or pale insipid ones, depends entirely on what the birds are being fed on (beware, there is an ingredient which can be added to their mash which colours the yolks without improving the flavour — too much of it and the yolks turn green). The fact that brown eggs cost a little more is usually because the birds that lay white eggs lay more often, but sometimes because we are illogically prepared to pay more for brown; they make us think of farms and birds pecking about in the sunshine.

A good partner for eggs is cheese, another slightly less temperamental standby in the kitchen. Cheese can harden if it is cooked too fast or too long, or can go into rubbery strings if melted and then allowed to get cool, so melt it gently and serve it hot. Cheshire cheese is among the very best cooking cheeses and melts to a beautiful creamy consistency; Cheddar is also extremely useful, but best of all are Gruyère and Parmesan. Cottage cheese can be boring food; cold and lumpy, it contains no cream, is curded, high in protein and just the thing for a diet. But in fact it is not as limited as it sounds and can be used quite successfully in recipes where a light cheese like ricotta is wanted, it should be sieved to get the right consistency, and if you like a spoonful or two of cream can be added. Cream cheese contains quite a lot of cream and is much heavier and richer — be sure to buy it unsalted if you are making a sweet dish with it — again sieved cottage cheese can be used as a substitute; mixed with $\frac{1}{3}$ to $\frac{1}{2}$ its weight in whipped cream.

In this book we have given instructions for making pasta — a laborious but enjoyable job and one that was once a daily tradition in Italian homes. It may be completely uneconomic to make your own noodles in terms of time consumed, but they are simply delicious once you have the knack, and anyway they are fun. But don't attempt to make them for a dinner party at your first try. They have a horrible way of sticking together until you know how to handle them and making them is a long job.

Rice was rather neglected in *Poor Cook* and we have tried to put this right by using it more often in this book. Get to know the three main types — long-grain for pilaus, curries and stuffed vegetables, oval Italian or Spanish (which is white or yellow) for risottos and round for puddings — do not try to use pudding rice for anything else. Cook rice carefully, plenty of rinsing beforehand to wash off the extra starch makes it almost foolproof. For most purposes 2 ounces of rice per head is the right amount.

Oeufs Mollets with Sorrel

Bring a pan of water to the boil. Put in a medium-size egg for each person and cook exactly 5 minutes.

Take them out and keep warm in a bowl of hot water. One at a time tap the egg shells all over to crack them and peel them *very* carefully. Put them back in warm water if you want to keep them warm.

Serve with a sorrel purée (page 134). Or allow to cool and make into œufs en gelée with a slice of ham underneath.

☐ *Nervous cooks may want to cook an extra egg in case one breaks.*

Poached Eggs in Wine Sauce

2 shallots chopped
2 oz button mushrooms, sliced
2 oz streaky bacon
1 oz butter
½ pint red wine
1 level tablespoon flour
4 eggs
2 slices white bread, crusts removed
olive oil, salt

Fry the chopped shallots, sliced mushrooms and bacon cut into little sticks, in half the butter for a minute or two. Pour on the wine, bring to the boil, skim, add a little salt and cook until reduced by half. Work the flour well into the remaining butter and dissolve the resulting paste into the hot sauce, whisking until it is all absorbed. Keep the sauce hot while you poach the eggs and fry four triangular sippets of bread in olive oil. Put the eggs on warm plates, pour the sauce over them (thinned with a little water if necessary). Serve with the sippets on the side of the plate. A glass of the wine you used in cooking is perfect with this.

☐ *Slightly sharp wine is good for this, so the last quarter of a bottle opened for a previous meal is fine.*

For 2

Poached Egg Salad

1 egg per person
lettuce
1 tablespoon mayonnaise for each egg
chopped herbs — any one of the following:
parsley, tarragon, dill, chervil, chives.

Poach the eggs very carefully till the whites are set but the yolks still soft, drain and trim them and leave them to cool.

Use only the best inner leaves of the lettuce, and break them up into pieces you can get on to a fork. Arrange a cushion of lettuce on each person's (small) plate. Put a poached egg in the middle of each — neither egg nor lettuce must be wet in any way — and cover just the egg with a thick spoonful of well-flavoured mayonnaise, into which you have stirred the chopped fresh herbs. Serve immediately.

□ *This is delicious as a first course or as one of several salads at a summer lunch.*

Scrambled Eggs with Spinach or Sorrel

large handful of spinach or sorrel leaves
3–4 eggs
a large knob of butter
a dash of cream or top of milk
salt, pepper

Wash the spinach, or sorrel, and put it wet, without salt or pepper, into a small saucepan. Cover and simmer until cooked (5 minutes for sorrel, 10–12 minutes for spinach) then put it in a small sieve to drain *really well*, then chop or sieve. Break the eggs into a pan with some butter, add the purée, cream, salt and pepper and stir very well. Scramble in the normal way. The purée will mix with the eggs evenly as they thicken. As soon as they start to thicken, turn down the heat and serve immediately. They should be as thick as whipped cream.

For 2

Brillat-Savarin's Scrambled Eggs

1 or 2 eggs per person
grated Gruyère cheese
butter
a little or no salt
pepper

Weigh the eggs. Take one third of their weight in grated cheese, and one sixth of their weight in butter. Melt the butter and add it to the beaten eggs with the cheese and a little salt and pepper. Cook gently in a saucepan stirring all the time until it resembles scrambled eggs and serve at once with sippets of fried bread.

Florentine Omelette

6 eggs
¾ pint cheese sauce (page 172)
1 lb fresh spinach, or one 6 oz packet frozen spinach, chopped
1 oz Parmesan
a little cream
salt, pepper, knob of butter

Strip the stalks from the spinach, wash well and cook, covered, with a little salt but no more water until tender. Drain very well and chop finely. If you are using frozen spinach melt it with a little butter, and salt and drain it very well. Stir the spinach into a little of the sauce and keep it hot while you make the omelette. Have the grill hot for the final stage before you begin. If you can, make a single omelette with all 6 eggs in one go, otherwise make 2. Just as the omelette is set (it should be under, rather than over-cooked), spoon the spinach filling into the middle, flip it over (opposite) and into a heatproof serving dish, stir the cream into the cheese sauce, pour the sauce over the folded omelette, sprinkle with Parmesan and leave under the grill until brown and bubbling. Serve at once.

For 3

Kidney Omelettes

2 lambs kidneys, or ¼ lb ox kidney
1 oz butter
salt, pepper
½ dessertspoon flour
dash of white or red wine } not more than ¼
a little stock or water } pint together
4 eggs
salt, pepper

Skin, core and slice the kidneys into small pieces. Sprinkle them with salt and pepper. Put half the butter into a small saucepan, and make a roux with the flour, add the wine and then the stock, and let it simmer while you briskly fry the kidneys in a small frying pan with the other half of the butter. As soon as they have changed colour from dark to pale pink, tip them with all their butter into the sauce. Taste for seasoning, and leave off the heat, but keep it warm while you make the omelettes. Just before each omelette is ready put half the kidneys in their sauce along the centre of it, and tip the whole thing onto a hot plate so that the omelette rolls neatly round its filling (see below).

For 2

Onion Omelette

1 onion
5–6 eggs
1 oz butter
salt, pepper

Chop the onion very finely, melt the butter in a pan and soften the onion, covered, until it is golden and transparent but not browned. It can take half an hour. Beat the eggs with salt and pepper, pour them into the pan, mix in the onions, turn up the heat, and finish like an ordinary omelette.

For 2–3

1

2

Tortilla

6 eggs
4 potatoes
2 onions
salt, fresh ground black pepper
olive oil

Peel and slice the potatoes and onions and fry them in your best frying-pan (one that doesn't stick and has a lid) in ¼ pint of olive oil. Cook them fairly slowly with the lid on, stirring often, until they are soft and cooked through but not brown, or only very slightly. Break the eggs into a large bowl and beat them with a rotary whisk until they are frothy. Season. Turn the heat up until the oil is really hot, then pour in the eggs and turn down the heat and let the tortilla cook on a moderate heat for 3–4 minutes, loosening the edges a little with a wooden fork. If it seems to be sticking slip a little butter down the inside of the pan. Put a plate over the frying pan and turn it upside down. Slide the omelette, uncooked side down, back into the pan.

The plate will have quite a bit of raw egg left on it. After two minutes put the plate on the pan again and turn it over, slide the omelette back into the pan — it will take most of the raw egg with it. Fry for 1 minute then repeat again. By this time the omelette will have re-absorbed all the raw egg. Serve the tortilla at once.

☐ *In Spain they use 1 egg for each person, but more is better. You can add bits of bacon and green pepper. Tortillas make very good picnic food, eaten cold.*

For 4

Curried Eggs

4 eggs
½ lb onions, very finely chopped or minced
4 cloves garlic
1 teaspoon chilli powder
1 teaspoon ginger
½ teaspoon cumin
1 piece cinnamon, 1 inch long
1 teaspoon ground coriander
1 teaspoon curry powder
1 14 oz tin Italian tomatoes
½–1 oz butter, salt

Preheat the oven Reg 3/325°. Hardboil the eggs. Fry the finely chopped onions and garlic in butter until soft but not brown. Add the spices and stir them round; let them cook for a minute or two, then add the tomatoes. Simmer the sauce until it has thickened a little; add quite a bit of salt. Slice the eggs across into ¼-inch slices, or cut them in halves or quarters, pour the sauce over them in a shallow ovenproof dish and heat through in the oven, Reg 3/325°. Serve with plain boiled rice.

☐ *This is very good, and although there are a lot of ingredients it is very quick to make.*

For 4–5

Spinach Soufflé

½ oz butter
6 oz fresh spinach purée or cooked frozen spinach
4 egg yolks and 5 egg whites
2 oz butter
1½ oz flour
½ pint milk
salt and pepper
1 oz grated Gruyère
1 oz grated Parmesan

Preheat oven to Reg 6/400°. Butter a 7″×3″ soufflé dish and dust inside with grated Parmesan. Heat the spinach gently in a closed pan with a little butter. Do not fry. Make a Béchamel sauce (page 183) with the flour, butter, milk and seasoning. Let it cool a little and add egg yolks one by one to the sauce, beating them in with a wire whisk. Stir in the spinach purée. Beat egg whites until stiff, stirring a quarter of them and most of the cheese into the spinach mixture. Fold in remaining egg whites, turn into the soufflé dish and sprinkle with the rest of the cheese. Place in middle of oven, and turn heat down to Reg 5/375°. Bake for 25–30 minutes.

For 4

Turkish Onion Eggs

4 medium onions, finely sliced
2 tablespoons butter
½ cup water
½ teaspoon sugar
4 eggs
salt, pepper, nutmeg

Sauté the onions in the butter in a heavy pan until tender (about 15–20 minutes). Stir in the water and sugar and cook until the water is absorbed and the onions cooked (about another 10 minutes). With the back of a spoon make four depressions in the onion mixture, each large enough to hold an egg. Break an egg into each depression and sprinkle with salt, pepper and nutmeg to taste. Cook the mixture over a low heat until the eggs are set and serve straight away.

☐ *This is a lovely lunch dish. It could also be cooked in individual dishes.*

For 4

Poor Man's Soufflé

3–4 large slices bread, crusts removed
2 oz grated cheese
1 oz butter
French mustard
salt, pepper
1 egg
a little milk

Spread the pieces of bread with butter and mustard, cut them into three and arrange them in buttered ovenproof dish, sprinkling cheese on and around each piece and seasoning lightly with salt and pepper.

Beat the egg with a small cup of milk — just under ¼ pint, and pour this mixture over the bread. Sprinkle with a little more cheese and allow to stand 20 minutes.

Preheat the oven to Reg 4/350° and bake for 45 minutes. The bread puffs up and rises to the top of the dish and goes brown on top.

☐ *This soufflé has the advantage of being unlikely to collapse and is a good teatime alternative to Welsh Rarebit.*

Cold Cheese Soufflé

4 oz grated cheese such as Parmesan, and Gruyère or Cheddar
2 egg yolks
whites of 3 eggs
salt, cayenne pepper,
1 teaspoon made mustard
¼ pint milk
2 teaspoons gelatine crystals
⅛ pint thick cream

Combine the egg yolks and finely grated cheese in a double boiler. Add salt, cayenne pepper and mustard. Add the milk and stir over very hot but not boiling water until it thickens like custard. If the water looks as though it will boil take the top pan off the heat immediately.

Dissolve the gelatine in 2 or 3 tablespoons of boiling water and stir into the warm egg mixture. Allow it to cool. When cold fold in the whipped cream and the stiffly beaten egg-whites. Pile into a soufflé dish, dust the top with cayenne pepper and chill.

☐ *This is surprisingly rich and should be served with a simple salad, before or after something very plain.*

For 4

Cheese and Ale

3–4 oz Gloucester or Cheshire cheese
1–2 teaspoons freshly made mustard
salt and cayenne pepper
a few tablespoons of brown ale
2 slices brown bread

Slice the cheese into thin slices and put them in a low oven in a small dish to melt like chocolate — overheating makes cheese tough and rubbery — Reg 2/300° for about 5 mins. Then spread with the mustard, sprinkle with salt and cayenne, pour on enough brown ale to cover. Mix and keep it warm while you make two pieces of brown toast and put them onto hot plates.

Now pour the ale and cheese mixture over the toast and serve straight away with a glass of ale.

For 2

Alsace Tartlets

For pastry
6 oz flour
3 oz butter
salt, iced water

For filling
6 eggs
salt, pepper
nutmeg
1 tablespoon fresh double cream
3 tablespoons Gruyère cheese, grated
1 tablespoon Parmesan, grated

Make the pastry well in advance. Preheat the oven to Reg 6/400°. Line 20 jam tart shapes with pastry rolled very thin. Beat the eggs with salt, pepper, nutmeg, cream and grated Gruyère or other cheese. Fill the pastry cases with this mixture but not too full as they puff up quite a bit. Sprinkle the tops with grated Parmesan and cook like jam tarts for 15 minutes until they are a good golden colour. Serve hot.

☐ *Eat these as an hors d'œuvre or at a party. They can be made in advance and reheated.*

Pancakes Stuffed with Ricotta

6 pancakes
8 oz ricotta (or cottage cheese)
6 oz chopped spinach, frozen or fresh cooked
1 oz grated cheese, preferably Parmesan
salt and pepper
1 pint cheese sauce (page 172)

Make the pancakes according to the recipe on page 185. Mix the ricotta, spinach, salt, pepper and grated cheese in a bowl, using your hands. Form into sausage shapes, lay one on each pan cake. Roll them up and put them in a fireproof gratin dish. Cover with the sauce and put in a hot oven for 10 minutes, until the sauce is bubbling and blistering with brown patches.

For 6

Cheese and Potato Casserole

4 largish potatoes
4 medium-sized onions, peeled and chopped
½ pint milk
½ lb grated cheese
salt and pepper

Boil or steam the potatoes in their skins till almost done, then make a thin well-seasoned Béchamel sauce, using half milk and half liquid from the potatoes. Peel and roughly chop the potatoes. Then put layers in a buttered casserole in this order: potato, chopped raw onion, sauce and a good layer of grated cheese. Repeat as required, ending with a thick layer of grated cheese. Cook in a moderate oven Reg 4/350° for about 1 hour to 1½ hours, till the top is beginning to brown.

☐ *Very good with pork chops or even as a meal in itself.*

For 4

Chinese way of Cooking Plain Boiled Rice

2 oz rice per person
salt, water

Wash the rice by running the cold tap over it until the water runs clear (this can be done in a tilted basin or pan, or sieve).

Using a saucepan with a perfectly fitting lid, put the rice in, with water to cover it by about $\frac{3}{4}$ inch, and add salt. Boil fast until the rice has absorbed all the water, and little holes appear on the surface of the rice (this should take 10–15 minutes).

Put the pan on an asbestos mat and turn the heat right down. Cover as firmly as you can with a lid, and leave, barely cooking, for 10 minutes. When you take the lid off, the rice should be beautifully separate and fluffy and not sticking at all to the pan. A lot depends on how well you washed it at first.

Cuban Rice

8 oz rice
4 bananas
4 eggs, or more according to hunger of the diners
1 clove garlic
salt, pepper
butter

Cook the rice in boiling salted water with the clove of garlic. When it is nearly ready for straining, peel and cut the bananas in half lengthways and fry gently in butter. At the last minute fry the eggs. Put a layer of rice on each plate, top with egg and banana and pour over some of the pan juices. Serve with green salad.

☐ *A very good dish for one person to make for themselves, especially if they are tired or hungover.*

For 4

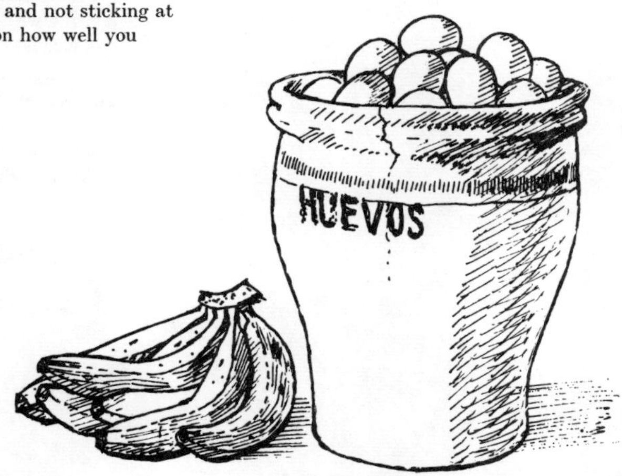

Potato Gnocchi

1½ lbs peeled, cooked potatoes
2 egg yolks
1 tablespoon flour
4–5 tablespoons grated Parmesan
salt pepper

Mash the very well drained, dry potatoes with a potato masher or fork. Beat in the egg yolks, flour, half the Parmesan, salt and pepper. Form lightly into ovals or rounds with floured hands and drop into boiling salted water.

Give the gnocchi four minutes cooking from the time they have all risen to the surface. Don't boil the water too furiously or they may disintegrate.

☐ *Serve with tomato or cheese sauce or simply with melted butter and plenty of Parmesan.*

For 4

Home-Made Pasta

½ lb plain flour
2 small eggs, beaten
2–4 tablespoons olive oil (if using large eggs cut down on the oil)

Make a dough with the flour, eggs and oil. Add more flour if it seems sticky. Knead well and if you have time leave in a cold place for at least 1 hour, covered. Roll the pasta out as thinly as possible *really paper thin* (it swells in cooking). If you haven't got a long Italian rolling-pin made specially for pasta-making, divide the dough into two before you begin. Transfer the sheets of what is now 'Pasta' to clean tea-towels and allow to dry for 1 hour (you can leave them flat or hang them over the back of a chair). Fold the sheets lightly and cut wide strips for lasagne or narrow strips for tagliatelle, squares for cannelloni, and so on. If you want to keep these before using them sprinkle lavishly with fine ground semolina (not flour as it makes them stick together).

To cook pasta bring a large pan of salted water to the boil and cook the strips of pasta for 10–12 minutes. This basic pasta is also used for Chinese dumplings and soup noodles (won ton for example). You can also use it for home-made ravioli.

☐ *Laborious to make but a great improvement on packeted pasta.*

For 4

Types of Pasta

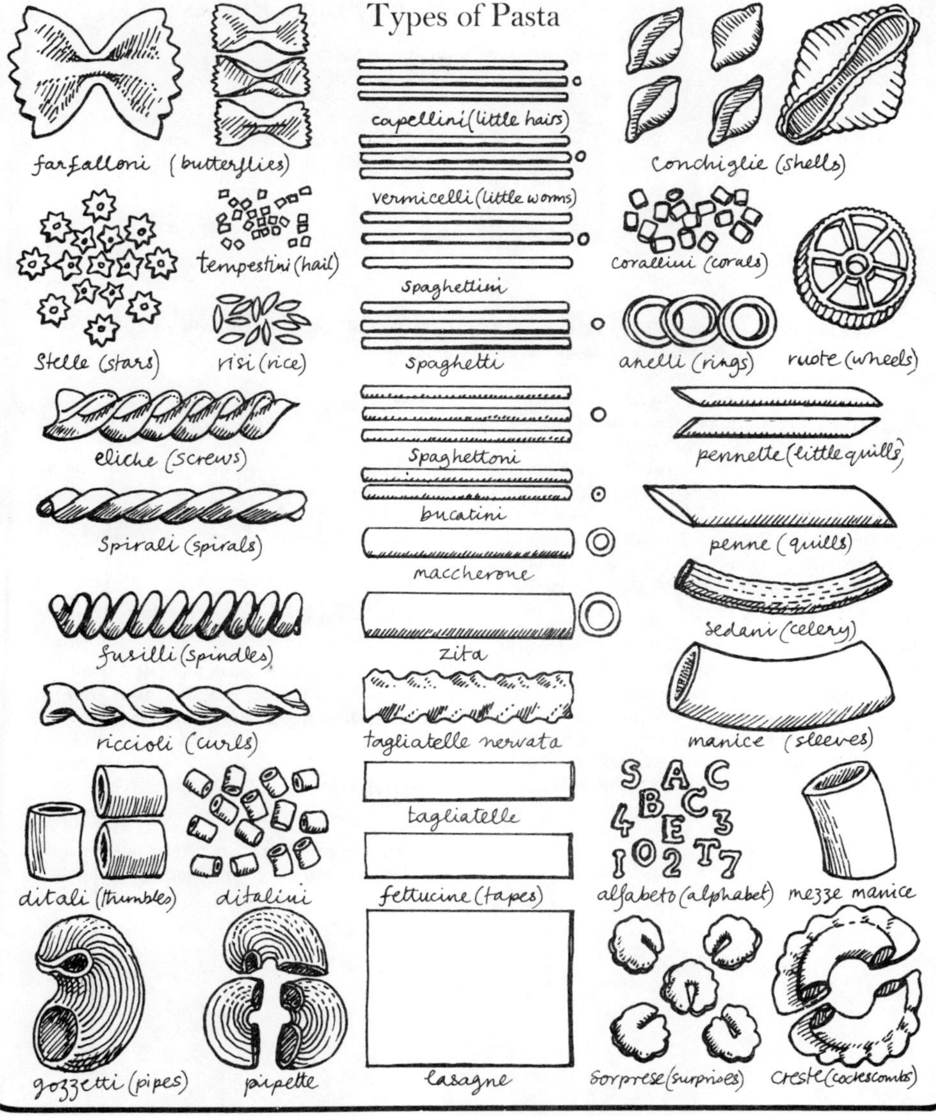

Ravioli

Roll out $\frac{3}{4}$ lb pasta (see Home-Made Pasta, overleaf) as thinly as you can. Make two sheets of equal size — don't let them get dry, cover them with a cloth if you have to fiddle with the filling. When it is ready, put teaspoons of the filling in rows about $1\frac{1}{2}$ inches apart on one sheet of pasta. Moisten the pasta between the fillings and lay the other sheet on top. Press between the blobs of filling with your finger tips to seal the little pockets. Run a pastry-cutter between the rows so that you make little squares. Do not lay them on top of each other as they will stick together.

Drop them into plenty of boiling salted water into which you have put a teaspoon of oil, which should prevent them sticking to each other or to the pan. Boil them for 15–25 minutes depending on how thin your pasta is and serve, well drained, with melted butter and grated Parmesan or with cheese or tomato sauce (pages 172, and 184).

Other Filled Pastas

Instead of ravioli, you can, with your sheets of thinly rolled pasta make:

Tortellini

Cut circles about $1\frac{1}{2}$–2 inches in diameter. Put a pea-sized amount of filling as shown on the circle (a). Fold it over as shown (b), curve the semi-circle round and pinch the ends together (c).

Capelletti

Make 2-inch squares of pasta and put a small amount of filling on each one. Fold them over (b) and pinch them together as shown (c).

Agnolotti

They are like ravioli but are two rounds pressed together with a teaspoon of filling in the middle.

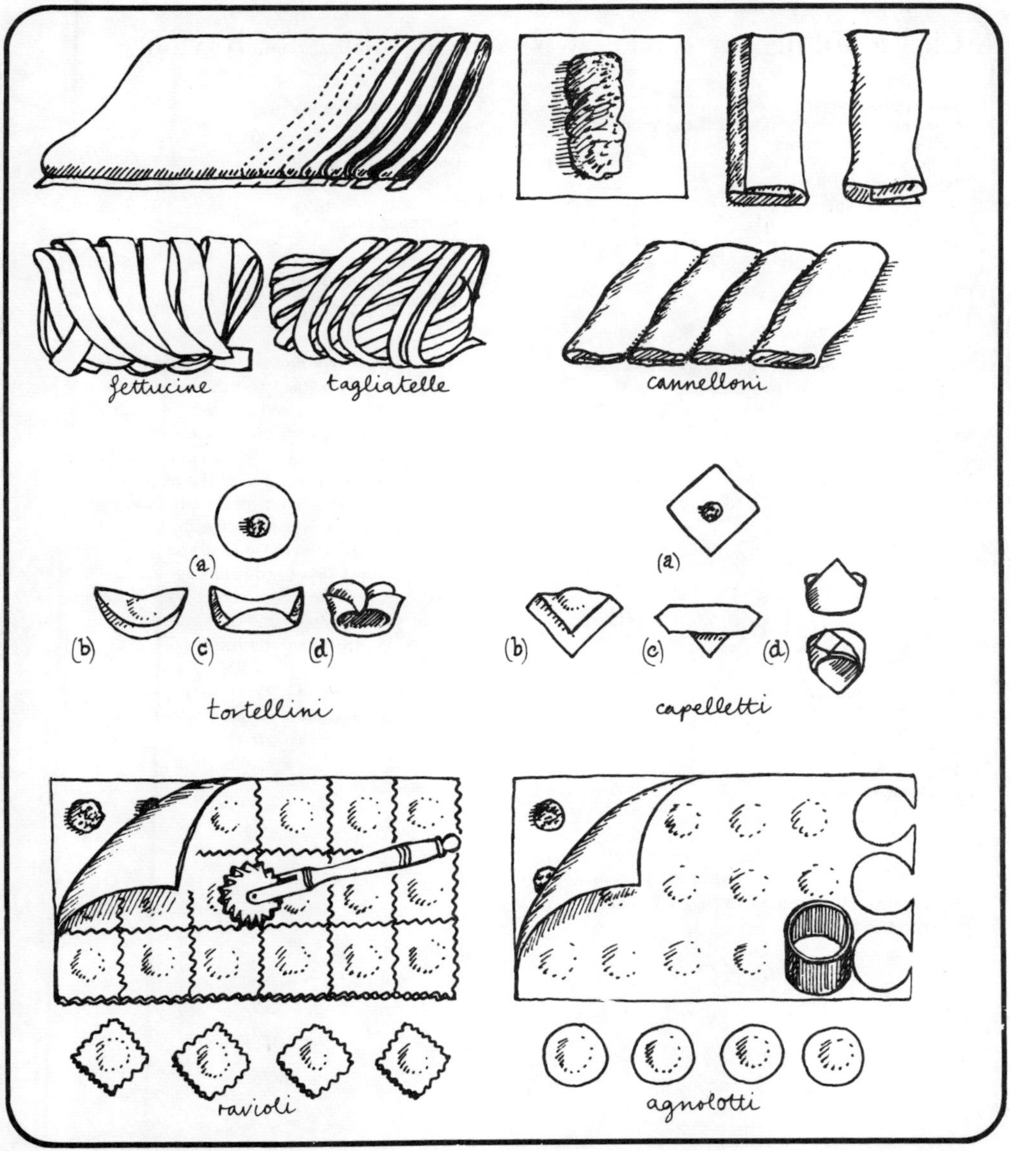
fettucine
tagliatelle
cannelloni
(a)
(b)
(c)
(d)
tortellini
(a)
(b)
(c)
(d)
capelletti
ravioli
agnolotti

Cheese Filling for Ravioli

4 oz ricotta cheese
4 oz cooked drained spinach (frozen will do)
1 oz Parmesan, grated
1 egg yolk
salt, pepper, nutmeg

Beat the egg yolk with ricotta, Parmesan and seasoning, including the nutmeg. Drain the spinach well and chop it finely or sieve it. Mix it into the cheese.

Spinach and Brains Filling

2 oz finely minced pork
2 oz cooked brains
4 oz cooked spinach
1 oz Parmesan, grated
1 egg yolk
salt, pepper, nutmeg

Fry the pork in a little butter to cook but not to brown it. Mix it with the rest of the ingredients, having previously beaten the egg yolks and mashed the brains.

Meat Filling for Ravioli

3 tablespoons olive oil
1 onion, chopped
1 carrot, chopped
1 stick celery, chopped
¾ lb freshly minced beef
salt, pepper, nutmeg
3 tablespoons tomato purée
dash of water
2 egg yolks
handful fresh breadcrumbs
2 oz Parmesan

Fry the onion, carrot and celery in the olive oil, until beginning to soften. Add the meat and stir it about until it is browned. Season with salt and pepper and moisten with the tomato purée, dissolved in a little water — just enough to bind it without making it wet. Cover the pan, turn down the heat and simmer for 1 hour. Allow to cool and then put this meat sauce through the finest blade of the mincer, so that you have a thick fine-grained sauce. Add the egg-yolks, breadcrumbs and Parmesan and check for seasoning. It should be a soft but firm paste. If it is too soft add more breadcrumbs.

☐*If you stop at the end of the cooking you can use this very good plain sauce for all kinds of ordinary pasta, spaghetti, macaroni etc.*

Makes about 1 lb of filling.

Filling for Cannelloni

½ lb minced pork
½ lb minced veal
1 onion
thyme, oregano
2 cloves garlic
1 8 oz tin Italian tomatoes or 4 tomatoes
¼ pint red wine
salt
1 tablespoon olive cil
2–3 tablespoons cream

Cannelloni can be made of 4-inch squares of your own pasta cooked, rolled around the filling and then covered with a thin layer of very cheesey Béchamel, sprinkled with more grated cheese and a pinch of ground mace or nutmeg. Bake in a hottish oven, Reg 6/400° for ½ hour or until brown and bubbling. Alternatively you can either buy cannelloni, but these are often broken in the boxes, or make them by cooking bought lasagne, rolling it round the stuffing and proceeding as above. Yet a third method is to use small thin pancakes (page 185) and roll them round the filling with the join facing downwards.

For 6

Noodles Alfredo

¾ lb dried noodles (tagliatelle) or 1 lb fresh
1 oz butter
½ oz flour
¾ pint milk
2 oz cheese, (Cheddar, Gruyère etc)
2 oz Parmesan cheese
¼ pint sour cream
1 clove garlic, bruised
1 bay leaf
salt, freshly ground pepper

Cook the noodles when the sauce is half made so that they both end up cooked and ready at the same time. Make a cheese sauce with the butter, flour and hot milk which you have infused with the garlic clove and bay leaf. Stir in three quarters of the cheese, add salt and pepper, and let the sauce cook, adding a little more milk if it gets too thick, for 5–10 minutes. At the last minute add the sour cream. Keep a third of the sauce aside, stir the rest into the hot drained noodles, first fishing out bay leaf and garlic clove. Turn it into a gratin dish, coat the top with the remaining sauce, sprinkle with the rest of the cheese and brown under the grill, or heat in hot oven 5–10 minutes.

☐ *Delicious but must be eaten at once. Is even better made with fresh pasta* (*see page* 36).

For 4

Macaroni in Pasticciere

1 lb tomatoes, fresh or tinned
2 onions
3 cloves garlic
¾ lb minced beef (finely minced)
small glass of red wine
1 tablespoon tomato purée
thyme, rosemary
¼–½ pint stock
salt, pepper
olive oil (2 tablespoons)
¾ lb macaroni

Skin the tomatoes and chop them. Peel, slice and chop the onions and garlic. Fry the onions and garlic in olive oil until soft and then add the beef and fry until nicely brown over brisk heat. Add the wine and let it bubble. Add the tomatoes, herbs, salt, pepper, purée and ¼ pint stock. Cook gently for 1 hour. Add more stock if necessary.

SAUCE

2 oz butter
3 oz flour
2 oz grated Parmesan
1 pint of milk (infused with bay leaf, sliced onion and salt)

Make sauce by melting butter, stirring in flour, adding strained milk gradually, then the grated Parmesan. It should be rather stiff.

Drop the macaroni into salted water. Allow to cook until just tender. Drain, mix with the meat sauce in a large bowl. Butter an oven dish and put in the macaroni mixture, level it out and then put the cheese sauce on top. Bake in the oven Reg 3/325° for ½ hour.

☐ *It is a rather quicker and easier dish to make than Lasagne. Children love it.*

For 8–10

Spinach Fritters

½ lb spinach leaves (fresh *not* frozen)
½ onion or 4–5 spring onions, chopped
4 oz flour (plain or wholemeal)
2 eggs
salt
1 teaspoon oil
Just under ¼ pint milk and water mixed
oil for frying (or lard)

Make a thick creamy batter by stirring the eggs into the flour and salt, then gradually adding the milk and oil, keeping the batter lump-free by beating hard with a wooden spoon.

Wash the spinach, shake dry in a cloth like lettuce, then chop it finely and stir it into the batter with the finely chopped onion. Allow to stand half an hour or more to allow the spinach and batter to marry together.

Heat oil to a depth of ¼ inch in a heavy frying pan. Drop the mixture, a spoonful at a time, into the hot oil and fry until a good golden brown, turning once. Serve these fritters, golden and green, crisp outside and soft within, as an accompaniment to roast chicken or on their own with grated Parmesan.

☐ *Children who wouldn't otherwise eat spinach love these. It is also good made with Swiss Chard.*

For 4

FISH
SELECTED MEDIUM
STEVE HATT
MACKEREL
CORNWALL

Fish

Fresh fish is disappearing at a very alarming rate, and as it becomes harder to find fish shops, so people find it easier and easier to buy and cook frozen fish, which can be cheaper, but is never as good as fish from a really good fish shop. Anyway the number of different frozen fish is very limited, mainly cod, haddock and plaice, and if you only buy frozen packets you are likely to miss all the interesting kinds that the fishmonger sells in small quantities at different times of the year.

Fish is a seasonable food and fishing depends on the weather, so find out from your fishmonger what is plentiful and what is in season, otherwise you may get fish in poor condition or pay vastly over the odds for what you buy. Try to shop for fish the day you are going to eat it; the shop has better conditions for keeping fish fresh than you have, so an extra day in the fishmonger's cupboard is better than one in your refrigerator. (There are three fish that are best not eaten the day they are caught anyway — sole, skate and plaice. But since it is extremely unlikely you will ever taste fish the day it is caught, unless you go out and catch it yourself, or live in a fishing town, this information is only useful if you do want to buy fish for the next day.)

If you have the choice between deep-sea and inshore fish, the deep-sea fish are possibly better quality (because they have richer feeding grounds). But they may not have been netted quite so recently, as deep-sea boats stay out for relatively long periods. If you eat a lot of smoked fish you may have wondered about the difference between smoked haddock on the bone, smoked haddock fillet, golden cutlets and golden fillets. The chief difference is that cutlets and fillets are dyed bright yellow before they are smoked, otherwise they get a white line across them where they hang on the line in the smokehouse, whereas the much more genuine-looking whole split haddock on the bone is strung on a stick through the collarbone and so has no white line. Golden cutlets are not usually particularly good quality and are correspondingly cheaper — they are usually haddock, but if cod is cheaper that week then they may be cod. They are probably cured and smoked in Scotland which means they are likely to be strong and salty; London smoked haddock are the best in the world if you can get them. Golden fillet may be haddock, whiting or possibly cod. When buying smoked fish watch out for a pinkish tinge or a slight smell, which indicate that the fish is in poor condition.

Although almost all fish is rather expensive now — skate, haddock, cod, turbot and shellfish are getting more expensive all the time — there are still cheap kinds to be found. Apparently the reason nobody likes coley (also called saithe or coal-fish) is because of the dingy grey colour, but it goes white when you cook it. The Billingsgate merchants use it for making fish pie, which is most children's favourite way of eating fish anyway. Red-fish, also known as Norway haddock, soldier and bergyld or sometimes misleadingly called bream fillets, is quite a good, little-known fish. Dabs and witch-soles, especially deep-sea ones, are tasty little fish and so are small lemon soles; fry them in crisp breadcrumbs to improve their texture. Small haddocks can be cheap and so can conger eel. In the south-east rock-salmon (or rock eel) is dogfish which is a variety of small shark, it is cheap but not really very special. In other parts of the country rock-salmon is a euphemism for all sorts of other unattractive fish. Officially, legislation is putting an end to this muddle over names as fast as it can.

Herrings, sprats and sometimes mackerel are still good cheap fish though not so plentiful as they were once. Try poaching mackerel instead of baking, frying or grilling them. Both smoked and tinned fish keep their nutritional qualities, and tinned tunnyfish, sardines and anchovies are useful standbys. Another useful preserved fish is salt cod which makes a base for some excellent dishes which we give in this book. It is not an easy taste to acquire, somewhere in the region of tripe as far as oddness of flavour and texture goes, but if you like interesting peasant food it can become a great favourite, especially made into a brandade. Don't be put off by the smell, and allow plenty of time for preparing it.

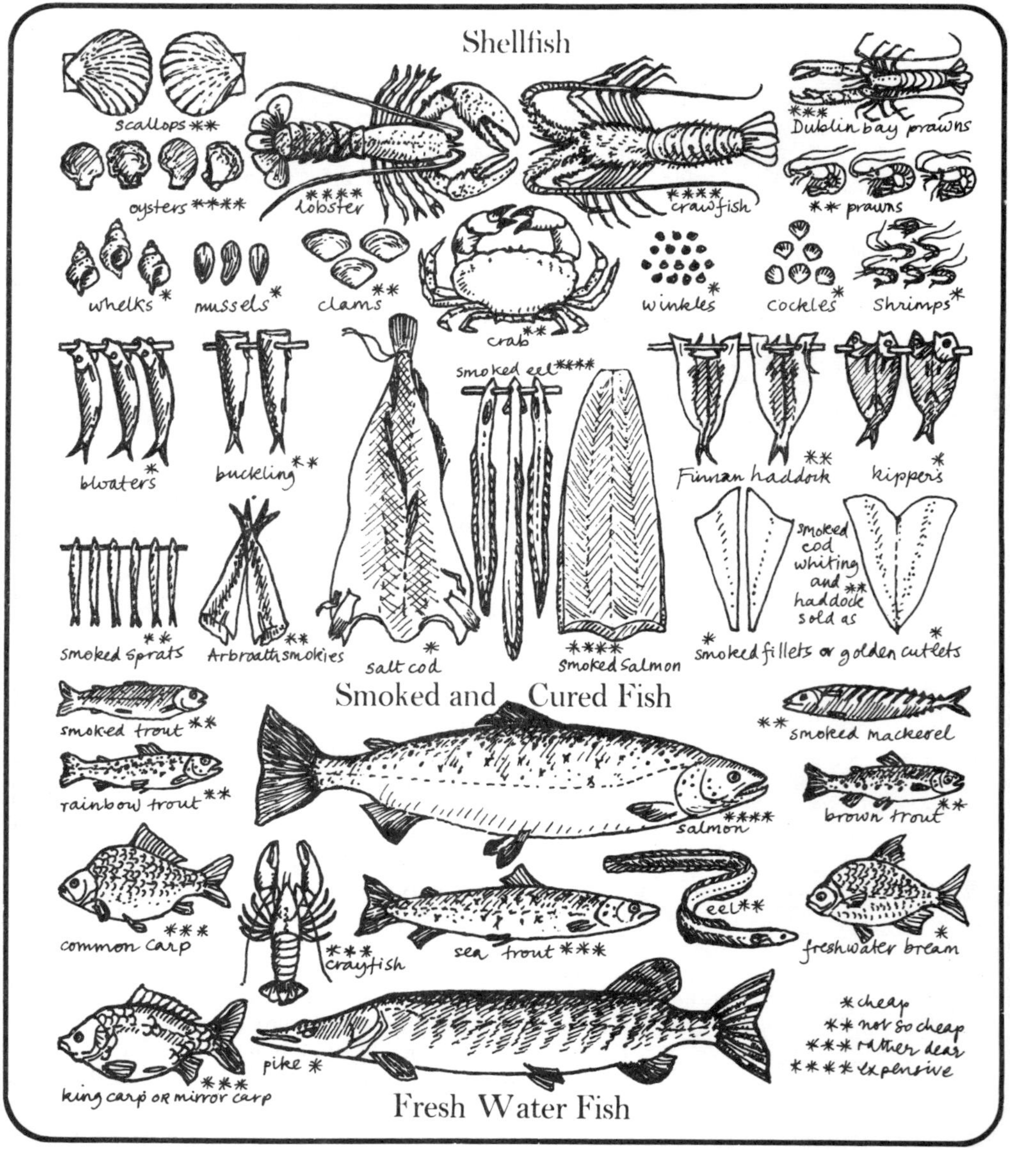
Shellfish
scallops **
oysters ****
**** lobster
**** crawfish
*** Dublin bay prawns
** prawns
whelks *
mussels *
clams **
crab **
winkles *
cockles *
shrimps *
bloaters *
buckling **
smoked eel ***
Finnan haddock **
kippers *
smoked sprats **
Arbroath smokies **
salt cod *
**** smoked salmon
smoked cod whiting and haddock ** sold as
* smoked fillets or golden cutlets *
Smoked and Cured Fish
smoked trout **
** smoked mackerel
rainbow trout **
salmon ****
brown trout **
common carp ***
*** crayfish
sea trout ***
eel **
freshwater bream *
king carp or mirror carp ***
pike *
* cheap
** not so cheap
*** rather dear
**** expensive
Fresh Water Fish

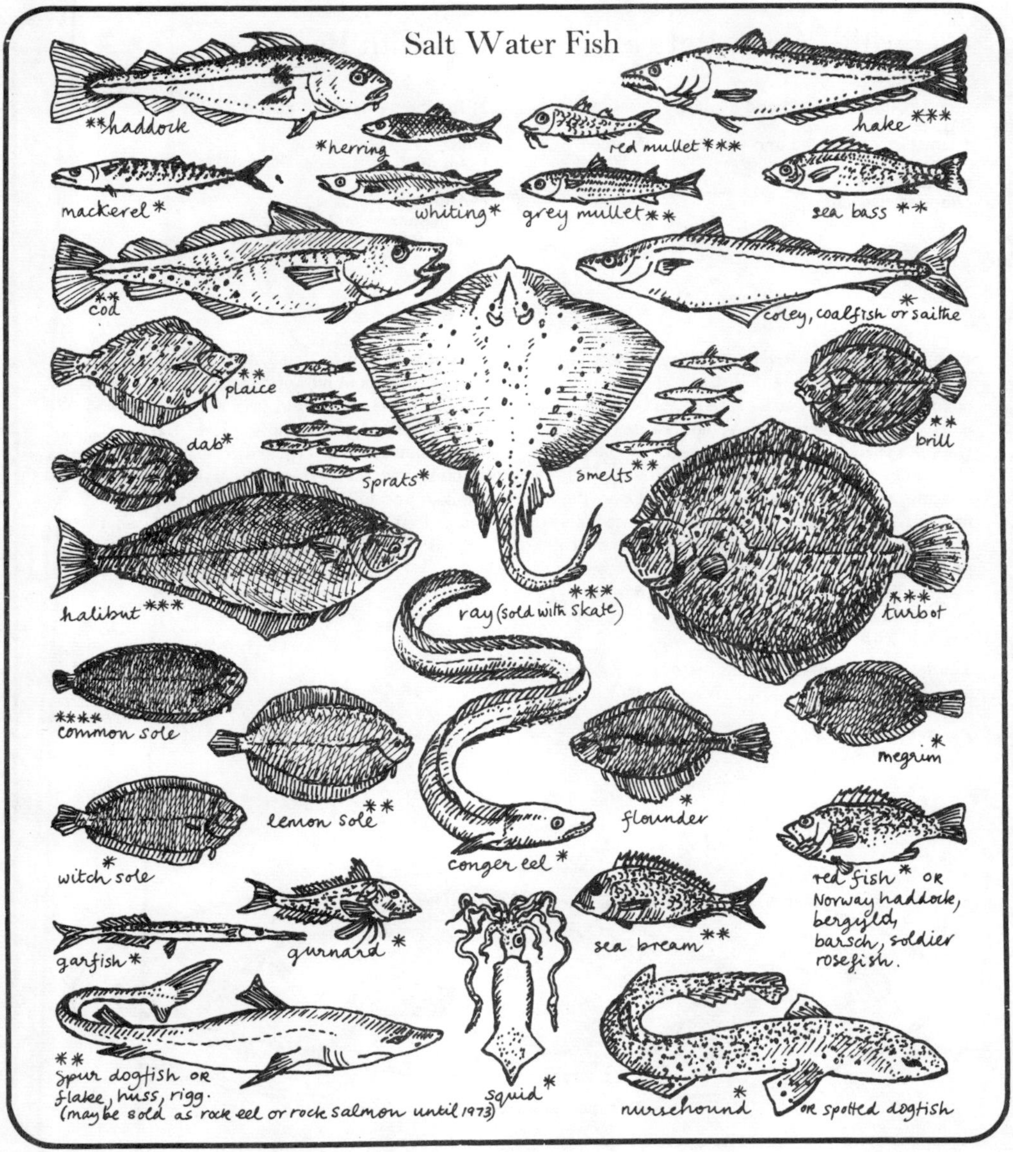

Salt Water Fish
**haddock
*herring
red mullet***
hake***
mackerel*
whiting*
grey mullet**
sea bass**
cod**
coley, coalfish or saithe*
plaice**
sprats*
smelts**
brill**
dab*
halibut***
ray (sold with skate)***
turbot***
common sole****
lemon sole**
flounder*
megrim*
witch sole*
conger eel*
red fish* OR Norway haddock, bergyld, barsch, soldier rosefish.
garfish*
gurnard*
sea bream**
** spur dogfish OR flake, huss, rigg. (may be sold as rock eel or rock salmon until 1973)
squid*
nursehound* OR spotted dogfish

Cod with Lemon Butter

8 cod cutlets (or 1½ lb cod fillets)
3 oz butter
1 small onion, peeled and very finely chopped
1 lemon
salt, pepper
chopped parsley

Preheat the oven to Reg 4/350°. Grate the rind of the lemon, and sauté it with the chopped onion in 1 oz of the butter (use a small frying pan). Don't let the mixture colour. Butter the base of a shallow fireproof oven dish, lay the fish in it, and spoon over the onion and lemon mixture. Season with salt and pepper. Cover the fish with foil and bake 20–25 minutes. Just before serving, melt the rest of the butter in the small pan and when it is on the point of turning brown add the lemon juice. Remove the foil from the fish, pour on the butter and lemon juice mixture. Sprinkle with chopped parsley.

You need lots of mashed potatoes or rice to sop up the juice.

For 4

Cod with Bacon

2½ lb whole piece of cod (preferably from a middle cut)
6 rashers streaky bacon
½ pint milk
½ oz flour
½ oz butter
salt, pepper
a dash of grated nutmeg

Preheat the oven to Reg 3/325°. Season the cod with salt, pepper and nutmeg and cover it crossways with the bacon. Put it in a baking tin and add milk to a depth of half an inch. Bake for 30–40 minutes. When cooked remove the fish and bacon to a warm serving dish. Make a roux with the flour and butter and gradually stir in the strained milk from the fish to make a sauce. Taste for seasoning and hand the sauce separately.

For 6

To Prepare Salt Cod

Choose 2 lbs of cod (middle cut if possible) and ask the shop to cut it into pieces about 3 or 4 inches across. Put these in a bowl a day or 2 days before you want to eat it, and stand the bowl overnight under a dribbling tap so that the water is slowly but constantly changing. When the cod is very soft it is ready. Drain and rinse, put in a pan of cold water, bring it slowly to the boil and as it reaches boiling point remove it from the heat and let it stand 10 minutes. It is now cooked and ready to use in a Brandade for example, or any of the salt cod recipes which follow.

Brandade de Morue

2 lbs prepared salt cod
1–2 cloves garlic
scant $\frac{1}{4}$ pint milk
scant $\frac{1}{4}$ pint olive oil
2 tablespoons mashed potato
2 eggs
a handful of chopped parsley
4 slices white bread and oil to fry it in

Skin the cod, which will be very gelatinous indeed, remove the bones and chop it with a large knife. Pound the garlic in a pestle and mortar, add the cod a little at a time, and as each lot is pounded to a rough fibrous paste transfer it to a wide bottomed pan.

Gently warm the milk and oil separately — they should be just over blood heat. On an asbestos mat on a *very* low flame add the milk and oil alternately to the cod. Keep the cod on one side of the pan, pour the liquids onto the other side a teaspoon at a time and draw them gradually into the mixture, mixing well with your wooden spoon. Add the mashed potato, stir it in then add the eggs and cook on, stirring as you would for scrambled eggs, until you have a purée the consistency of very creamy mashed potato. Meanwhile, cut the bread into triangular sippets and fry them. At the last minute stir the parsley into the cod and serve with the fried bread.

For 6–8

Salt Cod with Haricots

1 lb salt cod
8 oz haricot beans
2 tablespoons butter
2 tablespoons olive oil
2 onions
4 crushed cloves garlic
bouquet of thyme, bay leaf, parsley
pepper, salt if necessary
4 pieces fried bread

Soak and cook the cod as previously described. Soak and cook the haricots with no salt in case the cod is salty. Keep the water they are cooked in. Remove the bones from the cod and cut it into small pieces. Heat the oil and butter in a sauté pan, add the onions, finely chopped, and the garlic and soften them without browning. Now add half a pint of the water in which the beans were cooked. Crush several spoonfuls of beans with a fork or sieve them and use them to thicken the sauce. Add the herbs and pepper (no salt yet). Throw in the cod and the rest of the cooked haricots, simmer for 15 minutes, adding more liquid from the beans if necessary, and taste for seasoning. Serve on croûtons and sprinkle with chopped parsley.

For 4–6

Salt Cod with Tomatoes

1 lb cooked salt cod, skinned and boned
1 medium onion, peeled and sliced
¾ lb tomatoes, peeled and chopped
2 cloves garlic, chopped
4 oz black olives, stoned if possible
olive oil, salt, pepper

Flake the fish. Put it in an oiled shallow oven-proof dish. In another pan, cook the onion till soft in oil, add the tomatoes and garlic and cook until almost a purée. Season and pour over the fish and heat it through in the oven, or under the grill. Dot with black olives and serve with good fresh crusty bread.

☐ *More for grown-ups than for children, this is a very good lunch or supper dish, the black olives are the making of it, so don't be tempted to leave them out.*

For 4

Devilled Herrings

1 herring for each person
1 teaspoon Dijon mustard for each herring
dried breadcrumbs
olive oil
salt

Fillet the herrings and (if you can bear it) skin them so each one makes 2 skinless pieces. Spread mustard over one side, sprinkle with breadcrumbs and salt and then sprinkle with olive oil. Turn fillets over and do the same to the other side. Grill for about 4–5 minutes on each side and serve very hot, with mashed potato.

How to Skin a Fillet of Fish

Use a sharp, medium-sized, rather inflexible knife. Lay the fillet skinside down and hold the tail end. Starting from the tail end, with the knife blade flat, pull the skin while you cut the fish away.

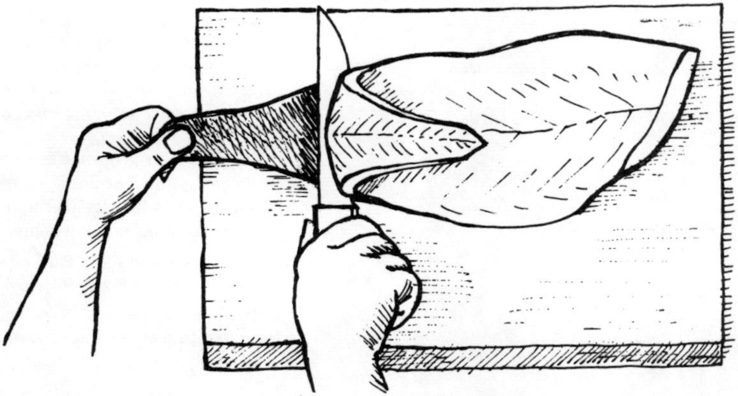

Pickled Herrings

12 fresh herrings
2 pints water
4 oz coarse or block salt
1½–2 pints distilled vinegar
1–2 tablespoons pickling spice
1 onion, sliced lengthwise
2 bay leaves
2 chillis
allspice, cloves, coriander, peppercorns, etc.

Cut the heads and tails off the herrings, and clean out the insides. Remove backbones (see diagram). Dissolve the salt in the water and soak the herring fillets in this brine for about 2 hours. During the soaking put the pickling spice into the vinegar, bring it slowly to the boil and leave it to cool. Drain the brine from the fish, and roll up the fillets, skin side out, wide end first, and secure with tooth picks. Slip a sliver of onion inside each roll. After you have rolled them, place in a suitable jar and strain the vinegar over them (it should cover them), add the bay leaves, chillis and spices, put a lid on.

Leave 10–14 days before eating. In a cool place they will keep for a month and more. Eat with sour cream, raw onion rings, brown bread and chopped apple.

☐ *A good standby for summer lunches.*

Makes 24 fillets

How to Fillet a Round Fish such as Haddock or Cod

Use a rather inflexible, not too pointed, sharp knife. Note: herring and mackerel are sold ungutted, so pull out their gut as you cut off the head. Also if you wish to stuff them, be careful not to cut along the stomach after stage 2.

1. Cut off the head to include collar bone and front fin.

2. Turn the fish on its side, insert the knife along the centre of the back, keeping the blade flat above the bones.

3. Keep your left hand flat on the fish while you detach the fillet from the bones with the knife. Don't cut through the stomach if you wish to stuff the fish (herring, sprats, mackerel).

4. If you are dividing the fish in two and not stuffing it, remove the first fillet completely, turn the fish over, and starting at the tail bring the knife towards you, along the fish rather than across it. Very slightly turn it up as you come to the central spine then flatten it again the other side.
(The fishmonger keeps his hand flat on the fish while doing this, but until you get good at it you might prefer to lift the fillet up as you go, so that you can see what you are doing.)

5. Remove second fillet, trim off fins and 'lug'. Use the head and bones for stock.

6. If you are stuffing the fish remove the backbone, starting at the tail as shown.

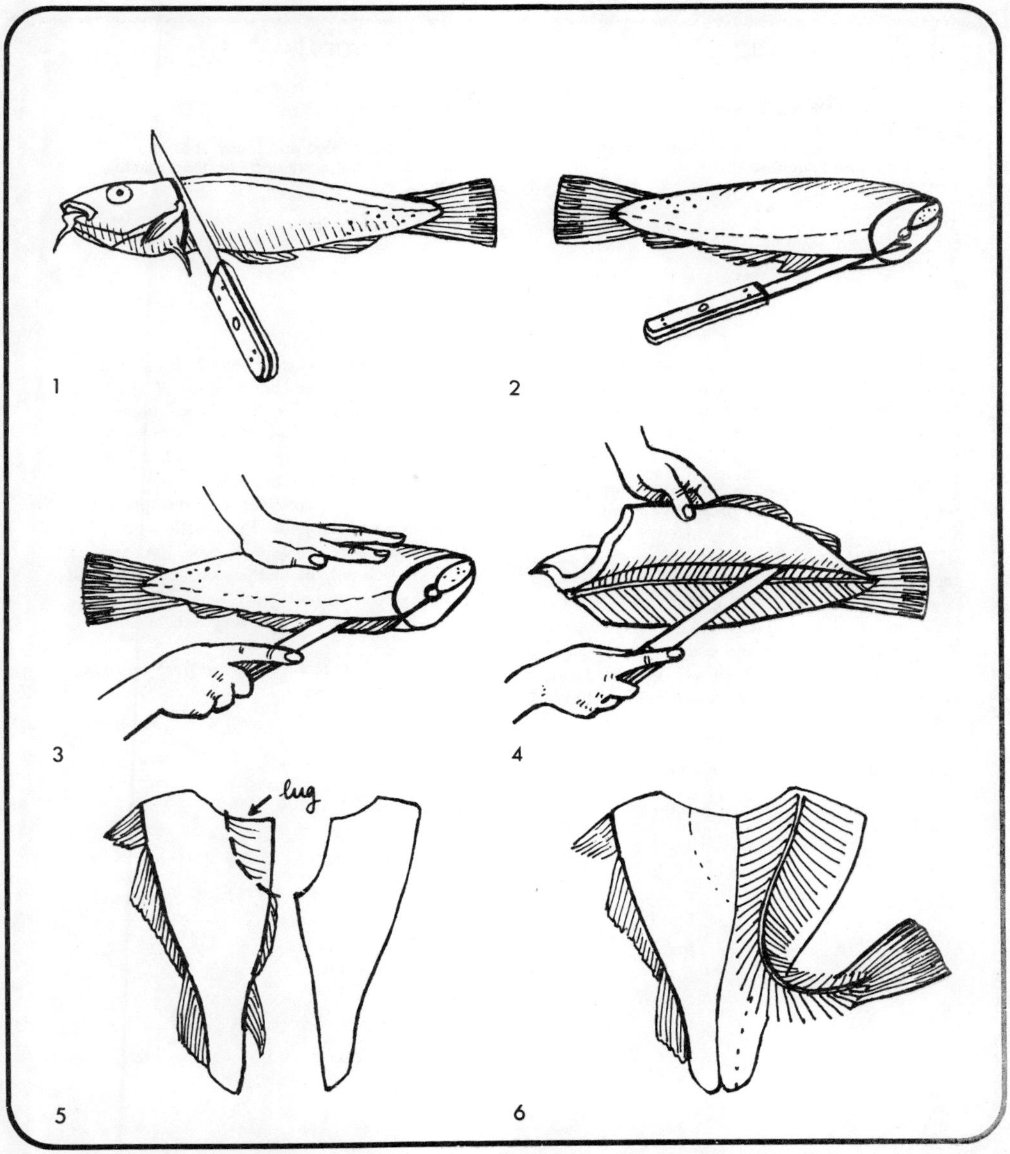
1
2
3
4
lug
5
6

Stuffed Herring

2 fine herrings with soft roes
a handful of parsley
1 slice white bread, crusts removed and soaked in water and squeezed dry
salt, pepper
½ oz butter
1 egg
2–3 tablespoons cream
1 teaspoon Dijon mustard

Clean and bone the herrings keeping them joined at the belly, like kippers (see page 53) and putting the roes on one side. Chop the parsley and crumble the bread, crusts removed. Chop bread, parsley and roes together.

Preheat the oven to Reg 4/350°. Melt half the butter in a small pan and break an egg into it, stirring it gently. Add the roe mixture, season and stir until the mixture is soft and creamy and holds together like scrambled egg. Remove it from the heat and stuff the fish with it. Bake them with a little more butter for half an hour in the oven. Remove them to a dish and pour a little cream into the butter in which they were cooked. Heat, add the mustard and pour this sauce over the fish and serve.

☐ *The stuffing rises like a quenelle mixture.*

For 2

Stuffed Sprats

1½ lbs fresh sprats
3 oz breadcrumbs
1 large onion, peeled and finely chopped
fresh or dried marjoram and chopped parsley
1 egg
salt, pepper
flour, fat or oil for frying

Choose large sprats as they have to be filleted, and small ones are very fiddly. Chop off the heads, split the fish and remove the tails and bones (see page 53). Mix the onion, breadcrumbs, marjoram, beaten egg, parsley and seasoning, adding a little milk if necessary, but the mixture must not be too wet. Lay the sprats out flat in matching pairs. Put a little stuffing between each pair of fish, as if making a sandwich, skin side out. Flour them on both sides and fry until golden on both sides. Serve with lemon wedges. They stay together very well.

☐ *You can also do this with filleted fresh sardines, small whiting, or herring.*

For 4

Soft Herring Roes

½ lb soft roes
1 beaten egg
fine dried white breadcrumbs
oil for frying (or butter)
salt

You need large whole roes for this.

Separate the roes and dry them a little. Beat the egg and dip the roes into it. Roll in breadcrumbs and deep fry until nicely browned. Sprinkle with salt and serve with tomato sauce (page 184), or simply roll them in seasoned flour and fry in 1–2 oz of foaming butter. Eat them on toast.

For 2

Breton Mackerel

4 mackerel

Court-bouillon
4 pints water
salt
¼ pint vinegar
a bunch of parsley
3 bay leaves
1 onion
1 carrot
6 peppercorns

Boil the ingredients for the court bouillon together for 10 minutes. Let it cool, add the cleaned mackerel. Poach them gently for 15–20 minutes. Remove them from the liquid and skin them carefully. When cold remove the fillets from the bones. Arrange on a dish and pour over them a Breton Sauce (page 171).

☐*These poached mackerel would also be delicious with a Salsa Verde (page 174).*

For 4

How to Fillet a Flat Fish

Use a sharp-bladed inflexible knife.

1. Cut the head off. Note the position of the hand and the direction of the cut, which leaves all the fish and takes away only the bony head.

2. Turn the fish over to the white side, insert the knife as shown. The knife is above the bone.

3. Slide the knife outwards and towards the tail taking care to leave the fins behind.

4. Work across the other side of the spine, using short cutting strokes, until the first fillet is freed.

5. Turn the fish over again, and score through the edge of the skin, starting at the tail end and leaving the fins attached to the bones.

6. Insert the blade at the tail end and cut the second fillet from the bone, working over the spine and across to the other side, again being careful to leave the fins attached to the bones.

7. You now have 2 fine fillets. Leave the skin on.

N.B. Sole have very little flesh along the spine, so it is easier to make 4 fillets, dividing each side along the spine. It is necessary to skin sole.

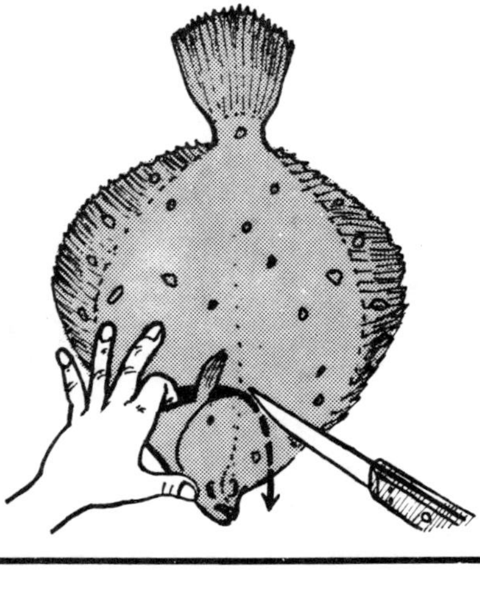

1

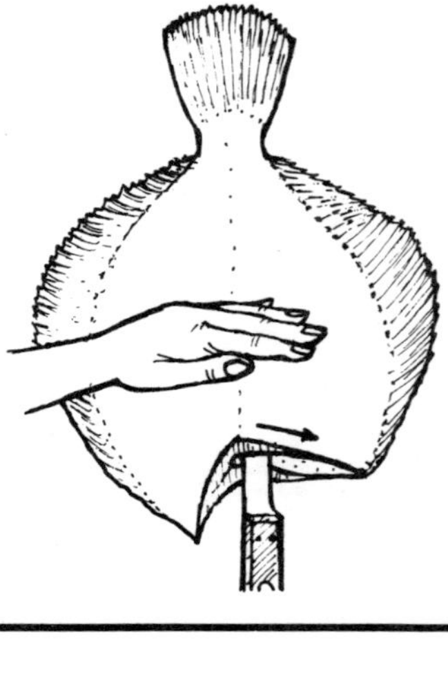

2

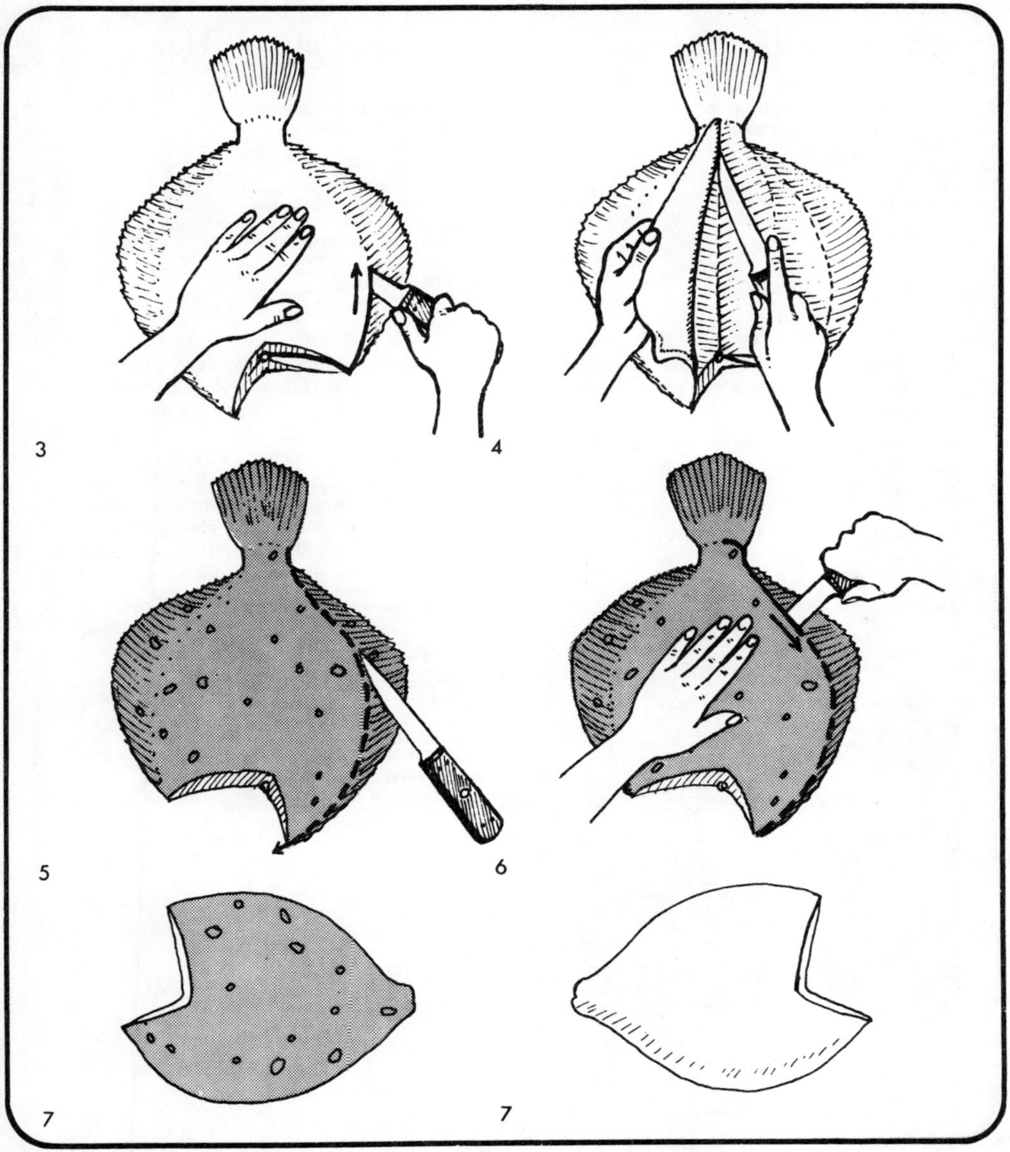
3
4
5
6
7
7

False Whitebait

4 large fillets whiting, or lemon sole
salt, pepper (white if possible)
flour
deep fat or oil for frying
parsley
lemon wedges

Leave the skin on the fillets and cut them into strips about the size of a large whitebait (about 2½ inches long).

Toss them in seasoned flour and fry them in very hot fat or oil until golden and crisp. Serve with fried parsley, and lemon wedges.

☐ *They are just as delicious as whitebait and have no bones.*

For 4 as a first course

Fish and Chips at Home

1 thick piece of fish per person
1 potato per person
1 egg, milk
3 tablespoons flour
½ teaspoon salt
2 tablespoons breadcrumbs
flour, salt
lemon juice, lemon slices
parsley
corn oil for frying

First make the batter. Mix the flour, salt and breadcrumbs. Beat the egg, add a little milk, stir into the flour mixture, beat well, let it stand half an hour. It should be thick. Skin the fish (see diagram on p. 51), season it with salt and pepper and lemon juice, dip fish into the flour, then into the batter and fry it to a nice golden colour when the fat is smoking blue (don't use a basket, the batter will stick to it). Keep fish warm on a dish with kitchen paper.

Peel the potatoes, cut into chips, wash them very well and dry them before frying, with a basket, in another lot of hot fat.

Keep them warm, and sprinkle with salt, like the fish. Serve with lemon wedges and parsley.

☐ *You should choose fillets of cod, coley, haddock, plaice or rock salmon.*

Fish and Chips (Another version)

2 egg yolks
$3\frac{1}{2}$ oz flour
$\frac{1}{2}$ teaspoon salt
2 tablespoons olive or arachide oil
warm water
1 egg white

Mix egg yolks, salt and flour carefully, add the oil slowly. Beat smooth, adding enough lukewarm water to make the batter like a thick sauce. Beat 10 minutes, leave in a warmish place for 2 hours (covered with a cloth). Just before using whip the white of egg and fold it into batter. Flour, salt, and pepper the pieces of fish. Dip into the batter then at once into hot deep fat. Don't use a basket or the batter will stick to the wires. Fry till crisp and golden.

☐ *Anyway, cheaper at home than going out.*

Fish Croquettes

1 lb firm fish — whiting or coley is ideal
2 oz rice, 1 oz butter
1 oz flour, salt, pepper
pinch curry powder
1 egg, dry breadcrumbs
oil for frying

For the court-bouillon
1 pint water, salt, pepper
1 onion, bay leaf
parsley
dash of cider or white wine

If you are using whiting ask the fishmonger to skin and fillet it, and give you the skin, bones and head. If he has no time, follow the directions on page 53. If using coley, buy fillet and use the skin to make the stock. Make a pint of court-bouillon with the fish trimmings, simmering them for 20 minutes with the other ingredients. Strain the liquid and poach the fish in it. When it is cooked, remove the fish and cook the rice in a little of the same liquid, reserving the rest for the sauce. Allow both to cool, while you make a thickish sauce with the butter, flour and $\frac{1}{4}$ pint of court-bouillon. Season it and flavour with the curry powder. Mix the rice, fish and sauce together and spread on a plate to cool and set (20 minutes in the ice-compartment of the refrigerator will do it). Form the mixture into cork-shaped croquettes with floured hands and leave again to get really cold. If you have time it is best to leave them overnight.

Finally, dip the croquettes first in beaten egg and then in breadcrumbs and fry in deep oil or fat until golden. Drain on kitchen paper and serve with Curry Sauce (page 174), Chilli Mayonnaise (page 171) or lemon wedges.

For 6 as a first course or 3–4 as a main course.

Fish Mousse

1 lb smoked haddock on the bone
2 eggs
½ pint milk, and ½ pint water
1 small onion
1 small carrot
1 bay leaf
½ oz butter, ½ oz flour
½ oz gelatine
¼ pint cream
a handful of parsley
salt, pepper

Hard-boil one of the eggs. Poach the haddock until tender in the milk and water (about 10–15 minutes). Save the liquid. Flake the fish and put the skin and bones back into the pan with the onion, carrot and bay leaf. Simmer, covered, for about 20 minutes. Make a roux with the butter and flour and slowly add about ¾ pint of the fish liquid, to make a Béchamel, add more milk if necessary and taste for seasoning. Separate the raw egg and stir the yolk into the sauce. Add the fish and some parsley and pound or liquidise. Add the cream (if it is thick enough, whip it first). Dissolve the gelatine in about 3–4 tablespoons of water over gentle heat, and add it to the fish mixture. Set aside to cool, and as it begins to set whip the egg white very stiff and fold it in to the mixture. Slice the hard-boiled egg and lay it in a pattern at the bottom of a wetted soufflé dish. Pour over the mousse mixture and leave it to set. Turn it out just before eating and serve with salad.

☐*Good weekend food.*

For 8

Hake or Haddock Patties

1½ lbs baby hakes (filleted) or fresh haddock fillet
1 large slice bread (a doorstep, crusts removed, soaked in ¼ cup water)
1 onion, grated
1 egg, beaten
pepper, salt
½ teaspoon sugar
Flour, oil

Skin the fish and cut it into small pieces, then, using a large board, and long sharp knife, chop it finely for 5 minutes. When it is soft and fine add the egg, grated onion, salt, pepper and sugar, and the soaked bread crumbled finely. Continue to chop for another few minutes so that it is of a well-mixed soft consistency adding water if necessary. Shape into flat round patties (a tablespoon is helpful for this) and flour them. Fry them gently in shallow oil until golden brown both sides. Serve with chips, and tomato sauce (page 184).

☐ *These make a change from fishcakes made with potato.*

For 4 (makes 12 patties)

Matelote Normande

2–3 lbs fish — hake, haddock or whiting (whole fish if possible)
2–3 quarts mussels
2 sticks celery
3–4 onions
4 oz butter
chopped parsley
juice of ½ lemon
2–3 teaspoons flour
salt, pepper

Keep the fish whole. Clean the fish but leave the skin on and, in the case of a whole fish, the head and tail. Clean the mussels. Chop the celery and the onions separately. Melt 1 oz of the butter in a large saucepan. Soften the celery, add a glass of water and bring to the boil. Throw in the mussels. When they are open remove them from the liquid and keep it on one side.

Meanwhile soften the onions in another ounce of butter for 20–30 minutes, with some chopped parsley.

Leaving the celery out, put the onions and the strained mussel liquid into a fireproof dish or pan, which will just hold the fish. Lay the fish in it, stomach up, and add water if necessary, to come halfway up its sides. Taste for salt — the mussel liquid may provide enough — add pepper and cook gently, basting frequently, until the fish is just done. Two minutes before serving, add the remaining butter into which you have worked the flour and more chopped parsley. Add the lemon juice, and the mussels from their shells. Allow to come to the boil and cook until thickened. This should be done quickly. The fish is served in its soup straight from the dish it is cooked in and sprinkled perhaps with more parsley. You can add a few shrimps with the mussels if you like.

☐ *This is a main course and could be served simply with bread and a green salad.*

For 6

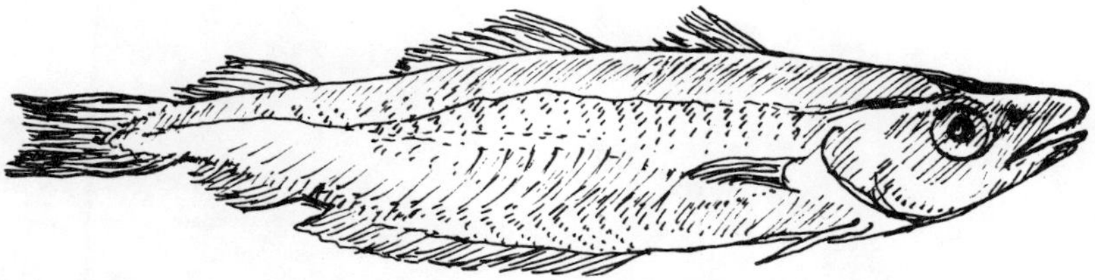

Spanish Fish Stew

1½ lbs of hard white fish with skin and bone on
1½ lbs potatoes
1 onion, salt
a sprig of parsley
4 tablespoons oil
2 teaspoons pimenton (Spanish paprika) or ordinary paprika plus 1 teaspoon sugar
2 cloves garlic, peeled and sliced
2 tablespoons vinegar

Peel the potatoes and cut them into halves. Pack them in a saucepan with the onion, parsley, salt and barely enough water to cover. Boil them until they are within 5 minutes of being done. Cut the fish into chunks with the skin and bone still on. Press the pieces in among the potatoes and cook for 5 minutes covered, by which time the fish should be done. Put the fish and potatoes on to a hot dish and reduce their cooking liquid a little. In another pan fry the sliced garlic till golden in a little oil, add the pimenton and then the vinegar. Let it sizzle, then quickly add the fish-potato liquid. Mix well, pour over the fish and potatoes as a sauce and serve. Rock eel conger or whiting can be used for this recipe. Good proportions would be 1 whiting to ½ lb rock eel and ½ lb conger or haddock.

For 4

Smoked Fish Pie

1½ lbs smoked golden fillet of haddock or cod
½–¾ pint milk
2 Spanish onions
2 oz butter
1 lb potatoes
1 oz flour
a handful of dried breadcrumbs
1 oz grated cheese (Cheddar)
freshly ground black pepper

Poach the fish in the milk until tender (5–10 minutes). Remove it and flake the fish, removing the skin and bones. Soften the onions in half the butter. Peel the potatoes and boil them in salted water until *just* tender. Drain, keeping some of the liquid. Cut them into small cubes. Remove the onions and add the remaining butter to the butter in which they were cooked. Melt over a low heat. Stir in the flour and make a smooth sauce with the milk in which the fish was cooked. Add plenty of pepper. (You will not need salt unless the fish has a particularly mild cure). If it is too thick add some of the water in which the potatoes were cooked.

Pre-heat the oven to Reg 5/375°. Butter a pie dish, mix the onions, potatoes and fish and put them in, pour the sauce all over the top, sprinkle with crumbs and then with cheese, dot with butter and bake for 25 minutes until bubbling and brown on the top.

For 6

Smoked Haddock Salad

1 large smoked haddock on the bone
1 pt mixed milk and water
1 bay leaf
⅓ pt mayonnaise
3–4 hard-boiled eggs
black olives
a few prawns to decorate if possible
5 oz rice

Poach the haddock in the milk and water with a bay leaf until you can take the fish from the bones (about 5–10 minutes). Reserve the liquid (discarding the bay leaf) and put aside the flaked fish. Cook the rice until just done (do not over-cook). Make the mayonnaise and dilute it with some of the liquid from the fish until you have just over half a pint of creamy sauce. Mix this with the fish and rice. Add some chopped hard-boiled egg. Fork it into a pyramid and if you want to be grand add some prawns and black olives for decoration. Serve with green salad.

□ *This is a sort of kedgeree, but for hot weather. You could mix curry powder into the mayonnaise for a change. Very delicious.*

For 4

Tunny Fish Salad

6 oz dried haricots, soaked and cooked
8 oz tin tunny fish
3–4 tablespoons olive oil
1 large tablespoon wine vinegar
½ clove garlic, crushed
a few onion rings
chopped parsley
salt, plenty of pepper
optional
a handful of black olives
1 hard-boiled egg

Mix the cooked drained haricots with the tunny fish broken into chunks. Make a vinaigrette with the oil, vinegar, garlic, salt and pepper. Mix it into the salad. Strew the top with onion rings and chopped parsley. If your onions are too strong in flavour, soak the rings in milk for half an hour before adding them to the salad. You can add black olives or sliced hard-boiled eggs.

For 4

Portuguese Tunny Fish Salad

1 lb potatoes (or 1 lb cooked chick peas)
3 eggs
1 8 oz tin tunny fish
1 small cup black olives
salt, pepper
oil, vinegar, mustard

Hard-boil the eggs and boil the potatoes in their skins. Cool and peel the eggs and peel the potatoes. Chop them both roughly. Make a vinaigrette sauce with pepper, salt, olive oil, wine vinegar and dash of mustard, using one part oil to one part vinegar. Add the broken-up tunny fish and oil from its tin. Season, pile in a dish with the potatoes or chick peas and eggs and decorate with olives. Serve chilled.

☐ *A very good picnic lunch.*

For 3–4

Tarama (Smoked Cod's Roe)

½ lb smoked cod's roe
1 slice stale white bread
milk
½ cup olive oil
a crushed clove of garlic
juice of half a lemon
pepper

Scrape all the roe carefully away from the skin and put it in a bowl. Squeeze the bread in milk, then mash it into the cod's roe with a wooden spoon, together with the finely-crushed clove of garlic, a little lemon juice and fresh-ground black pepper. When it has amalgamated add the oil little by little, beating it in with your spoon until the roe begins to shine. Then give it a last pounding, and pack it into a pot. Serve it with slices of hot toast and butter.

For 6

Meat

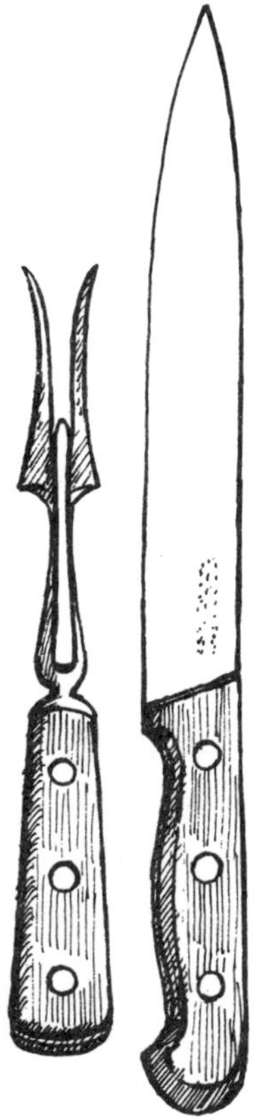

Meat

Meat is fiendishly expensive, but even so in this country we consume very great quantities of it. We buy and eat it rather wastefully in large lumps, and the reason for this is that good butchery is hard to find. If you go to a really good and careful butcher you will probably find he is also expensive, so the answer is to learn how to trim, bone and tie the meat yourself and also to carve it really expertly.

For both these operations you need extremely good sharp knives; the counsel of perfection is to get them reground every year or two — some ironmongers will do this or your butcher may be able to get it done for you: sharpen your knives every time you use them and use a separate set for carving which you use for nothing else. A chopper is also invaluable, it should be of a type that can be sharpened and it can be used for trimming bones on pork and lamb chops, for cutting up bones and carcases, and the flat side is useful for beating out escalopes and minute steaks. Keep a special ball of string for tying boned joints and get the butcher to show you how to make his special running knot (see the diagram on p. 85). Do your boning with a small strong-bladed knife which will also be useful for sneaking out sinews, and trimming cutlets and steaks. Well-trimmed meat goes much further and it makes a tremendous difference to young children's and most adults' appetites if the lamb chop on their plate is neat. Experts say that if you remove the sinews carefully from a rump steak it is twice as good as entrecôte and four times better than fillet. Cheap cuts of meat are cheap because they are fat, bony or tough, that is they come from the part of the animal that does the most work, and therefore they can be relied on to have masses of connective tissue which is the tough bit. But no matter how impenetrably tough a piece of meat may be, it can always be made tender by long, gentle cooking which gradually breaks down the tissue. Alternatively you can mince it finely; the meat can then be used for spaghetti sauce (but not hamburgers as the flavour only really develops with slow cooking).

Carving

All our information on carving comes from Mr Fred Knock of Simpson's in-the-Strand, who has been carving there for over fifty years. His demonstrations were revelations of just how much good carving matters. A skilful carver can get nine lavish servings of beautiful slices from a joint that a bad carver will hack up into enough tough chunks for four. He can give everyone their fair share of the best, with more fat or less, outside or tender pink underdone middle, according to what they like.

BASIC RULES FOR FINE CARVING

1. Have good knives; you will need two, which you should keep specially for carving and which are not to be used for cutting up dogs' meat or sharpening pencils; first a small poultry knife with a 6″ blade, which is used for cutting through joints and removing bones; second a carving knife with a 9″ blade for slicing. For sharpening them you will need a good long magnetic steel, and for holding the meat steady have a small carving fork with curved prongs and a shield to protect your hand if the knife slips. A board with spikes is a good idea as it stops the meat sliding about.

2. Keep your knives sharp and always either wrap them up in a soft cloth before putting them away or keep them on a magnetic knife rack.

3. Allow the meat to set after it is cooked. Let it stand in a warm place for 20 to 30 minutes for a small joint or bird, longer for large joints. This makes the texture firm and means that you can cut thinner slices. The perfect way to keep it warm is over hot water — special plates used to exist — with a loosely fitting cover. A tight cover causes the skin to lose its crispness. But if you just put it on a very hot dish on the table and leave it there until everybody has washed their hands and sat down it will lose almost no heat until it is carved. You can also leave it to stand in the cooling oven.

4. Put the meat in the correct position for carving — shown in the diagrams in this section. Professional carvers always keep the best-looking uncarved side toward the diners, so that they are appetised by the view of plump juicy meat rather than shown a row of bones.

6. Cut several slices before you begin to share out the meat, so that each person gets some of the best.

7. Stand boned and rolled joints on end and carve horizontally, otherwise you will blunt your knife on the dish.

8. Use very little pressure on the knife — if it is really sharp it should slice through the meat as you draw it backwards and forwards towards you, using the full length of the blade.

9. Hold the knife with your forefinger along the back of the blade, it gives you more control.

10. Take your time at first, you will speed up with practice.

How to carve a Wing Rib or Sirloin of Beef on the Bone

Use a sharp long-bladed knife and have ready your carving fork and a spoon for the juices.

1. Having got your butcher to chine the joint — which means sawing through the backbone about two thirds of the way down, but leaving it attached during cooking to keep the meat succulent and give it flavour — cut these chined bones away (a).

2. If there is a lot of fat trim it away at (b) and (c). Trim away gristle at (c). Run the knife carefully between the meat and the bone, keeping it completely flat against the bone, so you do not waste the meat.

3. Start carving at the wing (thick) end (d), cutting at right angles to the spine but at a slight angle, otherwise you are left with an upright piece too wobbly to slice (e).

4. Finish by carving the wedge you are left with (e) gradually flattening it out.

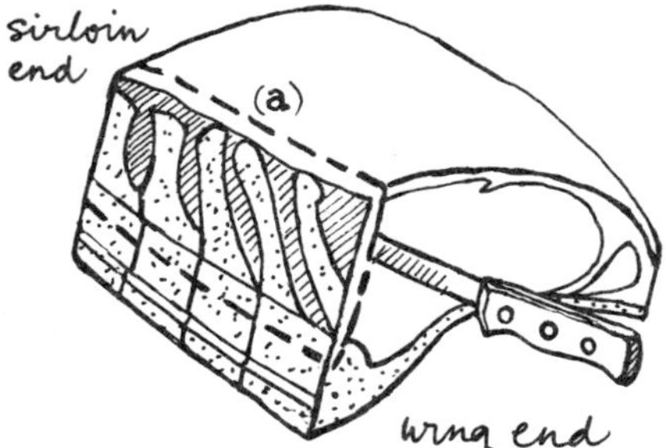

1

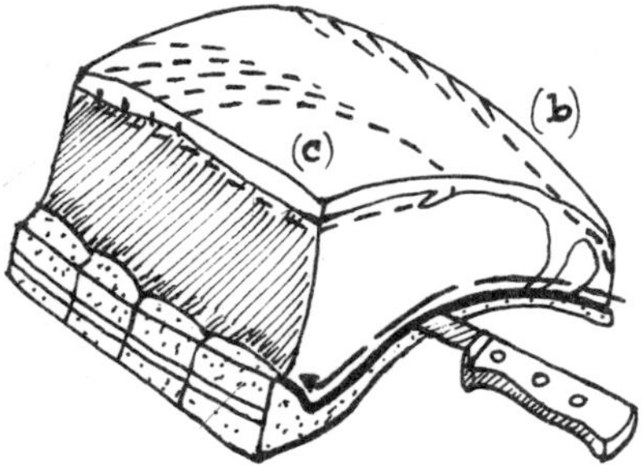

2

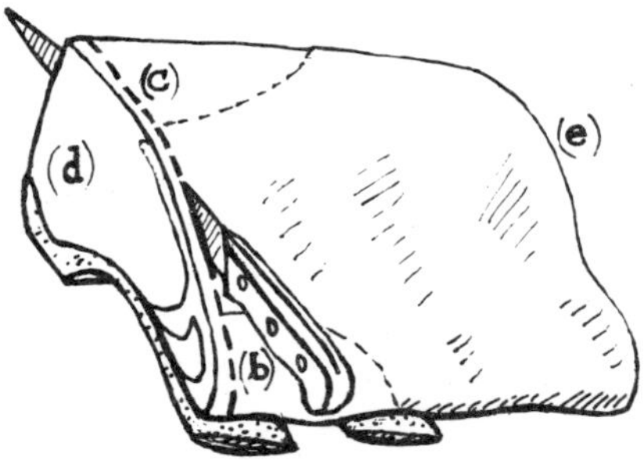

3

4

Roast Wing Rib of Beef or Wing End of Sirloin

12–14 lbs piece of wing rib of beef on the bone (4 ribs)
Salt, a little oil

Ask the butcher to chine the bone. Pre-heat the oven to Reg 8/450°. Rub the fat on the joint with salt and smear on a little oil. Put it to roast in the centre of the oven. After 15 minutes, reduce the heat to Reg 4/350° and, basting occasionally, roast it for 3 hours if you like the meat to be rare, 3½ hours if you like it more done. Leave it to stand in a warm place for at least half an hour before carving (see diagram opposite). Serve with horseradish sauce, gravy and English mustard.

☐ *This joint is half sirloin, half wing rib. It is rather expensive, but very good for a large party. Cooking it on the bone greatly improves the juiciness and flavour.*

For 10–15

Flat Rib of Beef with Runner Beans

4 lbs middle, top or flat ribs (not wing or forerib)
2 lbs of runner beans (or bobby beans)
1 onion
1 tablespoon tomato purée
salt, pepper
nutmeg

Ask the butcher to leave the bones in the beef and slice off the surplus fat which you will need. Tie the joint round with string. Preheat the oven to Reg 3/325°. Cut the fat into small pieces, put it in a frying pan and render it down, with a lid on, over a low heat, while you slice the beans and chop the onion finely. Brown the meat all over in the melted fat. As soon as the meat is browned put it in a covered casserole in the oven and start cooking, while you continue with the vegetables. Fry the onions until golden in the same fat as the beef. Bring some salted water to the boil and blanch the beans. Let them boil 2–3 minutes and drain, keeping ¼ pint of their liquid. Turn the beans into the pan with the onions and fry them gently until they have absorbed some of the fat. Stir the purée into the water which you have kept from the beans, and add it to the beans and onions. Season well with salt, pepper and nutmeg. Take the casserole out of the oven, put the meat on a plate. Pour the contents of the frying pan into the casserole and put the meat back on top of the vegetables, on its side. Cover again and cook (still at Reg 3/325°) for 2½–3 hours. Turn the meat over half way through. At the end it should have a roasted appearance and be tender, with a lot of gravy and some delicious beans. To serve, cut the bones off the joint first, then carve in neat horizontal slices. Remove the surplus fat from the gravy and strain into a jug, serve with the meat and beans.
For 6

How to Carve a whole Leg of Lamb or Pork

Sharpen your long-bladed carving knife, have ready your carving fork and a spoon for the juices.

1. Put the joint with the rounded meatier side (outside) uppermost. Shading indicates the bone.

2. Remove the shank bone (a) with a small knife if the butcher has not already done so. Using your fork to steady the joint, start slicing away from the knuckle (b). Make thin even slices and alternate them with closer-grained vertical slices from the front of the leg at (c).

3. When the 'eye' appears (a small oval disc of fat in the middle of all the lean) (d) turn the joint over.

4. Take off nice big flat slices from this new side (e) keeping the joint steady with your fork. Continue to carve slices from these three surfaces by turns until you reach the bone. Don't start serving until you have some of the meat from all three sides.

N.B. Carving the meat from a V-shaped cut in the middle is the most wasteful method of dealing with a leg of lamb.

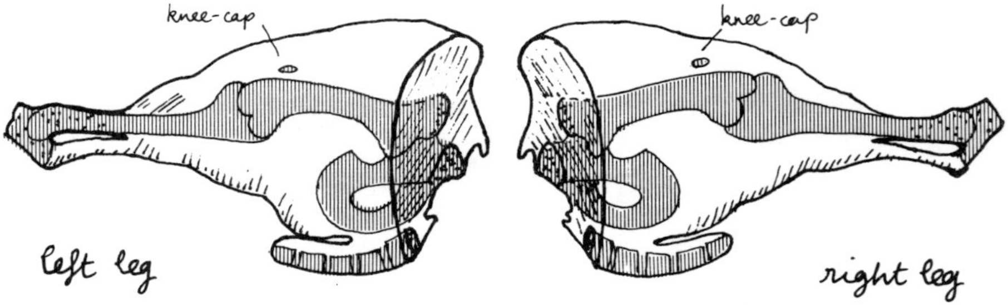

1

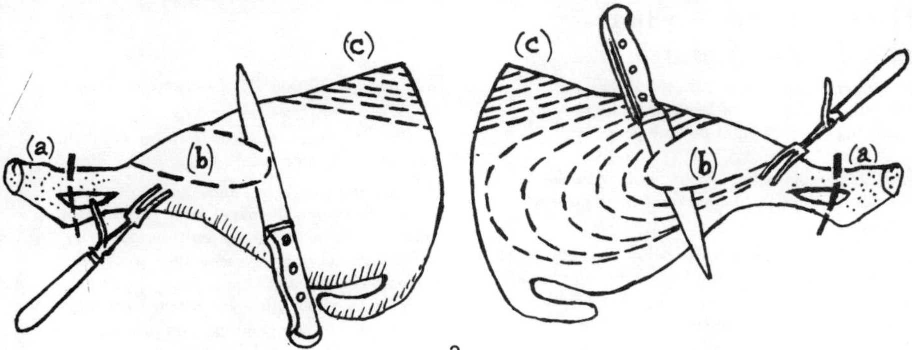

2

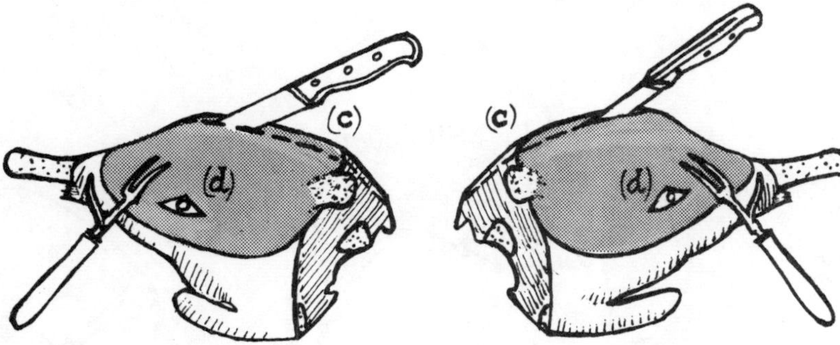

3

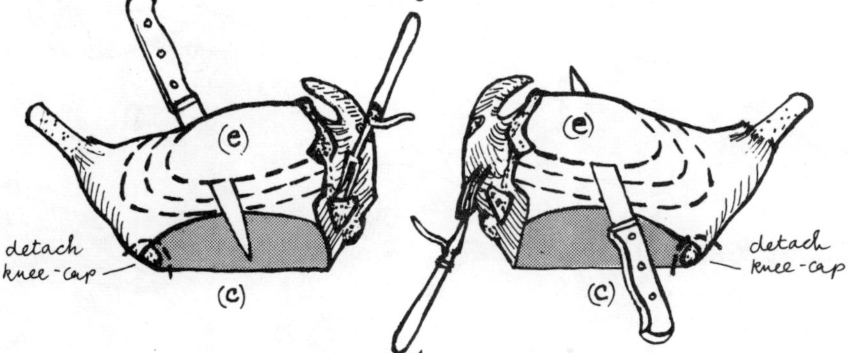

4

How to Carve a whole Shoulder of Lamb

The astonishing fact is that, if you carve it correctly, a shoulder of lamb provides enough good slices to feed eight or nine people.

1. Place the shoulder, left or right, with the knuckle to the left (shaded lines show position of bones).

2. Carve vertical slices from behind the elbow (a) parallel to the edge of the blade-bone and working towards it. Raise the joint off the plate with the fork or you will blunt your knife on the plate. Carve more vertical slices from the front of the blade-bone (b). These will be fattish slices, so find out who likes a bit of fat and give these slices to them.

3. Cut a few vertical slices from (c). Hold the knuckle with your hand to steady the joint.

4. Turn the joint over, and, starting halfway across the underside, carve large thin horizontal slices. This is a very good and juicy part, so don't start serving the meat until you have reached this point. There is plenty of meat under here: when you have reached the bone take a few horizontal slices from (d), the underside of the first leg-bone.

Left Shoulder

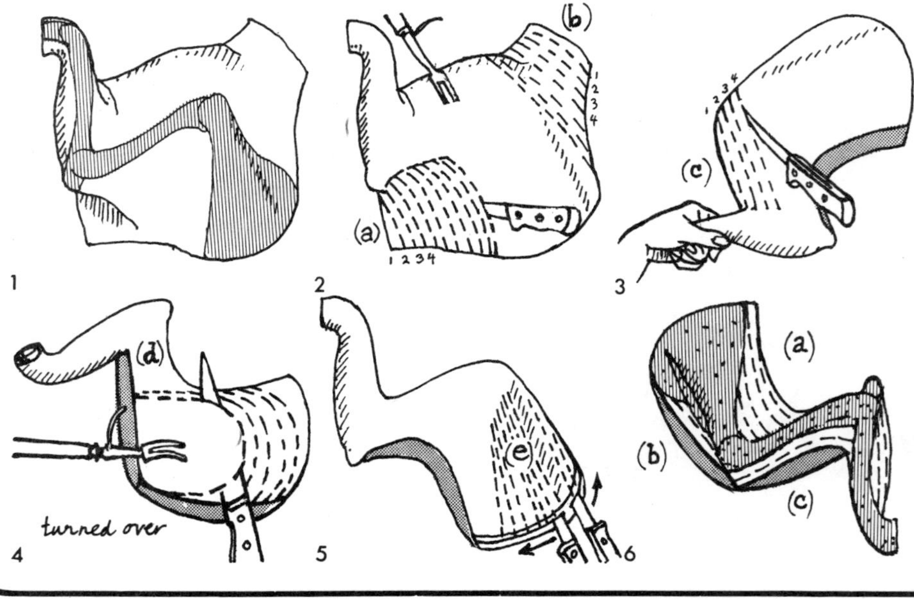

5. Turn the shoulder over again and insert the knife horizontally between the bone and the meat and slide it from the side of the vertical ridge in the middle of the shoulder-blade to the edge of the joint. This loosens the meat and enables you to carve nice vertical slices parallel to the ridge (e).

6. Finish by carving a few more vertical slices at (a), (b) and (c).

You will be left with nothing much but bones.

To roast a shoulder, follow the same general method as for Leg of Lamb (page 85).

Right Shoulder

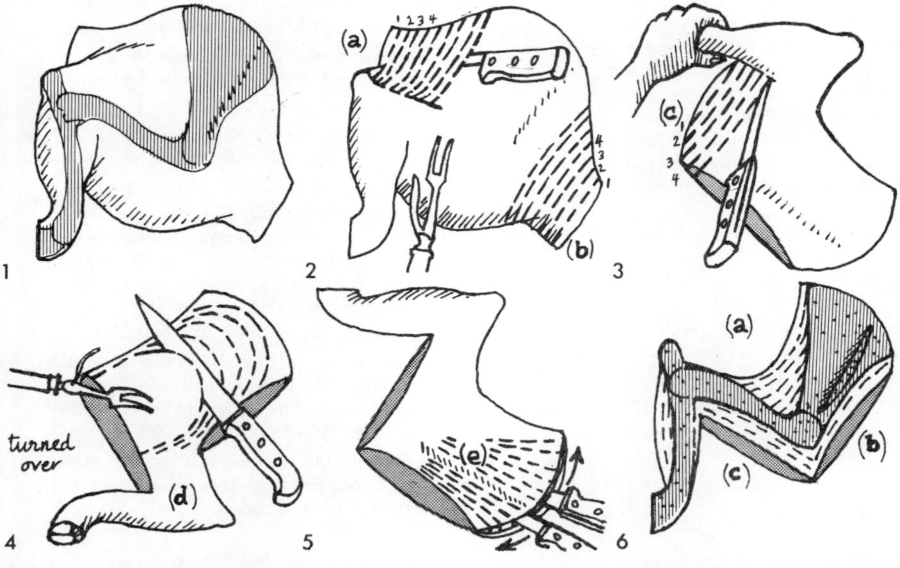

Roast Saddle of Lamb

5½–6 lbs saddle of lamb
salt, oil

Preheat the oven to Reg 5/375°. If the butcher has stuck the kidneys to the tail end of the saddle, remove them. He may also have scored the fat (having skinned it) in a pretty herring-bone pattern, but if he has tied the fatty side pieces together underneath the joint undo the string and lay the whole thing flat so that the sides get well cooked and it is easier to carve. Rub the top with salt and oil, stand the joint on a rack and roast it for 1 hour at Reg 5/375°, basting occasionally, then reduce the heat to Reg 4/350° for 20–30 minutes if you like it well done and less if you like it pink. Leave it to stand in a warm place for half an hour before carving according to the diagram opposite. Cook the kidneys, whole, with the meat for the last 20 minutes, or save them for breakfast (it is quite difficult to share two kidneys among ten people).

☐ *This is a small saddle.*

For 10–11

How to Carve a Saddle of Lamb or Mutton

A saddle is not an economical joint, it just looks very magnificent and tastes extremely delicious. To an inexperienced carver it is a complete puzzle, practically all bone with some long thin pockets of meat, and a lot of waste. If you just cut all the middle out you may find you don't have enough to go round, but with skilful carving you should be able to feed 8 to 10 people. Carve with the tail end to the left and the skin side up, and cut quite a few slices before you start handing it round.

1. The first cut is very important. Make it parallel to and at least 1″ from the backbone (a) to (b).

2. Cut slices to make a wedge shape at (a) and (b) as shown. Cut a few little slices (c), for those who like fat.

3. Continue to cut fairly thick slices as shown, turning the dish if necessary, long slices from the loin end and short slices from the chump or tail end. The projecting haunch bone (d) will gradually be uncovered.

4. Turn the joint over, still working on the same half, and carve long thin slices from the fillet (e) to (f). This is the best part and should go to favoured guests. There are some small chunks of well-done meat to be found at (g).

5. Finish one side before you start carving the other. A good carver makes a clean job of it and leaves very little but bones.

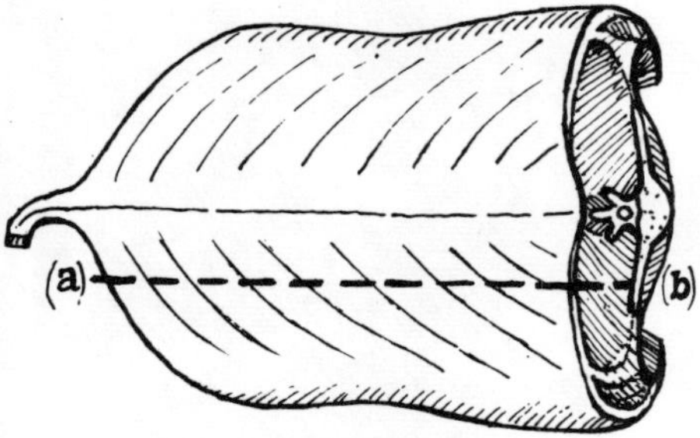

1

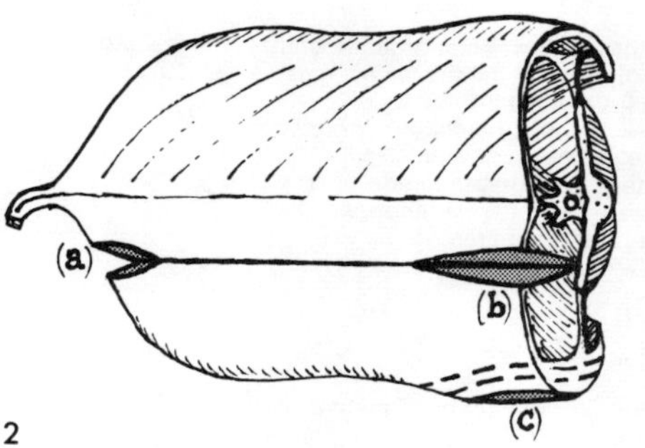

2

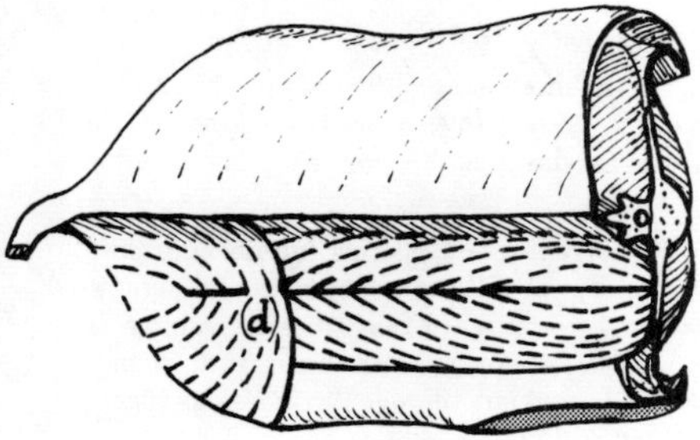

3

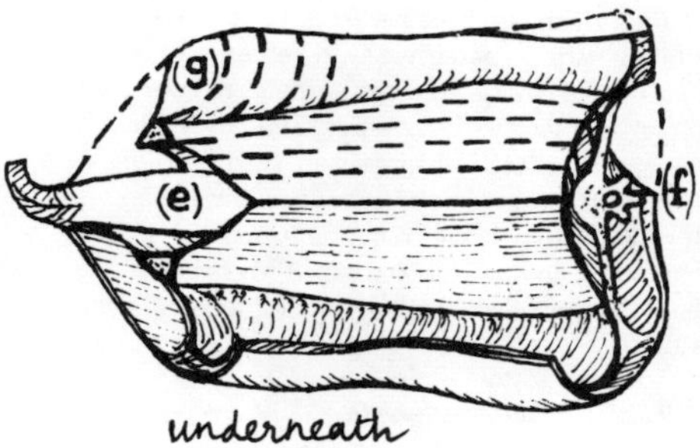

4

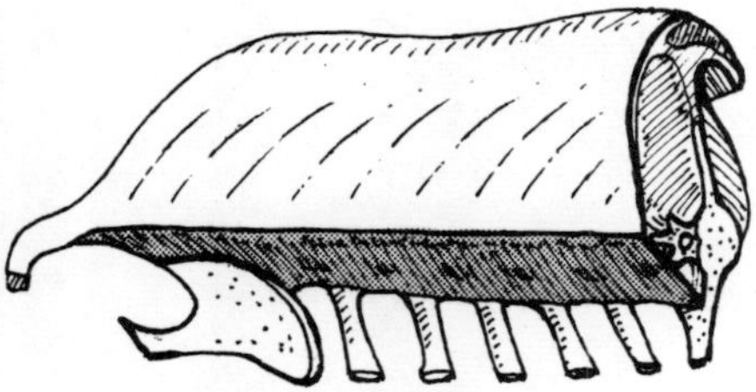

5

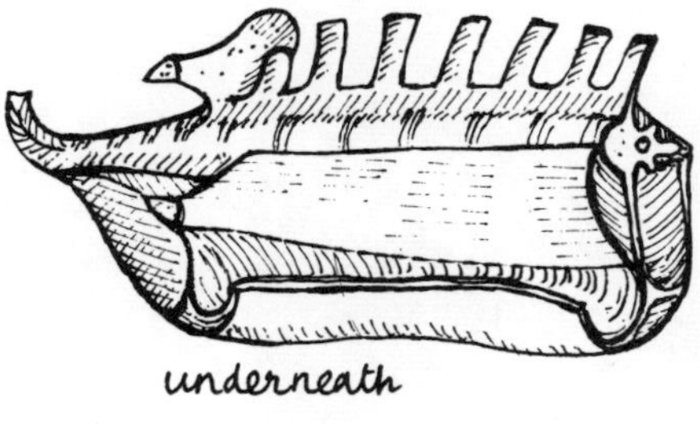

5

Guard of Honour

A pair of best ends of lamb, chined (consisting of about 8 cutlets each)
4–6 oz breadcrumbs
1–2 shallots, peeled and chopped
1 egg beaten in a little milk
½ teaspoon grated lemon peel
parsley and thyme, chopped
salt and pepper

Make up the guard of honour as shown. Chop or mince the trimmings, having removed some of the fat. Mix them with the breadcrumbs, herbs, seasoning, lemon peel and enough egg and milk to bind them. Preheat the oven to Reg 5/375°. Put the two prepared pieces together as shown and fill the cavity with the stuffing. Skewer the pieces together with 2 skewers and cover the bones with silver foil to prevent them burning. Rub a little oil over the outside of the lamb, sprinkle with salt and roast for 1 hour, or if it is stuffed 1½ hours. To serve cut down between the bones and give each person two cutlets and some stuffing.

☐ *This is equally good made with or without stuffing, and served plain or with red currant jelly.*

For 8

To Make a Guard of Honour

1. Take a pair of best ends of lamb, each consisting of 6–8 chops. Tell the butcher what you want them for, so that he can trim the bones, but don't let him separate them.

2. Skin them, if necessary.

3. On the inside score a line across the ribs about 2½″ down. Cut the meat out between the ribs as far down as this line. Keep the trimmings for stuffing or gravy-making.

4. Fit the two sides together interlocking the ribs as shown. Fill the cavity with stuffing if you like, or serve it, when roasted, with watercress in the cavity. Cover the rib bones with silver foil while cooking. Skewer the two sides together if using stuffing.

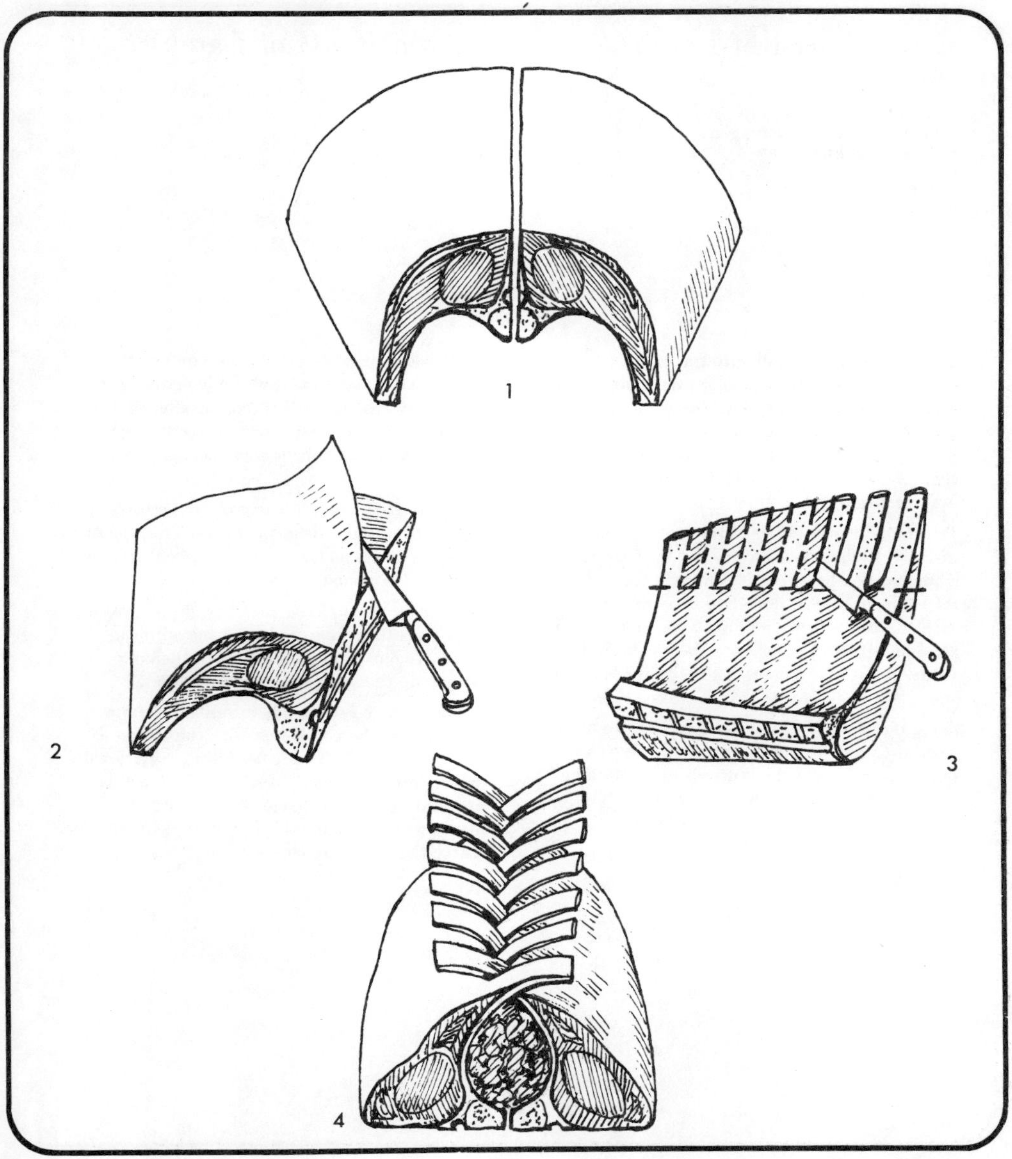
1
2
3
4

Crown Roast of Lamb (Stuffed)

Two best ends of lamb (a pair)
1 onion, peeled and chopped
thick slice of brown bread
marjoram
salt, pepper
1 egg, beaten
the trimmings from the lamb

Make the crown according to the diagrams (opposite). Keep the trimmings, removing all fat, then mincing the meat. Soak the bread in water, squeeze it dry, crumble it and add it to the minced meat, with the finely chopped onion, egg, marjoram, salt and pepper. Preheat the oven to Reg 5/375°.

Traditionally, the centre of the crown is filled with the stuffing, using a piece of fat from the trimming as a base, but if you prefer the fat on the chops to be well done, use the stuffing as a cushion for the crown and put a loosely crumbled piece of foil into the hollow to help it keep its shape. Roast for 1½ hours if the stuffing is inside, less if it is underneath.

Serve the crown on its cushion, the centre filled with watercress or green peas and perhaps a few button onions, or if the centre is full of stuffing serve the vegetables or watercress separately.

For 3–4

Crown Roast of Lamb

1. Choose a pair of best ends of lamb, with 6–8 chops in each side. English is better for this than New Zealand as it is more flexible. Tell the butcher what you want them for and he will trim them, but if time is short here is how to do it yourself.

2. Take off the skin if necessary and score a line 2″ from the ends of the bones. Trim the meat from the bones as far as this line (see diagrams for guard of honour, page 77).

3. Using a strong knife cut through the gristle that joins the chops. A sharp bang with the palm of your hand on the back of the knife should do the trick, or use a mallet (3a).

4. Bend the meat fat side inwards to form a crown. Join the two halves with thin string as shown, using a hefty needle. Fill the cavity with loosely crumpled piece of silver foil. Roast as for guard of honour (page 76), covering the bones with pieces of foil to prevent them burning. Carve the meat into chops.

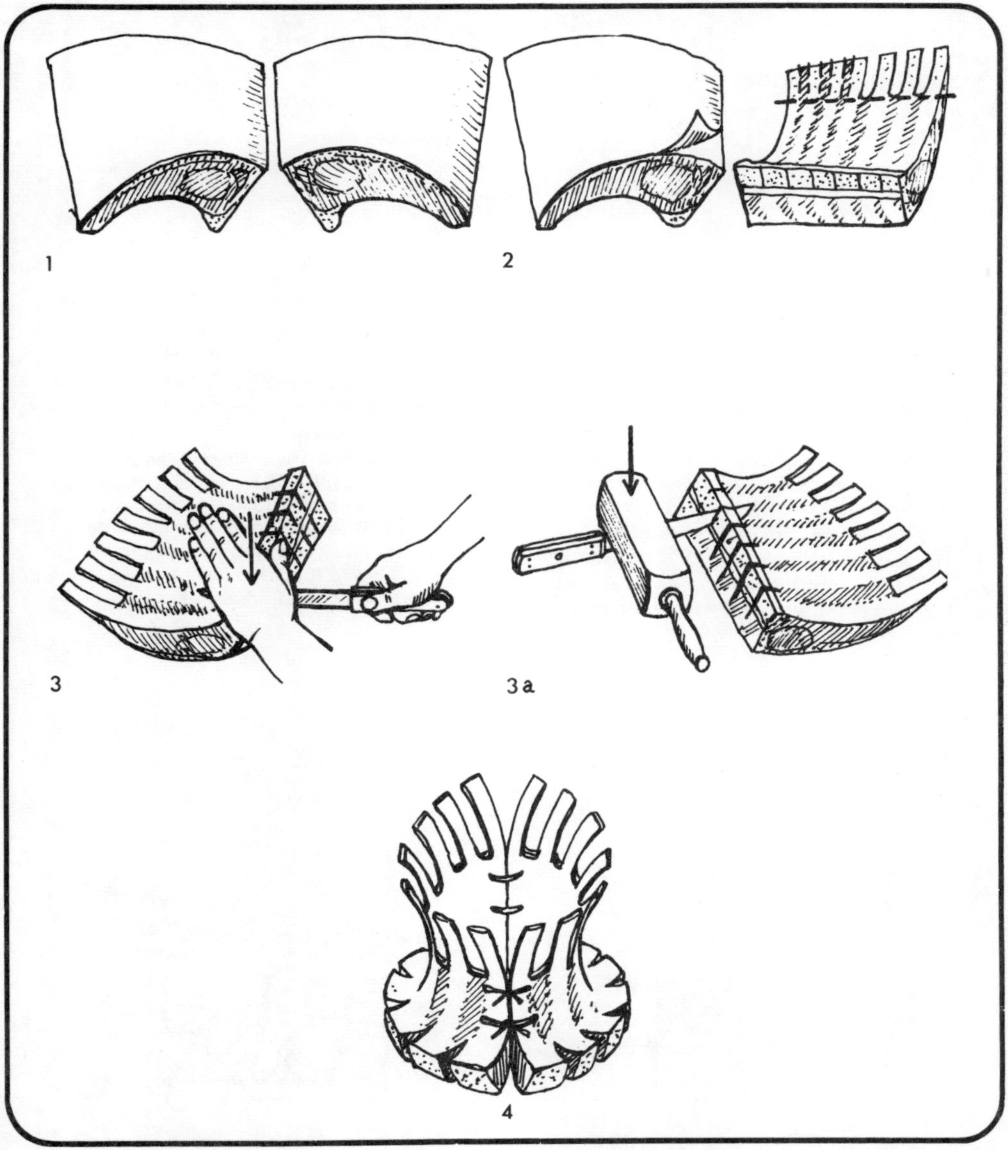
1
2
3
3a
4

How to Carve a Loin of Lamb, Pork or Veal

1. Have ready your short-bladed knife. The butcher may have wanted to chine the joint, but it is easier if he has just separated each chop where they are joined by gristle along the back.

2. Turn the joint upside down and carve it into chops by slicing between the bones and through the kidney, if it is still attached. You will have a little triangular chop at the chump end.

This is one of the simplest of all joints to carve as it is really just a long row of chops. They will be all the juicier for having been cooked in a piece rather than separately.

Roast Loin of Lamb

2½– 3 lbs loin of lamb
salt, oil
garlic, rosemary

Preheat the oven to Reg 5/375°. If the butcher has not already done so peel off the thin skin which covers the fat on top of the loin.

Rub the fat with salt, tuck slivers of garlic and a small sprig of rosemary underneath the joint. Rub it all over with a little olive oil, and basting occasionally roast it for 1 hour if you like it rather pink. If you like it well done reduce the heat to Reg 4/350° and cook it for another 20 minutes. Leave it to stand for half an hour, and carve according to the diagram below.

For 6

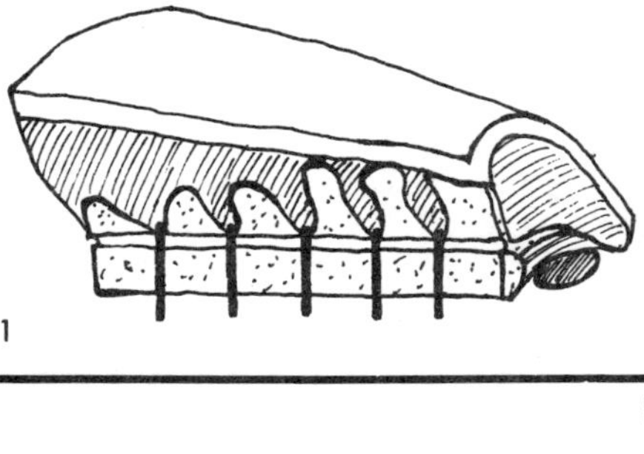

1

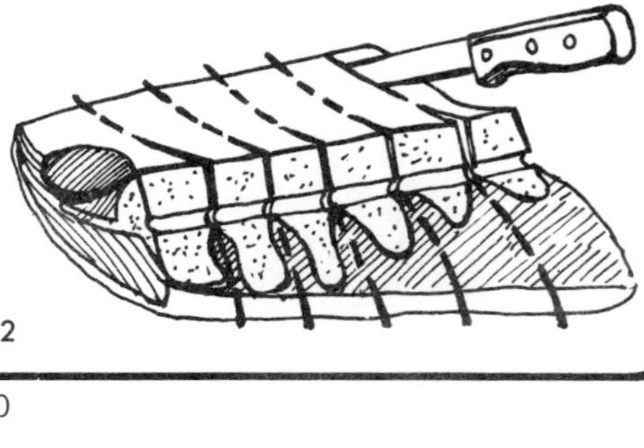

2

Navarin

2 lbs best end of lamb (or mutton if you can get it)
2 tablespoons butter
salt, pepper
a teaspoon of sugar
2 tablespoons flour
$\frac{1}{2}$–$\frac{3}{4}$ pint water, warmed
a bouquet of herbs
$\frac{1}{2}$ lb very small onions
1$\frac{1}{2}$ lbs new potatoes, or small old ones, peeled

Ask the butcher to separate each chop and cut off the ends. There should be 3 or 4 neat little chops for each person. Melt the butter in an ovenproof casserole, and brown the meat on both sides. Sprinkle with salt and pepper, and clear a little space at the bottom of the casserole. Sprinkle the sugar there, and watch it until it caramelises. This is very important as it gives the finished dish its golden colour. Next sprinkle the flour over the meat and stir it round well. Add the warm water and mix it well with the meat. Add the little onions and the bouquet and put the lid on the casserole. Let it simmer on top or in the oven (Reg 2/300°) for an hour. After this time remove as much fat as you can. Push the potatoes into the meat and return the pot, covered, to the heat, for at least another hour. Serve when the potatoes are soft and golden (remove the bouquet).

☐ *You can add turnip and carrot cut small, with shelled peas and beans at the same time as the potatoes. It then becomes Navarin Printanière.*

For 4

Pork and Cabbage

1$\frac{1}{2}$ lbs fresh belly of pork
1 savoy cabbage
$\frac{1}{2}$ lb boiling sausage
a little lard or pork fat
1 oz butter
1 oz flour
stock or milk for the sauce (about $\frac{3}{4}$ pint)
parsley, salt, pepper

Remove the skin from the pork with some of the fat. Sprinkle the remaining fat with a little salt and roast the meat with a little lard or pork dripping at Reg 4/350° for $\frac{1}{2}$ hour. Towards the end add the sausage twisted into short lengths.

Quarter and core the cabbage and shred it coarsely. Blanch it in boiling salted water for 5 minutes.

Make a parsley sauce with the butter, flour and stock and the chopped parsley. Season well.

Drain the cabbage and put it into a casserole. Lay the part-roasted pork and sausages on top; you can cut the pork into serving pieces first, and pour on the parsley sauce. Cover and cook in a slow oven, Reg 2/300° for 1 hour.

☐ *This is rather a rich and filling dish. It reheats well.*

For 4–6

Roast Hand of Pork

4–6 lbs hand of pork
a clove or two of garlic
salt, pepper, sprig of rosemary
oil

Preheat the oven to Reg 3/325°. Make sure the butcher has scored the skin all over. (If he has not a Stanley handyman's knife is the best sharp knife for this.) Insert the garlic and the sprig of rosemary, between the meat and the fat and rub the fat all over with salt. Roast, basting often for 3 hours or more. It should be well done and very crisp on the outside. Remove to a warm place to stand for at least ½ hour before carving. Serve with apple sauce and gravy.

This cheap but rather fat joint is good hot or cold.

For 4–6

How to Carve a Hand of Pork

1 & 1a. Remove crackling, and cut it up separately.

2 & 2a. Carve horizontal slices from the top of the joint, making the slices as thin as possible, as the grain is complicated and thick slices would be a bit chewy. Continue till you reach the bone.

3. Turn the joint over, and carve as many fine slices as you can.

4. Carve away from the sides of the bones. Use the knuckle for making stock as it does not have much in the way of carveable meat.

1 right side

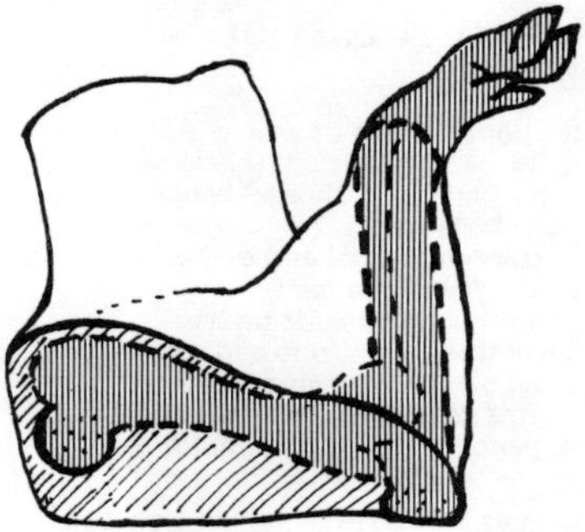

1a left side (showing bones)

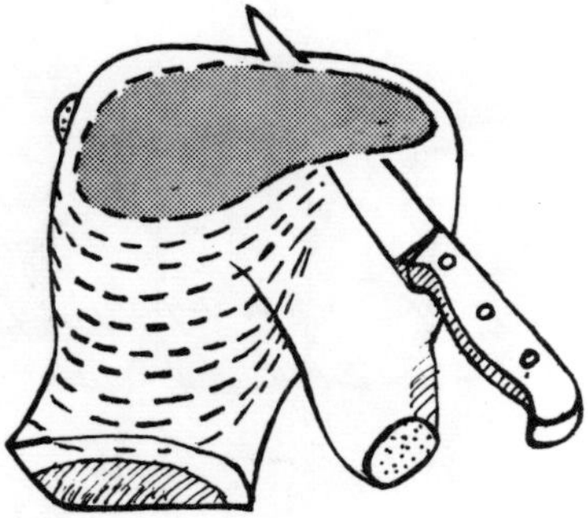

2

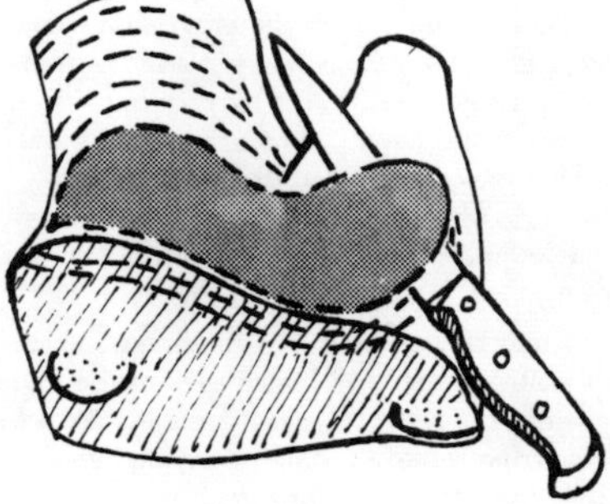

2a

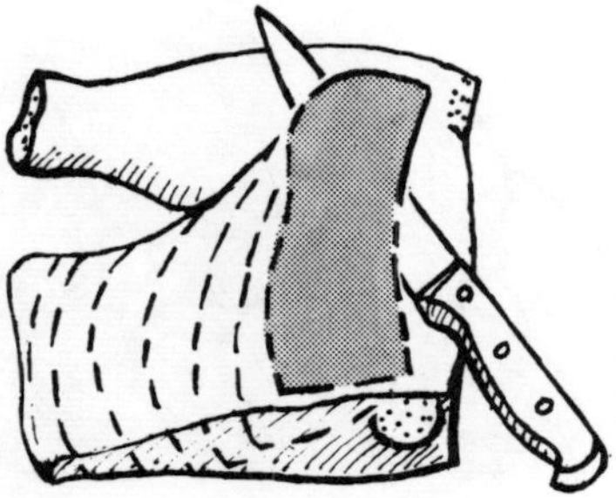

3 right side (turned over)

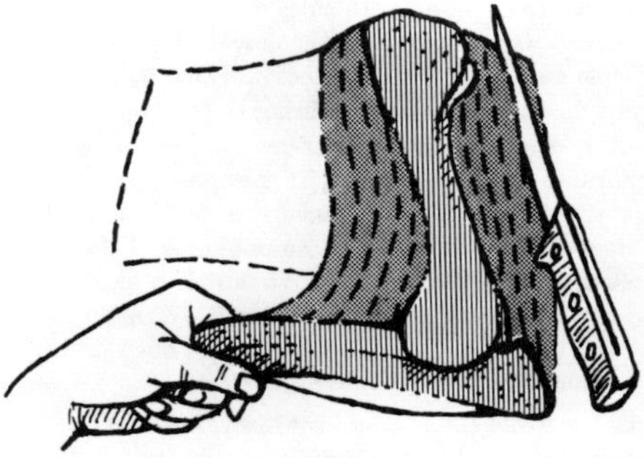

4 left side (turned over)

Stuffed Breast of Veal

4 lbs boned breast of veal in a piece
1 lb minced fattish pork (blade or other)
1 calf's brain, or 3 sheeps' brains
2 hard-boiled eggs, 1 raw egg
1 lb spinach cooked and drained well
1 onion, finely chopped
2 oz fresh white breadcrumbs
1 small teaspoon thyme and marjoram
1 small glass white wine
2 carrots, 2 onions, 2 cloves garlic
salt, pepper, nutmeg, 2 oz butter

Ask your butcher to bone the breast of veal and make a pocket in it for the stuffing. It must be good Dutch veal or it is not worth doing, as there is usually very little meat on English breast of veal. Make a stock with the veal bones. Soak, skin and blanch the brain. Hard-boil the eggs, chop the onions finely. Cook the well-washed spinach, drain it by pressing it well in a colander and chop it. Soak the breadcrumbs in milk and squeeze them dry. Mix the pork, brain, raw egg, spinach, onion, breadcrumbs, thyme, marjoram, salt and pepper and a heavy pinch of nutmeg.

Put half the stuffiing into the breast, pushing it in well. Set the hard-boiled eggs in the middle, push in the rest of the stuffing and sew it up. Tie string round to make it a good even shape. Melt the butter in a large heavy casserole and brown the veal on both sides with the sliced carrots and onions. Add the cloves of garlic, the wine and enough of the stock to come halfway up the meat. Season and bring to the boil. Turn down the heat and simmer covered for 2 hours, turning the veal halfway. It is important at the start of the cooking to make sure that the meat does not stick to the pan, so put some of the sliced vegetables under it. When it is cooked, allow it to cool on a plate. Keep it overnight or even longer and don't forget to take out the sewing thread and remove the string.

☐ *Serve cold cut in thickish slices. This is an impressive and beautiful dish for a summer lunch.*

For 8–10

1

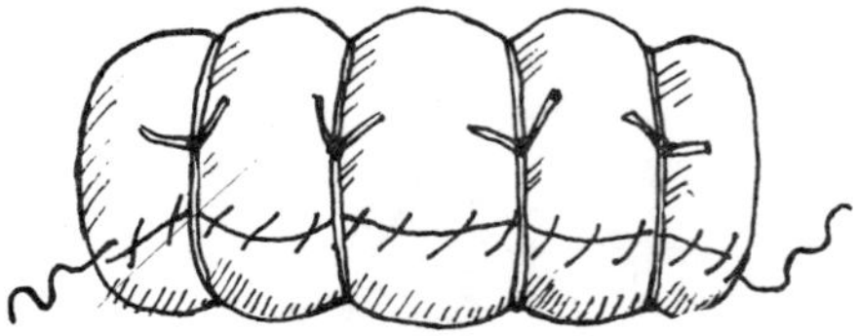
2

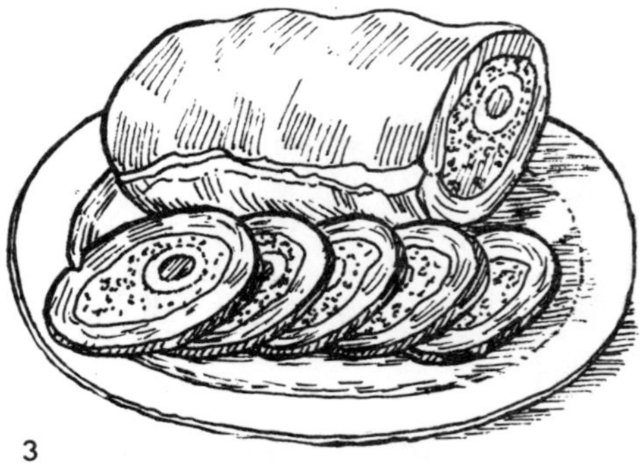
3

Roast Leg of Lamb

Preheat the oven to Reg 5/375°. Having chosen a fairly lean leg you will find that there is still quite a lot of fat at the top (tail) end. Cut most of this away. Make incisions here and there in the lamb and push in slivers of garlic or pieces of rosemary or thyme. Rub the outside with salt and oil or butter. Put an ounce of butter or 2–3 tablespoons of oil into a roasting tin, put in the lamb, thicker side upwards, and roast for from 1 hour 20 minutes for a small leg weighing 3 lbs and under, 1 hour 40 minutes for a medium sized leg up to 4 lbs, 2 hours for anything larger. Baste the joint once or twice during roasting.

This method should give a tender juicy joint with a great deal of rosy-pink meat but no red.

Leave it to stand in a warm place for ½ hour before carving according to the diagram on page 70.

How to sharpen a knife

Hold the steel horizontally in front of you with your left arm straight. Hold the knife in the right hand with the blade vertical and flat against the side of the steel. Draw the blade first down one side of the steel and then the other, keeping it as flat as possible and drawing it down the whole length of the cutting edge. If you don't keep the blade very flat you will bend the cutting edge.

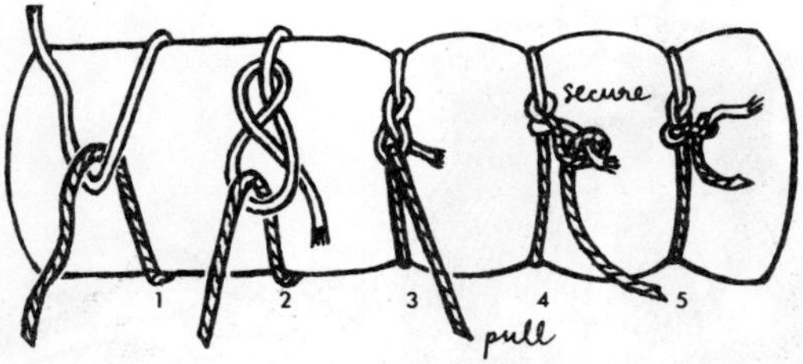

Butchers Knot

Beef Stew with Cloves

2 lbs stewing beef or veal
3–4 onions, peeled and sliced
2 cloves garlic, sliced
6 cloves
2 teaspoons cumin
2–3 tomatoes, peeled and sliced
a glass of red wine
salt, ground pepper
chopped parsley
olive oil

Cut the beef into large pieces, each weighing about 3 oz. Fry these pieces in oil until they are brown, remove them to a dish and fry the sliced onions, adding a little more oil if necessary. Return the meat, add the garlic, cloves and cumin. Stir well and cook fast for a minute or two. Add the tomatoes and red wine, salt, parsley and pepper. Bring to the boil and stew gently for 3 hours or until the meat is tender. If you prefer you can cook it in the oven at Reg 1½–2/275°–300°.

☐ *The very strong cumin taste makes this interesting.*

For 4–6

Beef and Tomato Stew

4 onions
2 oz pork fat or lard
2 lbs stewing steak in a piece
2 tablespoons tomato purée
2 fresh tomatoes, skinned and chopped
1 bouquet of marjoram, thyme, bay leaf and parsley
1 small glass water
salt, freshly ground pepper.

Chop the onions finely. Put them in a flameproof casserole with the pork fat and cook slowly for 5 minutes, stirring until they are beginning to soften. Meanwhile cut the stewing steak into large pieces, ½″ thick and 2″ square. Lay these over the onions, cover the casserole and cook gently for 10 minutes, until the meat has lost its redness. Mix the purée with a little water and add this, together with the chopped tomatoes, to the stew. Sprinkle with salt and pepper and lay the bouquet on top. Cover and cook gently on the top of the stove for 2½ hours, or until the meat is tender. (This can also be cooked in the oven at Reg 3/325° for 2–3 hours.) Serve with noodles or rice.

For 4

Bœuf à la Mode

3–4 lbs piece topside or silverside
2–3 tablespoons oil
2–3 old carrots, 2 large onions
2–3 sticks celery
1 leek if available
2 split pig's feet
½ bottle red wine, I clove garlic
a bunch of bay leaves, thyme, parsley, rosemary
sage
2–3 lbs new carrots
1 egg white, salt, pepper

Have the topside rolled and tied up with a thin layer of pork fat covering at least half the meat—this saves larding which is tedious. Season the outside of the joint with salt and pepper. Heat the oil in a deep enamelled iron casserole and fry the vegetables until lightly browned. Add the meat and brown the ends as well as the exposed parts of the meat. Add the pig's feet. Heat the wine and let it bubble, then pour it on and add enough water to cover, and throw in the herbs and clove of garlic. Add a teaspoon or less of salt, bring to the boil and turn the heat right down. Skim carefully, then cover the casserole and let it simmer very, very gently for 3½ hours. It is important to cook it very slowly or it will become dry. You can leave it on top, scarcely simmering, for an hour or so, then finish it off in the oven at Reg 2½/310°, or even lower.

When it is cooked and completely tender, take it out of the liquid and let it cool. Reduce the liquid with the pig's feet and vegetables, then strain and allow to cool. Skim off all the fat with a metal spoon (or as much as you can possibly remove). If you want a really crystal clear jelly, and have the time, clarify the stock using the method on page 184. Cook the small new carrots in boiling salted water, with a glass of red wine added if you like. Strain them (you can use their liquid and the pig's feet to make more stock for another dish).

Slice the cooled meat, all fat and string removed, and lay the slices, overlapping in rows, in a deep oval dish. Arrange the carrots around the meat and pour over the strained or clarified stock Allow to set in the refrigerator, preferably overnight.

☐ *Very good cold table food or summer lunch.*

For 8–10

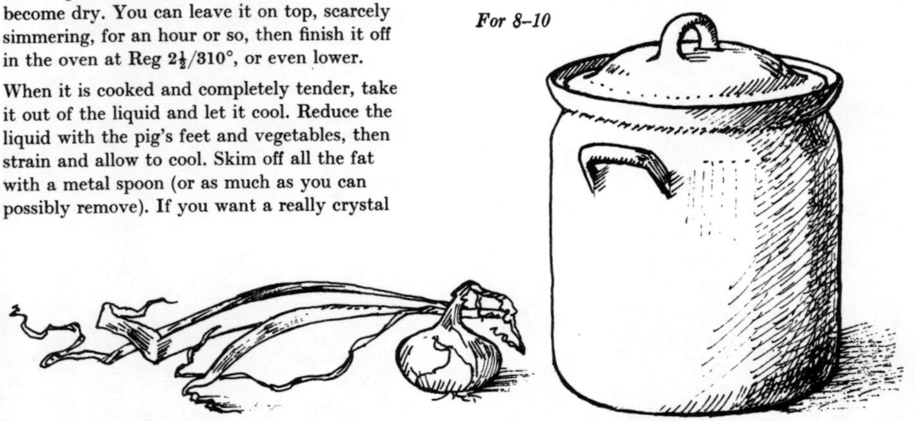

Spiced Brisket

3 lbs piece of lean rolled brisket
salt, pepper
6–10 cloves
a bouquet of herbs
1 carrot
1 onion
water

Rub the surface of the meat with salt and pepper and stick in the cloves. Check that the meat is tied firmly and put it in a saucepan with the bouquet, onion and carrot, and a little more salt. Cover with cold water, bring gently to the boil and allow to simmer quietly until completely tender (2–3 hours).

Remove from pan and drain well. Use some of the liquid for gravy and keep the rest for stock. Serve with potatoes or bread.

☐ *This is only worth doing with a large piece, as a small piece tends to get dry.*

For 6

Bollito Misto

1 small tongue, medium salted (soaked overnight)
2 lb piece topside, or silverside
1 lb belly of pork, salted or fresh (soaked if salt)
1 small 1½–2 lb chicken
2 large onions in skins (roast in the oven until slightly soft)
1–2 leeks, 2 sticks celery
3 large carrots, 1 lb new potatoes
1 lb baby turnips, 2 lbs new carrots
peppercorns, bay leaf, parsley
Parmesan, grated

Put the tongue, beef and pork belly in a casserole or large saucepan with the large onions in their skins, leeks, celery, large carrots, peppercorns, bay leaf and parsley. Cover with plenty of water, bring slowly to the boil, and turn down to simmering point. Skim *really well*, several times, this is important as the broth must be clear. Let it simmer until the tongue is almost tender (about 2½ hours) then add the chicken, and simmer on until everything is cooked (from 1–2 hours more).

Meanwhile cook — we think separately but do whichever you prefer — the new carrots, potatoes, and baby turnips. Serve the plain broth first with Parmesan, having put the meat (the tongue ready skinned) on a big dish to keep hot — it must be very hot. Now serve the meat, all four kinds to everybody, surrounded by young vegetables and with salsa verde (page 174).

☐ *Italian version of Pot au Feu.*

For about 10

Summer Veal Stew

2½–3 lbs boned breast of veal (make stock from bones)
1 large onion, chopped
butter or oil to brown meat in
1–2 oz flour
a dash of white wine or cider
stock or water, salt, pepper
parsley, slice of lemon peel
1 lb button onions, peeled and blanched for 10 minutes in boiling salted water
1 lb young fresh peas

Preheat the oven to Reg 2½/310°. Cut the veal into neat 1″ cubes. Brown the meat in a large flameproof casserole. Remove it to a plate. Add the onion and let it soften. Return the meat, sprinkle with the flour and stir until it thickens. Add the wine or cider, and stock gradually, and let it bubble 2–3 minutes. Add seasoning, parsley tied in a bunch, and a slice of lemon peel. Cover and cook in the oven for 1–1½ hours. Then add the shelled peas and onions, and cook until both are tender. Remove parsley and lemon peel and serve from the casserole with plain new potatoes or rice.

The sauce is very much improved at the end by the addition of an egg yolk beaten with lemon juice and slowly added. Do not let it boil.

For 6

Osso Buco

2 whole veal shins, including bones, sawn across into 1½″ pieces
2 tablespoons olive oil
2 anchovies
1 small glass white wine
1 lb tomatoes
2 bay leaves
a bunch of parsley, celery tops, sage or rosemary.
salt, pepper
To finish: 1 clove garlic, few sprigs parsley
2 strips lemon peel

Brown the meat all over in oil, in the casserole it is to be served in. The meat pieces should all stand side by side with the bone upright. Add the chopped anchovies, let them cook a minute, then add the wine and let it bubble up. Meanwhile skin and chop the tomatoes. Add them to the meat, together with the bunch of herbs and enough light stock or warm water to come half way up the meat. Season with salt and pepper and bring to simmering point before covering and putting the casserole into a moderate oven Reg 3/325° for 1½ hours. Turn the pieces of meat once. Just before serving remove the bunch of herbs and chop the parsley, garlic and lemon peel very finely. Sprinkle it over the meat and serve with Italian rice, risotto milanese or noodles, giving each person a fair share of marrow bones.

☐ *English butchers don't always understand what you need veal shin bones for and unless it is cut correctly the dish will not work. So tell him exactly how you want the bones — cut across into slices (looking somewhat like oxtail) with 1 to 1½ inches of marrow-bone through the middle of each. There should be a decent amount of meat on each, and one shin should make four good slices.*

For 4

Vitello Tonnata

2 lbs leg of veal, boned and rolled
12 anchovy fillets
7 oz tin tunny fish
3 carrots
2 onions
1 stick celery
1 small glass white wine
2 tablespoons wine vinegar
bouquet thyme, parsley and bayleaf
salt, pepper, olive oil
½ pint stock
lemon juice
tablespoon of capers

Make cuts in the veal with a sharp pointed knife, and push half an anchovy fillet into each one as you make it. When it is well larded with anchovies put it in a fireproof casserole on a layer of sliced carrots, onions and celery. Add the white wine, vinegar, herbs, salt (not much because of the anchovies), pepper and stock. Braise the veal, covered, at Reg 3½/3350 for 1½ hours, turning it once.

Allow to cool in its liquid, remove it to a dish, put in the tunny fish and allow the liquid to reduce for 20–30 minutes.

Skim off any excess oil and sieve the sauce through the fine blade of a moulin-légumes together with any remaining anchovies.

Gradually stir a tablespoon or two of olive oil into this sauce — like mayonnaise it can curdle, so take it slowly.

Finally add lemon juice and stir in the capers, it should be a fine, fairly sharp pale pinky-beige sauce.

Carve the veal into thinnish slices and arrange them one at a time on a serving dish, giving each one a spoonful of the sauce. Spread the remaining sauce over the top, and allow to stand for several hours or overnight.

For 8

Steak and Kidney Pie

For the pastry
4 oz self-raising flour
4 oz plain flour
4 oz butter (or lard if you prefer)

For the filling
2 lbs chuck steak
½ lb ox kidney
bay leaf, 1 medium onion
1½ oz seasoned flour
water, 1 egg
2 oz dripping
pinch salt, water

Make the pastry and leave it to rest in a cold place. Preheat oven to Reg 7/425°. Trim the steak and kidney and cut it all up into nice pieces. Toss the meat in seasoned flour (you can add a pinch of dried mustard to the salt and pepper if you like) and brown it in good dripping. Brown the chopped onion. Mix the steak, kidney and onion, adding a bay leaf. Put it in a 12″ pie dish with a pie funnel in the centre. Add water to come almost, but not quite, to the top of the meat. Cover with pastry. Decorate and glaze with beaten egg, to which is added a pinch of salt and dash of water. After 15 minutes reduce heat to Reg 4/350°, after another 10 minutes look to see if the pastry is coloured yet. If it is, cover firmly with damped double greaseproof paper to prevent the pastry burning. Give the pie 1½–2 hours cooking in all. This is a much better way of making steak and kidney pie than recipes which tell you to pre-stew the meat.

☐ *If you can add a pigeon or two it is a great luxury and much improves the flavour.*

For 6

A Pastry Rose for the Steam Hole

Put four scraps of very thinly rolled pastry one on top of the other with flour between each layer and cut a 2″ square (a).

Make sure the layers are still separate, then pinch the corners together (b).

Take a sharp pointed knife and cut a deep cross in the centre (c).

Turn back the points and stick the rose over the steam hole (d).

It is easier if there is a funnel inside the pie.

Lamb Hot-Pot

3 lbs neck of lamb
2 large onions, peeled and chopped
1 lb carrots, scraped and sliced
1 lb turnips, scraped and sliced
1 lb potatoes, peeled and sliced
stock or water to cover
salt and freshly ground pepper
parsley, roughly chopped

Put the lamb, cut in chops, and with excess fat removed, in alternating layers in a casserole with the cleaned sliced carrots and turnips and the chopped onion and parsley. Season the layers with salt and pepper. Cover with a layer of sliced potatoes. Pour in stock to come just to the top of the potatoes, and cover. Cook in a very slow oven Reg 3/325°, for 2½ hours. Remove the lid for the last ¾ hour, to brown the potatoes. You can put young broad beans in this when they are in season. Add them, raw, by lifting the crust of potatoes and spooning them in about 45 minutes before serving.

For 6

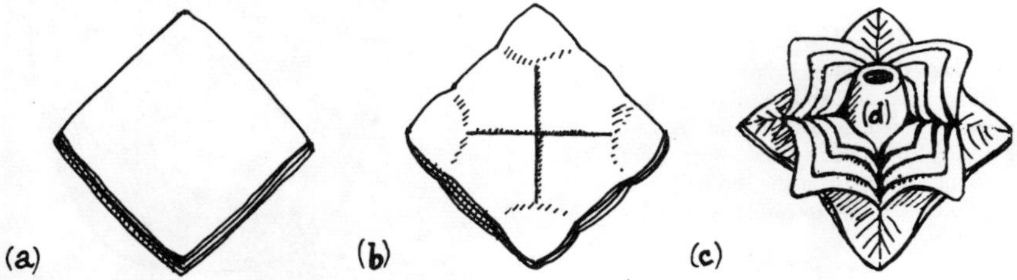

Couscous

1 lb couscous
1–2 lbs lean stewing lamb (neck, fillet or shoulder)
3½ lbs boiling chicken (not too old and tough)
½ lb chick peas (soaked overnight)
1 turnip, 1 onion, 1 carrot
12 dried apricots (or 2 handfuls of raisins) soaked
1½ lbs vegetables, from among the following: courgettes, peas, runner, french or broad beans
2 red or green pimentoes, 1 cauliflower
½ lb tomatoes, peeled and chopped
a sprig of mint
salt, pepper, olive oil, water, butter
harissa (or cayenne red chilli), ground ginger, saffron, paprika

TO MAKE THE STEW

Cut the meat into convenient pieces and put it with the whole chicken, pre-soaked chick peas, onion, carrot, turnip, salt and pepper into the bottom half of the *couscousier*, or a large saucepan. Just cover with water and add a little olive oil. Simmer, covered, for 2 hours. One hour before the end start cooking the couscous (see method below). ½ hour before the end add the fruit, tomatoes, cut-up vegetables and mint, with saffron or ginger if wished. Before serving drain off most of the liquid which can be served separately as an extra sauce or kept for reheating at another meal. Pile the meat, vegetables and cut-up chicken on a dish and serve the couscous and sauce in separate bowls.

TO MAKE THE SAUCE

Take ¼ pint of the liquid from the stew, and add cautiously a little harissa or cayenne or chilli for a fiery sauce, or paprika with tomato purée for a milder one, in which case use ½ pint of liquid as people will take more.

TO COOK COUSCOUS

Start 1 hour before the stew is finished. Turn the couscous into a bowl and moisten it with 1 or 2 cups of water — it will go rather solid. Mix it very well with your hands, to make sure there are no lumps at all. Put it in the top half (with the holes) of your steamer or *couscousier* and set it over the slowly cooking stew or boiling water for ½ hour, without a lid. Do not press it down.

When ½ hour is up, turn it back into the bowl again and add 1–2 cups of cold water with a little salt and pepper. Stir well, this time with a wooden spoon (it will be hot) and make sure there are no lumps. Return it lightly to the steamer. After another ½ hour over the simmering stew or water it should be ready, light and fluffy with each grain soft and separate. Finish by stirring in an ounce or two of butter and turn it into a warm dish.

For 6–8

Notes on Couscous

Basically a North African dish, it translates rather well into English, now that the actual proper grain, or couscous, is available in many shops, not only delicatessens but also health food shops, as is harissa, for the sauce. Moreover it is not at all difficult to cook if you have a *couscousier* or perforated steamer which fits tightly over a pan in which you can boil water or cook a stew. The steamer doesn't need a lid, but it does need to fit tightly into the pan below. You can fix a cloth all round the join of the two pots to help keep in the steam if need be. Ideally the meat and vegetables cook below the couscous, but if the lower pan is too small to hold everything, the stew can cook separately, and the couscous cooks just as well over water. Don't worry about it falling through the holes, it stays together in a mass.

Pork and Apples

4 good spare rib pork chops
1 large onion, chopped and peeled
1–2 sharp cooking apples, chopped and peeled
2 tablespoons cider vinegar (or wine vinegar)
1 glass of cider
¾ pint hot water or mild stock
dripping, or bacon fat for frying in
3–4 sage leaves
Parsley
salt, pepper, 2–3 cloves
2 cloves garlic, sliced

Melt some dripping in a frying pan, and fry the onions and garlic until they just begin to turn golden. Put them into the bottom of an ovenproof dish that has a lid. Brown the chops, and put them aside. Fry the apples in the same pan, adding more fat if necessary. As they soften and colour, add the vinegar, stirring well to collect all sediment in the pan. Add the cider and let it bubble 2 or 3 minutes. Mix the apple with the onions in the casserole, add the sage and parsley, and cloves. Put the browned chops on top, add salt and pepper and then a little hot water. It should not swamp the meat. Cover and cook in the oven Reg 3/325° for 1–1½ hours. Remove the chops and sieve the remaining apples, onions and gravy and serve the thick resulting sauce with the chops, having checked seasoning and removed cloves.

For 4

Pork and Beans

1 lb dried haricot beans
2 lbs salt belly of pork, lean end or 2 lbs hand of bacon or gammon
1 onion
2 tablespoons vinegar
2 tablespoons brown sugar
2 tablespoons treacle
2 tomatoes
1 teaspoon mustard
pepper, salt

Soak the beans, and if necessary the pork or bacon too (ask the butcher). Parboil the beans in plain unsalted water for ½ hour or more, depending on how fresh they are (see the note in the introduction to vegetables). Add the pork in a piece and the whole onion, just cover with cold water and simmer until the skins of the beans begin to split, about 1½ hours. Then drain, keeping the liquid, put the beans in a buttered casserole and add the vinegar, sugar, tomatoes, peeled and chopped, the boiled onion which you chop roughly, black treacle, mustard and pepper. Add a little salt only if the beans need it — there may have been enough in the pork or bacon. Remove the skin and put the meat in with the beans. Add 2 or 3 tablespoons of the cooking liquid and bake, covered at Reg 4/350° for 2 hours, then remove the lid and bake for a further hour or more, until the beans are soft and tender and the liquid creamy. Add more liquid during cooking if it is needed.

☐ *This reheats extremely well.*

For 4–6

Pork Spare Ribs

2 lbs really cheap proper spare ribs, largely bones

For the marinade
juice of 1 large lemon
1 tablespoon olive oil
chopped fresh herbs (chives, marjoram, thyme rosemary)
salt, black pepper
1 clove garlic, crushed
1 large teaspoon Barbados (soft brown) sugar

Ask the butcher to cut the ribs in half across. Mix the ingredients for the marinade together and pour them over the pieces of meat. Leave it to soak in for at least 1 hour, turning them about from time to time.

If you have a barbecue or charcoal grill cook the ribs over a grid, wiping excess moisture off them first.
If you are roasting them in the oven, set it at Reg 6–7/400°–425°, turn the pieces once, and baste with the marinade. Allow them ½ hour. Serve with salad, Barbecue sauce (page 170), French bread and spring onions.

☐ *Very messy to eat, but easiest with hands and no knives and forks*

For 4

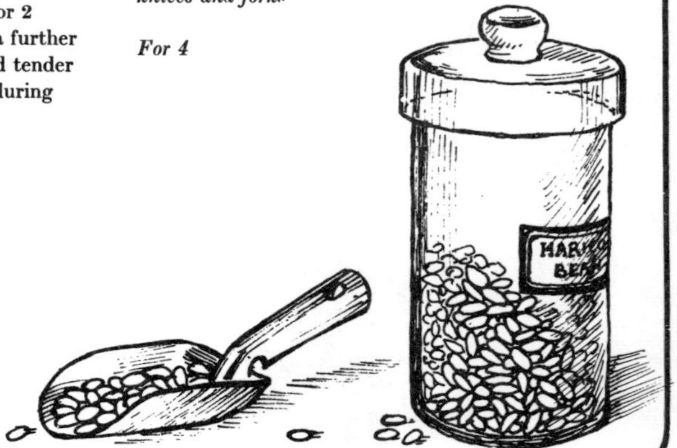

Pork Epigrams

4 thick slices of belly of pork (about 1 lb — fresh, not salt)
seasoned flour, 1 egg, beaten
dry breadcrumbs
good pork dripping or oil, fat for frying
1 large onion, peeled and finely chopped
Sweet-sour sauce
1 oz butter
2 tablespoons tomato purée (or 2–3 fresh peeled tomatoes, or a small tin of tomatoes)
2 tablespoons vinegar
1 tablespoon soft brown sugar

Trim the meat of skin and bone and cut into neat ½" cubes. Toss them in seasoned flour, coat in beaten egg, then cover with breadcrumbs (this stage can be done in advance). Fry very gently in shallow oil or fat, until golden brown and crisp. Drain on kitchen paper and keep warm.

Meanwhile make the sauce by gently cooking the finely chopped onion in butter till soft, add sugar, tomatoes or purée, and vinegar, and bring to the boil, stirring. If using fresh tomatoes simmer for a further 10 minutes before serving (or use Barbecue sauce, see page 170). Serve pork with plain boiled rice and the sweet-sour sauce.

☐ *A great success with children, and very very cheap*

For 4

Pork and Prunes

½ lb prunes
lemon juice or rind
1½ lb lean belly of pork (without bones) or 2 lb with bones
2 oz seasoned flour
salt, pepper

Soak the prunes overnight, then stew them with a little lemon juice or rind until tender. Strain them, and reserve their liquid. Stone them. Take the skin off the belly of pork, and also as much of the fat as possible, which you can melt down for the next process. Preheat the oven to Reg 3½/335°. Cut the meat into small chunks, roll them in the seasoned flour and brown them well in the melted pork fat, in a frying pan (add a little dripping if there isn't enough fat). Put the meat and prunes into a casserole. Stir any remaining flour into the remaining fat in the pan and add ½–¾ pint prune-juice to make a thin gravy. Add this to the casserole. Cook in the oven for 1¼ hours. Taste for seasoning and serve.

☐ *This stew tastes incredibly of chestnuts. It is even more delicious if you add ½ lb, skinned and peeled, at the very beginning, or a few whole tinned ones at the end.*

For 4–6

Cassoulet

1 lb haricot beans
pieces of pork skin or bacon rinds cut in large squares
4 large onions
4 cloves
1 large carrot
2 large bouquets of herbs
several cloves garlic
1 lb salt pork
1–2 lbs blade, spare rib or hand of fresh pork
whole or ½ shoulder of mutton (depending on number of people to be fed)
a small duck, or 1–2 wild duck
4 large tomatoes
1 lb Toulouse or other boiling sausage
salt, pepper
6–8 oz fresh breadcrumbs

Soak the beans overnight. Take a large iron pan with a lid, or a deep thick earthenware one. Line it with the pork rinds, including those from the salt pork. Drain the beans, put them in as well, cover with more fresh water, add 1 onion stuck with 4 cloves, the carrot, the bouquet, 4 cloves garlic, and the salt pork cut into big cubes. Bring gently to the boil, skim and simmer in the oven or on top until the beans are nearly done but not splitting (about 1½ hours).

Meanwhile set the oven at Reg 3/325°. Cut the boned lamb and pork into largish pieces, and roast them with the whole duck, for ¾–1 hour, while the beans are cooking. Strain off the fat, and use two or three tablespoons to fry the remaining three onions, peeled and chopped. Keep the rest of the fat for later. When the onions are soft and golden add the peeled and chopped tomatoes. Add the rest of the gravy from the meat tin, and plenty of salt and pepper. While this is cooking cut the duck into six pieces.
Cut the sausages into pieces as well if they are big.

Drain and reserve the liquid from the beans, throw away the original onion, carrot and bouquet and re-fill the pot in which the beans were cooked, or use a new larger one, as everything has to go in this time. Put the pork rinds first, then a layer of beans, then meat, sausage, duck, onions and tomatoes, then beans with a fresh bouquet and two or three cloves of crushed garlic, then the remaining meats and vegetables. Finish with some beans and a good cupful of their liquid, and finally strew the top thickly with fresh white breadcrumbs and drip a little roasting fat on to the breadcrumbs. Put it back to cook uncovered in the oven at Reg 2/300° for 1½ hours.

Traditionally, at least three times during the cooking you push down the breadcrumbs as they turn golden and sprinkle more breadcrumbs on. This makes a really delicious thick crust, and is a very important part of every cassoulet. Add more liquid if the whole thing seems to be going dry.
A fresh green salad is all that you need to follow.

☐ *The traditional French recipe uses preserved goose (confit d'oie) but it is perfectly acceptable to use wild or tame duck instead. It is not cheap but very filling for a large lunch on a cold day. If you cannot buy pork or bacon rind separately use strips cut from the outside of the pork in this recipe.*

For 8–12

Cold Pickled Pork, or Salt Pork

A hand of salt pork with its trotter, boned, tied and rolled (about 4–6 lbs when ready)
2 onions
2 carrots
2 bay leaves
a sprig of thyme, some peppercorns
1 clove garlic

Depending on the strength of his brine, the butcher will take 2–5 days to salt the pork for you. If he has a hand of pork already salted, ask him to bone, tie and roll it in a sausage shape for you. Soak it for 6–12 hours when you get home, no matter how perfect the butcher says it is. Change the water once or twice. Put it in a casserole or baking tin with the trotter, bones (if you have them), carrots, onions, herbs, garlic and pepper and just cover with water. Cover the dish and bake in the oven Reg 3/325° for 3 hours.

Leave it to cool in its own liquid for 1 hour, then put it in a bowl, with greaseproof paper over it and a weighted board or plate on top of that. Keep stock for soup. Next day the pork is ready for cutting. Eat with salads and as you would ham.

☐ *Belly of salt pork can be cooked in the same way. Remove the bones when nearly cool. Wrap in greaseproof paper and press till cold.*

For 10–12

Sausages or Sausage Meat

Caul fat (optional) 1 tablespoon vinegar
1½ lb belly of pork
2 tablespoons fine fresh breadcrumbs
a handful of parsley, finely chopped
1 level teaspoon ground mace
a large pinch of ground coriander
a large pinch of black pepper
½–1 teaspoon salt
2 rashers lean bacon
2 tablespoons finely chopped onion
2 oz lard

Soak the caul fat in hot water with a tablespoon of vinegar. Put the pork, skinned and boned, and the rashers of bacon twice through the fine blade of the mincer. Mix it with the breadcrumbs, parsley, spices and salt. Soften the finely chopped onion in half the lard and add it to the mixture.

To make the sausages, dry and skin (if necessary) the caul fat and stretch it by easing it with the flat of one hand and the fingers of the other. Cut it into 4″ squares. Shape the sausage meat into little sausage shapes, wrap them in caul fat, like little parcels. When you want them, fry them very slowly in lard or pork dripping.

Caul fat is not very easy to get, but sausage skins can be obtained if you know of a butcher who makes his own sausages. You then only have the problem of filling them, which is possible with a mixer with a sausage-filler. Otherwise make skinless sausages which, however, tend to be dry.

☐ *10 times better than average bought sausages.*

Makes just over 1½ lbs.

Stuffed Peppers

4 medium peppers (round dumpy ones)
2 large onions
1 thick slice bread
½ lb minced pork or beef
1 clove garlic
a small bunch of parsley, ½ teaspoon oregano or marjoram
1 egg yolk
1 dessertspoon tomato purée
2–3 tablespoons olive oil
salt, fresh ground black pepper
breadcrumbs

Slice the stalk off the peppers and scoop out the core and every seed. Plunge into boiling water with a drop of oil in for 3–5 minutes according to how thick they are. Remove, refresh in cold water and drain dry. Fry the finely chopped onions in olive oil until slightly brown. Soak the slice of bread in a little water. Crush the clove of garlic and add it with the meat and a handful of chopped parsley and oregano or marjoram to the onions. Brown, stirring for a few minutes, then remove the pan from the fire and add the egg yolk. Mix well then add the bread with the water squeezed out, tomato, salt and fresh ground pepper and mix very thoroughly. Stuff the peppers with this mixture with a teaspoon and put in an oiled baking dish. Sprinkle the tops with bread crumbs, pour a little olive oil over this and bake 40 minutes at Reg 5/375°. If the tops aren't brown finish off under the grill.

For 4

Stuffed Tomatoes

The mixture above is good for stuffed tomatoes and is enough for 3–4 large tomatoes. Cut off lids, scoop out seeds and pulp and use the pulp in the stuffing (add after meat is browned, sizzle till liquid is reduced to a thick purée). Stuff generously and replace lid. Smallish marrows can also be stuffed with this method.

Stuffed Cabbage

1 fine cabbage — Savoy is good for this
½ lb sausage meat or minced pork
4–5 chicken livers (½ lb)
1 thick slice bread, crusts removed and soaked in milk
2 egg yolks, salt and pepper
plenty of nutmeg or mace, thyme, parsley
a few dill seeds if liked
1 oz butter, 1 oz flour
¾ pint stock
3–4 cloves, handful capers

Make a stuffing with the sausage meat or pork, finely chopped chicken livers, bread, crusts removed, soaked in milk and squeezed dry, egg yolks, herbs, seasonings and spices. Let it stand. Wash the cabbage well and drop it whole into a large pan of boiling salted water.

Let it boil 8–10 minutes, remove and drain it very carefully. Now open it out leaf by leaf. Lay a light layer of stuffing over each leaf, starting from the middle and carefully pressing them back into place to re-form the cabbage.

Tie it up (strips of silver foil or tape are good for this) and put it into a casserole in which you have previously made a thinnish sauce with the flour, butter and well-seasoned stock.

Stick the cabbage with 3 or 4 cloves, spoon some of the sauce over it, cover the pot and cook over a low heat for 1½–2 hours adding more water if necessary, or bake at Reg 2/300° for 2–3 hours. To serve, remove the foil strips or tape, and throw a few capers into the sauce.

If you can spare it a tot of rough brandy poured over it at the last moment is delicious. Do not ignite it.

☐ *The number of people it will feed depends on the size of the cabbage. This amount of stuffing can be used in a small cabbage or a large one.*

For 4–6

Dolmades

½ onion
2 tablespoons olive oil
1 pepper (preferably red)
½ lb minced lamb (or beef)
2 oz raw rice
2 tomatoes
salt, pepper
chopped mint and parsley
30–40 fresh vine leaves

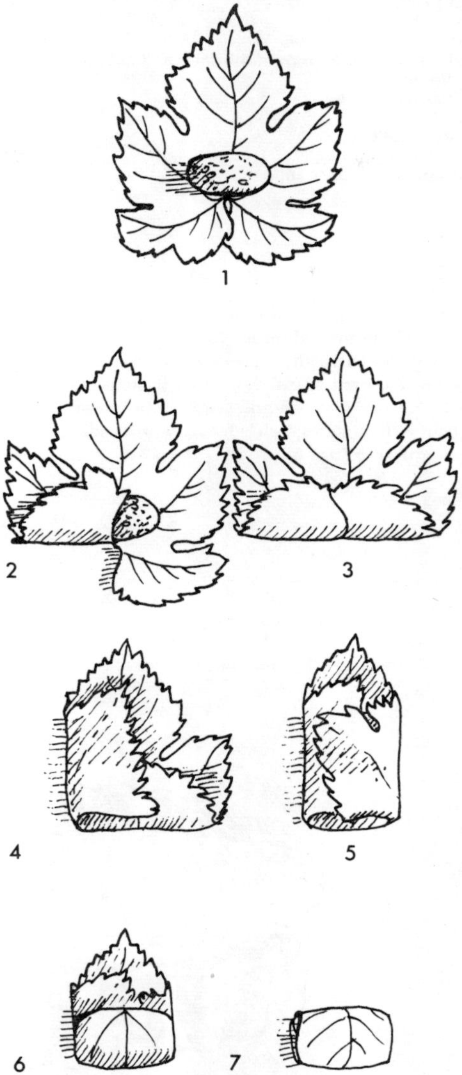

Fry the onion, finely chopped, in the oil until soft, add the finely chopped pepper and fry a minute or two. Then add the meat and when it has crumbled and separated add the rice. Finally add the skinned and chopped tomatoes, seasoning and herbs. You want a dryish mixture that sticks together. Remove the stalks and blanch the vine leaves in boiling salted water until they go limp. Choose the leaves that are not split or indented too deeply, keep the rest for lining the pan. Lay the good leaves out flat, inside up, one at a time, and put a teaspoon of stuffing in the middle. Fold the leaf round the stuffing to make a little parcel. Squeeze it lightly to make it stick together.

Line a shallow pan with the extra leaves and put the dolmades in close together, add a cup of stock and a spoonful of tomato purée, squeeze of lemon juice and a tablespoon of oil. Cover with another layer of vine leaves, then a plate or saucer to keep them from moving about, and simmer for ½ hour.

For 3

Grilled Tripe

1 lb thick dressed tripe, well-dried and cut into fingers
4 tablespoons oil
juice ½ lemon
pepper, salt
parsley
breadcrumbs for coating

Cut the ready-prepared tripe into strips about ½″ by 2″. Marinate them for 1 hour in the oil, and lemon juice with salt, pepper and parsley. Just before you want to eat them drain them, coat with breadcrumbs and grill gently until brown, about 8–10 minutes each side. Serve with salad and grilled or fried tomatoes.

For 2

Liver with Sour Cream

2 large onions, finely chopped
oil for frying
1 lb pig's liver, cut into ½″ cubes
5 oz carton of sour cream
1 tablespoon flour
½ pint water
marjoram, parsley, salt

Fry the finely chopped onions in a little oil until they are transparent. Add the liver and fry, turning often, with the onions for 5 minutes. Mix the sour cream with the flour, add the water slowly, stirring, and add this to the liver and onion, cooking and mixing for another 5–10 minutes. Add the marjoram. Keep warm till ready to serve, and only add salt and pepper just before doing so, otherwise the liver becomes tough. Sprinkle with parsley. Serve with boiled or mashed potatoes, and sweet-sour gherkins or cucumber salad.

For 4

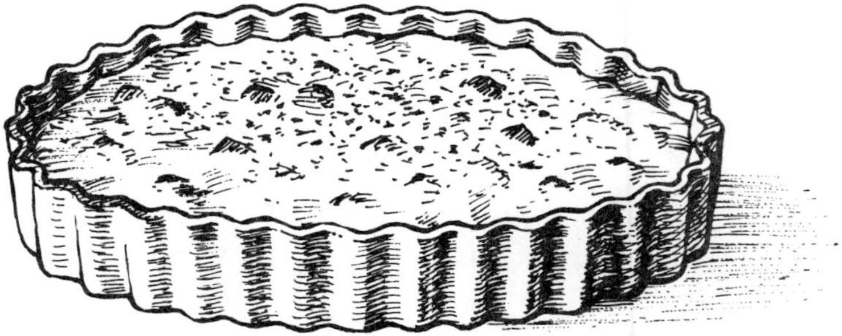

Liver with Raisins

2 lbs liver (pig's or lambs') thinly sliced
1½ oz butter
1 onion, chopped
2–3 rashers bacon, or salt pork
salt, pepper
1 tablespoon wine vinegar
1 dessertspoon Demerara sugar
2 tablespoons seedless raisins (previously soaked in water)

You need a large frying pan with a lid for this dish. Season the slices of liver with salt and pepper, and fry briefly in the butter. Remove the slices and keep them warm. Cut the bacon or salt pork into small pieces and fry lightly with the onion in the same pan. Add the vinegar, sugar and raisins. Return the liver to the pan, and cook gently, with the lid on for 1 hour. Serve with mashed potatoes.

☐ *Some people hate liver cooked for a long time in any form, but for those who like it this is a good recipe.*

For 6

Brains in Cider

1 lb brains (calves' or lambs')
2 glasses cider (dry)
2 glasses of stock
1 small onion, peeled and sliced
salt, pepper
1 oz butter
1 oz flour
the yolk of an egg
juice of ½ lemon
a grating of nutmeg
chopped parsley

Soak and skin the brains (see below) and put in a pan with the cider and stock, the onion and some salt and pepper. Bring to the boil, skim and cook them gently for 30 minutes — or less if using lambs' brains. In small pan melt the butter, stir in the flour with a wooden spoon and gradually add ¾ pint of the liquid in which the brains have cooked. Stir until smooth and allow to simmer 15 minutes. Put the egg yolk into a small bowl, add the lemon juice, and a little nutmeg, and mix together, and add little by little to the sauce. Stop cooking as soon as it thickens. Put the brains on a dish, pour the sauce over them and serve sprinkled with parsley.

For 2

The Preparation of Brains

Calves' brains are the best; you need one set per person. Lambs' brains are much smaller, so buy three sets for two people. Soak the brains in tepid water for half an hour or more. Remove the skin and membranes and all the red threads. Blanch in simmering salted water, acidulated with lemon juice, for 15 minutes or more. If they still seem too slippery and fragile to handle you can firm them up by chilling in the refrigerator for an hour or so, or even freezing in the ice-compartment before slicing or cooking them in batter etc.

Brains Vinaigrette

4 sets lambs' brains
stock
vinaigrette dressing
parsley, capers

Soak and skin the brains (page 101). Poach for 20-30 minutes in good stock and allow to cool in their own bouillon.

When they are quite cold remove them carefully and allow them to drain for 5 minutes. Serve sliced with a good vinaigrette poured over them and sprinkled with chopped capers and parsley.

For 4

Brains in Black Butter

Prepare the brains as above but as soon as they are cooked drain them very well, slice them and serve them very hot with black butter (page 172) poured over them.

Courgettes and Brains Fried in Batter

1 lb courgettes
2 sets calves' brains, or 3 sets lambs' brains,
batter (page 186)
deep oil for frying

Soak the brains in cold water for 1–2 hours. Cut the courgettes lengthwise into quarters and cut these in half. While the brains are soaking, salt the courgettes. When you have soaked the brains, skin and blanch them for 15 minutes or more (page 101). Rinse and dry the courgettes. Cut the brains which are fairly firm if you have prepared them well, into pieces about 1″ across. Put the oil in a pan and heat it. Put the prepared brains and courgettes on a board by the side of the cooker and the batter at the side of the board. Dip the courgettes into the batter and drop them into the sizzling hot oil. (They only need a very light coating of batter.) When they are light brown and tender put them in a dish lined with draining paper and keep them hot in the oven. After you have fried all the courgettes add a small beaten egg, if you like, to the batter, beat it well and fry the cubed brains covered with this slightly thicker mixture. The courgettes should not be dropped into the batter in handfuls as their moisture makes it too wet. Serve the two things together with tomato sauce or with lemon quarters and fried parsley.

For 6

Poultry Game Pâtés

Poultry, Game and Pâtés

If you eat a lot of chicken you are already economising, as it is the cheapest meat you can buy, although for your peace of mind and pleasure it really is worth spending a few pence more on a free-range bird. It is also imperative to buy a fresh rather than a frozen bird — the flavour and texture of a freshly-killed fowl is delicate and it should be moist, succulent and fragrant. If you like game, life is more difficult, for while chickens get more and more prolific, game becomes scarcer and more expensive every season. Pheasant, partridge and grouse are now in the realms of ultra-extravagance although there are sometimes shops that will sell them unplucked and undrawn for just possible prices, and of course older birds are cheaper. If you are buying pheasant, hens cost less than cocks because they are smaller, which is lucky as they are also better, being plumper and juicier; in all game-birds it is plumpness rather than largeness that counts. If your bird is large and old don't attempt to roast it. If you bought it cheaply and you think it might be young but can't tell either by the pointed spurs or darkened feathers of your pheasant, the oval wing-tips of your partridge or the hard skull of your grouse, all of which are indications of an old bird, then make a pudding, pie or casserole rather than ending up with a piece of intractable rubber on your plate. If you are looking for much cheaper game, pigeon and hare are both quite good value, they are meaty and their strong flavour, like that of pheasant or grouse, will not suffer from being cooked a long time, so an old beast or bird can be turned into really delicious food. Rabbit is not particularly cheap, and wild rabbits have a strong but not a wonderful flavour. However, if you find a good source of supply for tame rabbits, they are worth buying not as an economy but for their taste and their beautiful texture. Stewed, they give the sauce a really marvellous smoothness and velvetiness and they keep their moisture much better than chickens which tend to become dry when sautéed or stewed in pieces.

Fried Chicken

1 small chicken, cut in 8 pieces (page 107)
3–4 tablespoons oil
1 lemon
salt, pepper
1 clove garlic
1 onion
parsley
2–3 tablespoons plain flour
pork dripping or butter and oil for frying

Make a marinade with the oil, lemon juice, salt, pepper, sliced garlic and onion, and sprigs of parsley torn up small. Marinade the pieces of chicken in this for 2–3 hours. Take the pieces out, dry them and shake them well with flour, seasoned with more salt and pepper, in a paper bag.

Heat pork dripping or oil to a depth of about 1″ in a heavy saucepan or sauté pan. When it is very hot put in the pieces of chicken and brown them evenly on all sides. Then cover the pan and turn down the heat, cooking the chicken gently and turning the pieces from time to time, for ½ hour or until the chicken is cooked.

Serve with quarters of lemon. If you prefer the chicken to be very crisp on the outside take the lid off the pan again 15 minutes before serving.

For 4

Chicken with White Wine Sauce

1 chicken cut in 8 or 10 pieces
4 shallots, 1 oz butter
2–3 tablespoons oil, flour
salt, freshly ground pepper
1 glass white wine
6 juniper berries
2 cloves garlic
3 good strips orange peel
a large bunch of thyme
1 glass stock made with the giblets

Dust the pieces of chicken with flour, salt and pepper. Brown in fat and oil in a heavy pan or flameproof casserole. Do this fairly slowly, about 5 minutes each side. Remove the pieces to a plate. Soften the chopped shallots in the butter and oil. When they start to brown return the chicken, pour on the wine and let it bubble. Add the stock, crushed juniper berries, sliced cloves of garlic, orange peel, thyme, salt and pepper.

Simmer uncovered on top of the stove for ¾ hour, turning the pieces of chicken from time to time and tipping the pan to mix the sauce. When tender remove the thyme and taste for seasoning and serve sprinkled with chopped parsley.

☐ *This is also good with rabbit.*

For 4–5

Plain Roast Chicken

3–4 lb chicken with its giblets
½ lemon
1–2 ozs butter
salt, pepper
sprig of thyme, or better, tarragon
small shallot, onion or, if preferred, clove of garlic
bouquet of herbs, carrot, onion, salt and pepper
for the stock for gravy

Preheat the oven to Reg 5/375°. Roll half the butter in some salt and pepper and put it into the chicken with the onion, shallot or garlic and herbs. Squeeze the juice of quarter of the lemon into the cavity and then put in the peel.

Rub the outside of the bird with the remaining quarter of the lemon, cover the skin with the rest of the butter and sprinkle with salt. Put the giblets in a small pan with the bouquet, carrot, onion, salt and pepper and simmer while the chicken roasts.

Roast the bird first on one side for 20 minutes, then on the other side for 20 minutes and finally breast upwards for 20 minutes, basting thoroughly. The object of putting it on its side is to cook the drumsticks and the thigh more thoroughly and to keep the breast moist.

Put the chicken onto a serving dish and keep it warm while you make the gravy with the juices in the roasting tin and the strained giblet stock.

For 4 or more

Chicken Salad

Mix leftover chicken, shredded neatly, with home-made mayonnaise, capers and chopped hard-boiled eggs and decorate with borage flowers and more capers.

To Carve a Chicken for Four People

This is a useful way of dealing with a small roaster if you have four people to serve. Otherwise follow instructions for carving a turkey (page 109).

1. Place the chicken with the legs to the left. Remove all the string and skewers. Insert the fork into the nearest drumstick and pull it down towards you cutting it at (a).

2. Insert point of knife into ball and socket joint (b), severing it. Slice through and remove in one piece. Divide into thigh and drumstick.

3. With a knife halfway down the breast cut through to the carcase at (c) removing wing and a good share of breast in one piece. You will encounter and sever the wing joint at (d).

4. Holding the knife blade vertical, cut the carcase in half from (e) to (f).

5. Separate the breast by cutting through the ribs in a line from (g) to (h).

6. Turn the other half of the chicken over, remove the leg and wings as before and cut through from (g) to (h) as before. Give everyone either a drumstick and a piece of breast, or a thigh and a wing. Set aside the bony lower portion for soup or gravy.

You can use this method for pheasants and also for cutting up uncooked birds.

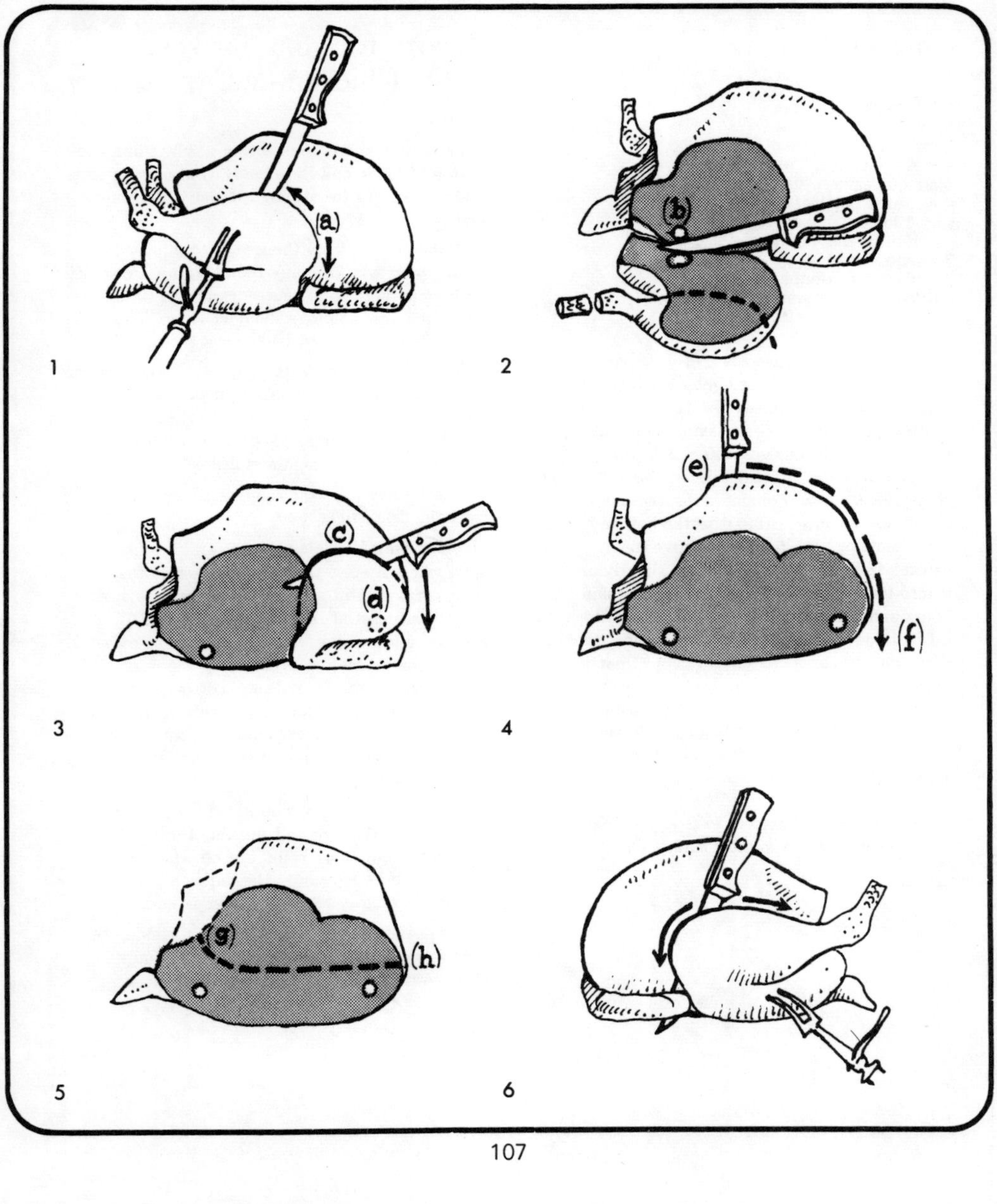
(a)
1
(b)
2
(c)
(d)
3
(e)
(f)
4
(g)
(h)
5
6

Chicken Waterzöi

1 6 lb boiling chicken
butter
8 stalks celery, 1 small onion
4 leeks, 1 carrot
4 sprigs parsley
4 cloves, ½ bay leaf
salt, 1 lemon
pinch of thyme, nutmeg
3–4 egg yolks
2 tablespoons double cream
chicken broth or water to cook it in

Melt the butter in a very large frying pan and turn the chicken in it until golden all over. Put it in a large saucepan, cover with water or chicken broth, bring to the boil and skim before adding vegetables, herbs and seasoning. Add the celery, leeks cleaned and cut in 4″ pieces, the peeled and chopped carrots and onion, herbs, seasoning, cloves and nutmeg. Bring it to the boil and poach for 2 hours or until tender. Remove the chicken from the stock, let it cool slightly and cut it into large serving pieces. Remove the skin and bones and keep the meat hot. Strain the stock into a large saucepan and add the lemon thinly sliced and 1 tablespoon finely chopped parsley. Heat the stock until it is almost boiling, stir in 4 egg yolks beaten with the double cream and let the sauce thicken without boiling. Add the chicken meat and serve with thin slices of buttered brown bread.

☐ *This is soup with chicken in it — you need a knife, fork and spoon to eat it with.*

For 6

How to Carve a Turkey, Large Chicken or Capon

Sharpen two knives, one with a 6″ blade and one with a 9″ blade and have ready your carving fork and a spoon for the stuffing. Remove all strings and skewers.

1. Remove the merry thought or wishbone by feeling your way carefully round its outside edge with your short knife, and snicking the sinews where it joins the bird's shoulder-bones. This helps to carve fine, straight breast slices.

2. Place the bird with its legs to the left, stick the fork firmly into the drumstick, make cut (a) and pull the drumstick towards you so that you can cut through the ball and socket joint. Slice through to remove thigh and drumstick.

3. Carve slices from the thigh and more slices from the drumstick.

4. Using your long-bladed knife and leaving the wing where it is, so that the bird does not tip over, carve careful vertical slices starting halfway down the breast at (b). A horizontal cut (c) across the top of the wing through to the carcase helps to make neat slices and keep the wing intact. The reason for starting halfway down the breast and making your cuts vertical rather than slanting is that any meat remaining after you have carved what you need stays nice and moist under its skin.

5. Remove the wing as you did the leg, levering it away with the fork and snicking through the joint with your short knife. Cut off wing-tips if they have been left on by the butcher, and divide the wing in two if it is a large bird.

6. Carve the other side as before but keeping the meaty side towards your guests and tilting the bird towards you with the help of your fork.

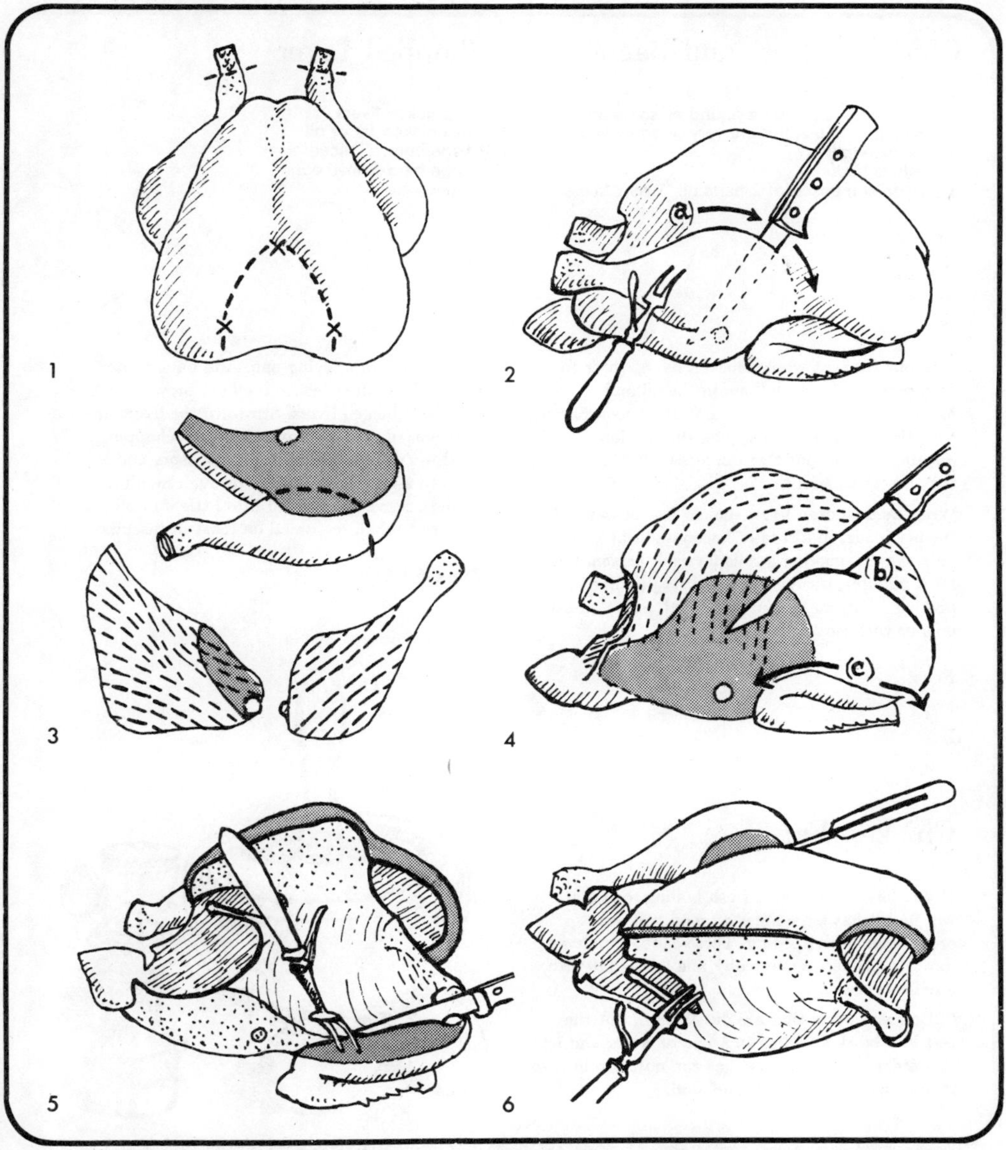
1
2
(a)
3
4
(b)
(c)
5
6

Chicken Livers and Bacon

¾ lb chicken livers (buy a pound as some are too sloppy to use but are very good in pâté after marinading)
12 rashers bacon
marinade composed of 2 parts oil, 1 part Madeira

Pick out the best whole chicken livers, three for each person. Marinate them in the oil and Madeira for 1 hour at least. Lay the bacon rashers, with the lean part overlapping the fat, in a roasting tin and put them in a low oven until they are transparent.

Wrap each chicken liver, shaken free of most of the marinade, in a slice of bacon and impale it on a skewer, making 3 rolls for each person. Grill for 5 minutes, turning once — it is just like making toast, no basting is needed. Serve on their own or with rice.

For 4

Chopped Liver

1 lb chicken livers
6 oz chicken fat or oil
2 large onions, sliced
2 large hard-boiled eggs
pepper, salt

Melt the fat in a frying pan. Add onions and soften them. Just before they get brown add the chopped chicken livers. Stir until the livers are well cooked. Put the mixture into a chopping bowl with the hard-boiled eggs, season, and chop to a fine paste (or put through mouli, or pound). Serve cold, rolled into little dumplings, with rice salad, or spread on toast or biscuits.

For 4–6

Chicken Fat

If you have a nice large fresh boiling fowl you will find it has large areas of good yellow fat around the back opening. These can be rendered down to produce some really fine frying fat with a delicate flavour.

Cut off any parts that are discoloured, put the rest in a bowl, standing in a pan of water and let it simmer until all the fat has run out. Strain it to remove any bits of fibre, and chill.

Chicken Croquettes

a few mushrooms peeled and chopped, if available
½ lb left-over chicken, chopped up (no skin or gristle)
Béchamel – 1½ oz flour, 1½ oz butter, just under ½ pint milk (see page 183)
1 egg yolk
salt, pepper
flour
1 egg, beaten
dry breadcrumbs
deep fat

Fry the mushrooms, if any, in butter. Make the sauce, which should be very thick, and season it. Add the chicken and mushrooms and egg yolk. Stir over low flame until the mixture is really thick. Put it on a flat dish to cool and solidify (leave all day, or overnight). Take a floured board and shape croquettes (like fat sausages). Dip in beaten egg, then breadcrumbs, and fry in smoking hot deep fat, until golden. Serve with tomato sauce.

☐ *These are also very good made with left-over pheasant or turkey.*

For 4

Poule au Pot de bon Roi Henri

1 cabbage, 1 lb carrots
½ lb turnips, 4 sticks celery 1 onion
1 large boiling fowl, not too fatty
1 bacon hock (preferably smoked)
2 slices stale white bread
6 oz ham or boiled bacon with its fat
3–4 sprigs parsley, 3–4 sprigs tarragon
1 clove garlic, salt, pepper
plenty of nutmeg
2 fresh eggs and 2 oz butter
or the eggs from inside the fowl and its own fat melted down (economy)

Prepare the cabbage, cut it in half, and put it in a very large saucepan with the scraped carrots, turnips, celery and onion. Cover with 6–7 pints cold water. Stuff the chicken with a stuffing made by chopping the boiled bacon or ham, the bird's liver and the heart very finely. Mix with the grated bread, chopped herbs, garlic and beaten eggs. Add salt, pepper and nutmeg, and the melted butter, and stuff the bird with this mixture. Skewer it well or sew it up to prevent the stuffing escaping. Put it in the pot, bring it to the boil, skim, and simmer for 1½ hours. Add the bacon hock and simmer another 1½ hours or less if the chicken is small. Serve the strained bouillon, skimmed of most of its fat and with a handful of finely chopped parsley or cooked rice thrown in. You can serve it with the vegetables but they are pretty soggy by now. Traditionally pieces of bread toasted in the oven are served with it, but new bread or fried bread croûtons are good too (croûtons are not necessary if you have added rice).

The next course is the chicken with its delicious stuffing and the boiled bacon hock, followed by a salad or accompanied by a green vegetable such as beans.

For 8

Poulet en Cocotte

2½–3½ lbs roasting chicken
butter
¼ lb streaky bacon in a piece
15–20 button onions
15–20 walnut-sized new potatoes
salt, pepper

Cook the chicken in a deep casserole, uncovered. Start to roast it in the usual way (page 106).

Peel the onions and scrape or peel the potatoes. Cut the bacon into cubes and sauté it in a heavy frying pan with a nut of butter. When there is a fair amount of fat and the cubes are brown, lift them out and keep them on one side while you brown the potatoes and onions gently for about 20 minutes. Then add them to the casserole with the bacon, season with salt and pepper and cook on until the chicken is cooked and the vegetables tender, about 30–40 minutes. Put the chicken on a dish surrounded by the vegetables, you can carve it up first if you like. Make giblet gravy and serve it separately.

For 4–6

Old English Pigeons

2 plump pigeons
6 medium onions, chopped
salt, sugar, pepper
bouquet of herbs (parsley, bay leaf, thyme)
juice of 1 lemon
½ oz butter
½ oz flour

Buy the pigeons well in advance (as this recipe entails marinating them for 3–6 days). Make a mixture of equal parts of salt and sugar, about a dessertspoonful of each and rub it well into the birds, inside and out. Leave them in the refrigerator or cool place (covered with a cloth and turn ing occasionally) for 3–6 days. Take them out, wash them well and dry them. Put them into a bowl, or casserole with a tight fitting lid, with the chopped onions, herbs and a little salt and pepper. Cover tightly with foil, or a cloth and greaseproof paper and steam (as you would a suet pudding) in a large covered pan of constantly boiling water for 4 hours. (Young birds may be done after 2–3 hours, so test occasionally.) A great deal of gravy is produced by the onions and birds, by the time they are done, which you turn into a sauce with the flour, butter and lemon juice. Remove the pigeons and onions to a warm dish and discard the bouquet. Work the flour and butter together thoroughly and add bit by bit to the gravy stirring constantly over a low heat till the sauce thickens. Add the lemon juice and check seasoning. Serve birds, cut in half with sauce and onions poured over them.

For 4

Stuffed Duck for a Party

1 7 lb duck
1 glass brandy } (if possible)
1 glass white wine }
salt, pepper, marjoram, thyme, parsley, pistachios (if possible) truffles if you have any
1 fresh pig's foot
1 carrot
1 onion
½ lb pigs' liver or chicken livers
¼ lb bacon rashers (rinds removed)
¾ lb pie veal

Choose 2 things from any of these, according to the amount you have to spend, and availability.
1 pigeon
1 very small roasting chicken
½ lb cooked tongue in 1 piece
½ lb cooked ham or boiled bacon in 1 piece
1 small rabbit
2 cloves garlic

Start two days before the party. Bone the duck according to the diagram in *Poor Cook* for boning a chicken, leaving its lower leg bones in, and wings. Salt and pepper its inside and sprinkle with brandy or wine. Leave to rest while you prepare the stuffing and stock. Put its bones into a large saucepan with a bouquet of herbs, the pig's foot, the carrot and onion, and add to it any other bones and scraps you may encounter from making the stuffing — e.g. rabbit, pigeon, or chicken bones. Aim to make almost 1 gallon of stock, which will give 20 people delicious consommé for a first course.

Make the stuffing. Stiffen the liver by cooking it in a little butter before mincing it with the bacon rashers and pie veal. If you are using pigeon, chicken or rabbit, take the slivers of meat from the tenderest parts and mince the rest putting the bones in the stock-pot. Marinade the slivers in brandy.

If you are using the tongue, ham or bacon, cut strips about ½" square and 4" long. Mix the minced meats well and add salt, pepper and crushed or finely chopped garlic. Add chopped parsley, thyme leaves and marjoram if you have it. Add pistachio nuts and truffles if you are feeling the party is worth it. Add brandy and wine and 2 ladles of stock, which should be getting good by the time you have done all this boning and mincing. Taste a teaspoon of the mixture for seasoning after frying it in a little butter. Drain the liquid from the marinading strips into the minced mixture. Stuff the duck with alternate layers of mince, and fillets, or strips of meat. Sew it up. Cool about 1½ pints of stock and place the duck in it. Use an oval tin or steel fishkettle with a lid if you have such a thing, if not use a baking tin and cover it with silver foil, but the shape of the finished duck will spread in a tin, so tie tapes round it. Braise it in the oven 1½ hours covered, Reg 3/325°. Finish by draining off the stock, but keep it separate and turn up the oven to Reg 5/375° for the duck to brown, uncovered, for ½ hour. Allow it to cool completely before removing threads. Scrape the sediment from the pan with the stock from the cooking of the duck, this will improve its colour and flavour. Strain it through a sieve and put it to cool in the fridge. There will be a great deal of fat on it. Also strain the consommé from the big pan and put it to cool.

NEXT DAY. Remove the threads from the duck and take all the fat from the cooking stock, which should be jellied enough to use as a glaze. Pour a little at a time over the duck, to coat it with a nice shine. Decorate if you like, with strips of green cucumber skin, slices of tomato or red pimento, and pieces of white cucumber. Serve with its dark jelly chopped up all round it, and slice it as you would a loaf of bread. Serve the soup first, clarified with egg white if need be (page 184), but straining through a cloth is usually sufficient. Add as much sherry to it as you can for flavour.

For 20

Roast Duck

3 lb duckling with giblets
½ an orange
leaf of sage
salt, pepper, oil
a bouquet of herbs
onion, carrot

Preheat the oven to Reg 3½/335°. Put the orange, sage and a sprinkling of salt and pepper into the duck. Rub the outside with oil, and sprinkle on some salt. Put the giblets, all but the liver, into a saucepan, with water to cover, and the bouquet, onion and carrot, and salt and pepper. Simmer while you roast the duck. Lay the duck upside down in a roasting tin and roast, basting occasionally for ¾–1 hour. Turn it over the right way up and drain off most of the fat which has run from it. Pour the giblet stock into the pan and give it another hour, basting as you go, until the skin is crisp and dark gold. Put it on a warm serving dish and make the gravy in the following way.

Remove most of the fat from the roasting tin with a large spoon. Put it over a low heat and put in the liver to cook whole. When the juices are bubbling add a sprinkling (just a touch) of flour and ½ glass of wine if you can spare it. Then add a little water and cook, stirring, turning the liver over from time to time. Remove the liver to the serving dish and serve the gravy in a sauceboat, having tasted it for seasoning. Leave the duck to stand in a warm place for at least ½ hour before carving.

For 4

How to Carve a Duck or Goose

You can deal with a small duck by cutting it into 4 portions as described for a small chicken (pages 106–7). A larger duck or a goose will need to be carved.

Sharpen your short poultry knife and your long carving knife, use the short one for jointing and the long one for carving slices. Remove all string and skewers.

1. Remove the wishbone by carefully feeling your way round its outside edge with your short knife and snicking through the sinews at the shoulder joints.

2. Turn the bird over onto its breast and insert your knife under and behind the leg, which lies well underneath the bird (a). Prize it away with your fork, sever the ball joint with the point of your knife and continue the cut towards the tail-end of the bird (b) as there is a nice piece of meat here to include with the leg.

3. Cut the leg in two; the joint is off to the side so feel for it carefully.

4. Turn the bird the right way up and make vertical slices with the longer knife, carving the bird from about quarterway up its breast (c). These will be thin slices that end just above the wing. When you have finished the breast remove the wing. It has hardly any meat on it but somebody might like to chew it.

5 & 6. Carve the second side as you did the first, keeping the meaty side of the bird towards the guests.

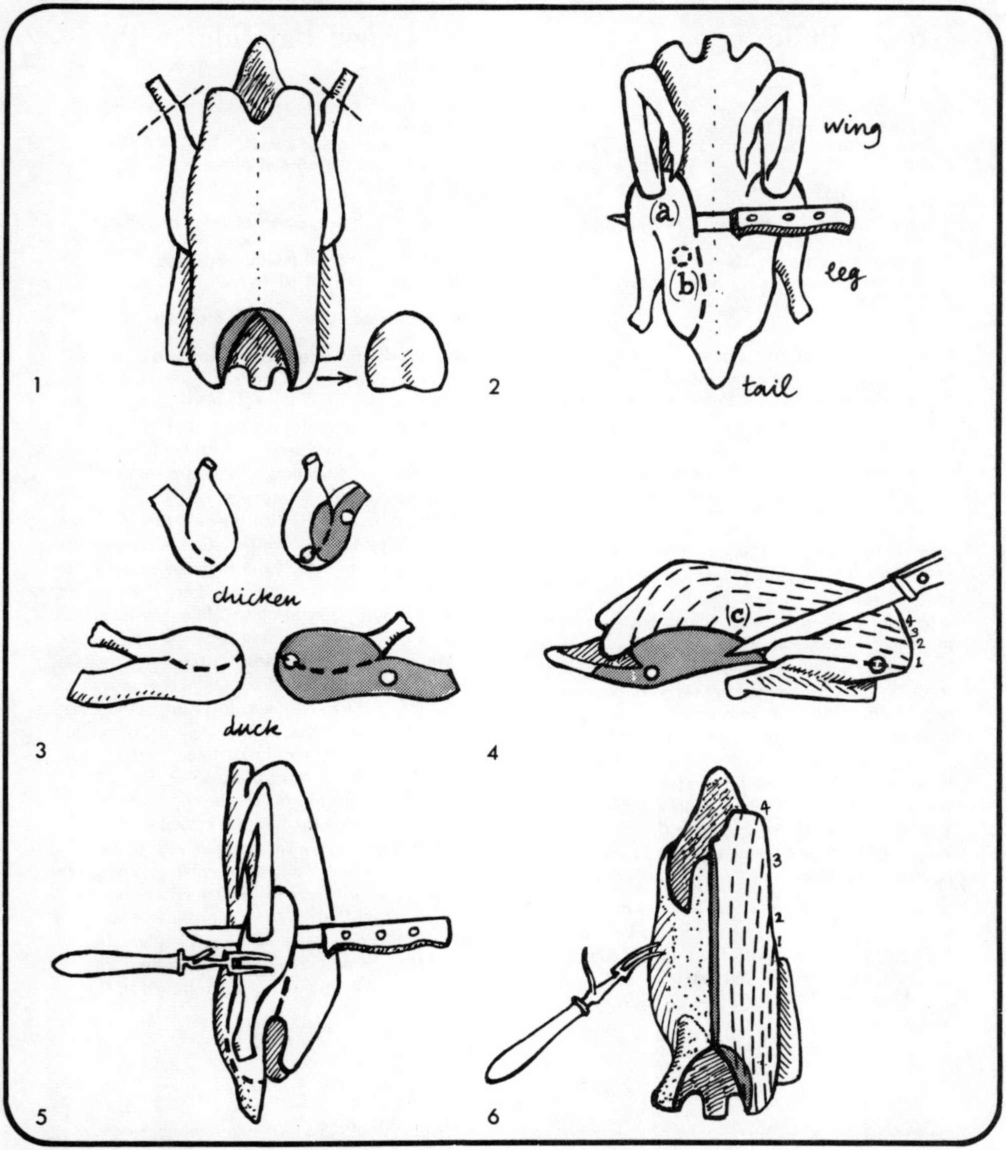
1
2
wing
(a)
(b)
leg
tail
chicken
duck
3
4
(c)
4
3
2
1
5
6
4
3
2
1

Grouse Pudding

1 old grouse
¾ lb chuck or skirt of beef
1 onion, with a clove in it
1 carrot, sliced
a bouquet of herbs, salt and pepper
} To make stock with bones of grouse
¼ lb mushrooms, tossed in butter or bacon fat
1 oz seasoned flour
6 oz self-raising flour
3 oz shredded suet
Salt, a little water
} Suet pastry

Start several hours, at least six, before dinner. Strip the grouse from its carcase, leaving the legs and wings whole, quarter the breast meat. Cut the beef into thin slices. Make stock by covering the onion, carrot, herbs, salt and pepper, grouse carcase and beef trimmings with cold water and simmering, covered, for 2 hours. Let it cool, and strain it.

Make the pastry with the suet, flour, pinch of salt and water. Take ¾ of it to line a greased pudding basin. Wrap each cooked mushroom (quartered if large) in a strip of the beef, which has been tossed in seasoned flour. Put grouse and beef alternately in the lined basin and almost cover with strained stock. Cover with remaining pastry, damping the edges to make it stick. Cover the top firmly with doubled greaseproof paper or silver foil, tucked under basin's rim and tied with string. Have a large pan ready with boiling water and put the basin into it, so that the water comes about ⅔ of the way up the basin. Cover the pan and keep it boiling for 4 hours, replenishing with boiling water as need be.

To serve, heat the remainder of the strained stock and cut a wedge from the pastry lid. Pour in the boiling stock, mixing with the pudding contents, so that each serving is well gravied.

For 4

Casseroled Partridge with Cabbage

2 oz pork fat, fresh or salt, pork dripping or lard
2 old partridges
2 carrots, peeled and sliced
1 small onion, peeled and sliced
1 savoy cabbage
4 oz bacon or salt pork
a bouquet of herbs, pinch of mace or grate of nutmeg
4 pork chipolatas, or boiling sausages
salt, pepper, dash of white wine
½ pint stock
½ oz flour, ½ oz butter worked together

Cut the pork fat into cubes, and put it in a large iron or earthenware casserole to give out its fat or alternatively melt the lard or dripping. As the fat begins to run, dust the partridges with flour and brown them on all sides, turning frequently. While they are browning slice the onion and carrots and shred the cabbage finely.

When the birds are golden brown, remove them to a plate and keep them hot while you soften the onion, bacon and then the cabbage in the same fat in a separate pan. Turn them over a few times until they are glistening and starting to brown. Cover the bottom of the casserole with carrot slices, place the birds on top, bury them in the cabbage, onion and bacon, and season well with salt, pepper and mace or nutmeg. Add the bouquet and the wine, and let it sizzle, then add enough stock or water almost to cover the birds. Put on the lid and leave in the oven, Reg 2/300° for 3–4 hours. 1 hour before the end brown the sausages, and put them in the casserole with the partridges. Serve each person with half a partridge, a sausage and some cabbage and gravy thickened with beurre manié before serving.

If it suits you to cook them more slowly use Reg 1/275° for 4 hours or more. They are done when the legs pull easily from the bodies. They will stay moist if you keep them buried in the cabbage.

For 4

Roast Rabbit

1 fine tame rabbit
2–3 cloves garlic
a small bunch of parsley or thyme
salt, pepper
2 oz butter
2 tablespoons stock
½ glass white wine

Put the skinned and cleaned rabbit ribs upward on a piece of butter in the roasting tin. Chop the garlic and parsley finely and press these into the rabbit all over the underpart (now uppermost). Spread very soft butter over all. Season and roast at Reg 5½/390° for 45 minutes–1 hour, basting very frequently. When it is cooked remove the rabbit to a hot dish and make a gravy with all the juice (including the butter), 2 tablespoons of good stock and ½ glass of white wine plus salt and pepper. Strain and hand separately.

□ *Sweet young turnips braised in butter are very good with this followed by a green salad.*

For 4–6

Notes on Rabbit

The only cheap rabbit is that which you shoot yourself, or deep frozen Polish, Australian or Chinese. All these need long slow cooking (unless the rabbit you shoot yourself is a tiny one and therefore young).

Good butchers stock large, tame, tender young hutch rabbits. These are delicious, need little cooking, and are rather expensive. They cost more per pound than roasting chicken or shoulder of lamb.

If you do use these rabbit recipes on a wild English or foreign rabbit, double the cooking times.

Civet of Rabbit

1 rabbit, cut in pieces
½ pint red wine
3 rashers bacon
1 oz butter, flour
salt, pepper
½ pint or less stock, made with head, etc.
4 cloves, 2–3 blades mace
4 juniper berries, 4 peppercorns
1 onion or 3 shallots
a bunch of thyme, parsley and bay leaf

Cut the rabbit into pieces and save the blood and liver. Mix the blood with a little vinegar to keep it liquid. Marinate the rabbit pieces overnight in the red wine. Remove the rabbit pieces and shake them dry. Put the liver aside till later, with the blood.

Cut the bacon into squares and brown them in the butter in a flameproof casserole. Pat the rabbit pieces with flour, salt and pepper and brown them a few at a time quite slowly. Remove them to a plate as you brown the other pieces. Then return all the pieces, pour on the marinade and enough stock to cover the rabbit. Add the chopped onion or shallots, spices, herbs and a *little* salt (the bacon and the stock provide most of it), bring to the boil, cover and simmer for ¾ hour. Add the liver and simmer a further 10–15 minutes. Turn off the heat, remove the liver, pound it with the blood until it is a paste, gradually add several tablespoons of hot stock. Then return this to the pan, stir it in, allow to stand covered 3–4 minutes, then serve.

□ *If you don't have the rabbit's blood, put any blood clots found in the neck area into a bowl with a couple of teaspoons of vinegar. Hare can also be used for this recipe but needs at least an extra hour's cooking time.*

For 4

Family Pâté

½ lb fat salt pork
½ lb veal (odd lean pieces but cheap)
¾ lb chicken livers
2 cloves garlic
6 juniper berries
8 peppercorns, salt
small glass red wine (½ gill or just over)
2 bay leaves
a bunch of thyme, 1 egg
a dash of brandy
butter for frying

Chop or mince the pork and veal together. Carefully remove the strings from the chicken livers and sauté them quickly in sizzling butter for a minute or two. Mince them. Put all the meat in a bowl together with the butter, in which the livers were fried. Crush the peppercorns, juniper berries and garlic in a mortar and stir them into the meat.

Add the salt, wine, a good sprinkling of thyme leaves, beaten egg and a dash of brandy if you can spare it. Stir thoroughly and allow to stand for about 1 hour if possible. Turn the mixture into a terrine. Stand it in a tin of water and cook in a slow oven, Reg 2/300° for 1½ hours covered with foil and a further ½ hour uncovered with a bay leaf laid on top. Allow to cool, pour melted bacon fat over the top and cover. Best kept overnight before eating and will keep at least a week in the refrigerator.

☐ *Very rich and good. You can equally well cook these in small glass preserving jars, which you seal with rings and clips as you remove them from the oven. They make very good presents.*

Makes 1 × 2 lb pâtés

Hare Pâté

The back legs of a hare (or 1½ lbs boned hare meat)
the liver of the hare
6 oz salt pork
1–2 cloves garlic
glass of wine
a little stock, salt, pepper, pinch of mixed spice
thyme, bay leaf
4–5 rashers of thin streaky bacon
a marinade as for the one in game pie

Marinade the hare and liver for 24 hours (see the marinade in game pie, opposite). Take out the legs and simmer them in a little stock or water for 20 minutes. This is not to cook them, but just to make the meat easier to bone, chop and mince. Slice the best meat into neat fillets and chop or mince the rest, with the pork. Stiffen (sauté briefly) the liver in a little pork fat or butter, and mince that too. Add the crushed garlic, wine, salt, pepper, spice and thyme to all the meat, and if it needs a little more moisture add some stock or some of the marinade.
Preheat the oven to Reg 2/300°. Fill a pâté dish with the mixture and press it well down. Cover it neatly with bacon rashers and put a bay leaf on top. Cover with silver foil. Put the pâté in a bain marie and cook for 2 hours. Take the foil off for the last ½ hour to brown the top. Press and cool. Eat when set next day.

Game Pie

All the pieces of a jointed hare except the saddle, which you can eat at another meal
2 pigeons
6 oz fresh belly of pork
6 oz salt pork
salt, pepper, 6 juniper berries, nutmeg or mace
a small glass of brandy, small glass of red wine
1 pig's trotter, onions, carrots, celery, bay leaf for the stock

For the marinade
1 glass red wine, $\frac{1}{2}$ glass vinegar, blade of mace, sprigs of thyme, rosemary and bay leaf

For the pastry
1 lb flour, 6 oz lard, $\frac{1}{4}$ pint milk and water, salt

Make the marinade by mixing the ingredients together and pour it over the pigeon breasts and pieces of hare. Turn the pieces after an hour or so and allow to marinate overnight.

Make a stock from the pigeon carcases and odd parts of the hare such as head, heart and so on and the pig's trotter. Keep the liver for the pie filling. Put in some carrots, onions and celery, a few peppercorns, bay leaf and some salt. Cover with plenty of water and skim when it comes to the boil and afterwards until the stock becomes clear. Let it simmer gently, uncovered for several hours until you have about a pint of liquid left. The day you make the pie, drain the meat from the marinade (which you can keep to marinate the saddle), dry it and cut the best bits, pigeon breast and top part of the hare's legs, into thin fillets. Mince the rest with the pork both salt and fresh and hare's liver. Mix the minced meat with the crushed juniper berries, nutmeg or mace, brandy and red wine and season well with pepper but go easy on the salt, because the salt pork will add almost enough.

Put the flour and salt in a bowl, bring the lard and milk and water to the boil and pour it into the flour, mix well, first with a spoon, and then with your hands. Knead it well until it is smooth, but do this as quickly as you can and in a warm place, as unlike ordinary pastry this sort is only workable while it is hot.

Preheat the oven to Reg 7/425°.

Grease a game-pie tin or cake tin with a removable base and line it with $\frac{2}{3}$ of the pastry. Put in a layer of the mince, a layer of fillets, more mince, more fillets and so on until it is full, pressing it down fairly well. Cover the pie with the remaining pastry, leaving a hole in the middle into which you fit a little greaseproof paper funnel if you are a perfectionist, to prevent any juice bubbling up and spoiling the look of the crust. Glaze and decorate the pie and cook at Reg 7/425° for 20 minutes, then at Reg 4/350° for 1 hour 40 minutes. Cool thoroughly, then pour in enough of the strained, cooled stock (it should be poured into the pie in a just-melted state) to fill it to the top. This is done through a small funnel stuck into the hole in the middle. Allow to set and keep overnight before cutting.

☐*This is very good picnic or journey food provided your jelly is quite firm — if you doubt its holding powers add some gelatine to the stock before you put it in the pie.*

Faggots

1 large onion, peeled and chopped
1 clove garlic
1 lb pigs' liver
½ lb fresh belly of pork
2 oz pure pork fat
sage or thyme, and parsley if you like
salt, pepper, scrape of nutmeg
1 large egg
4 oz breadcrumbs (fresh, not dry)
pigs' caul (see page 97)
good stock or left-over gravy

Mince together the onion, garlic, liver, pork and fat. Season it with the herbs, nutmeg and a little salt and pepper. Lightly grease a large pan and cook the mixture *very slowly* for about ½ hour, turning it often so that none of it burns. Tip the pan and pour the mixture of fat and gravy that runs from it into a bowl. Add the beaten egg and breadcrumbs to the meat. Mix to a fairly firm mixture that you can form into balls about the size of a small apple. Wrap each ball in a piece of caul fat, and place them closely together in a gratin dish or baking tin. Heat the oven to Reg 3/325°. Mix the stock or left-over gravy together with their own gravy and pour it into the tin to come halfway up the faggots. Bake them for about 40 minutes, until they are nice and brown on top. Serve them with peas or pease pudding (page 139) and mashed potatoes. Leftovers will reheat well, but will need more gravy.

If you cannot obtain caul fat, roll the balls of mixture in flour and bake as described above, without adding the gravy, which is served separately.

For 4–6

Rillettes of Pork

2 lbs belly of pork (skin removed)
¼ lb flare fat (sold in a strip for larding by the butcher)
salt, pepper
grating of nutmeg

Cube the fat and pork into 1½" pieces. Put them into a heavy pan with a little water. Cover and cook in a very low oven for 4 hours (Reg 1/275°). Strain off and reserve the liquid and pull the meat to pieces with 2 forks, or better still, when cooled, with your fingers, removing any bones there may be. This is a lengthy job but there is no better way. You are aiming at fine soft threads of meat in a creamy spicy body. Season well and return the liquid to the meat. Reheat until it bubbles, then put it, if possible, into stoneware jars or nice china or earthenware dishes. Cover with melted lard, about ½" deep and put paper covers over that. Rillettes will keep for months in a cool place.

☐ *Eat as a snack with wholemeal bread. Good for Christmas presents. You can add pieces of rabbit or pigeon at the beginning, if you like, but it should be mainly pork.*

Vegetables

Vegetables

The mark of a cook worth her salt is that she doesn't mind spending time and trouble on boring details, and unless you do take time and trouble with them boring details are just about what vegetables become. But a good cook can make even perfectly plainly cooked vegetables into a well-loved part of the meal. She learns how to cook them properly, to drain them for long enough and reheat them briefly so that they are dry and hot. They can then be tossed in plenty of fresh butter, a few spoonfuls of cream or some olive oil and lemon juice, or smothered with a cream sauce or shaken with some fried breadcrumbs or crumbled fried bacon to make them into something special. Of course really fresh vegetables from the garden don't even need this, but from the minute they break contact with the ground vegetables start to lose their vitamins, their tender creamy texture and their flavour. So, if you haven't got a garden, buy the very fresh looking over-sized sprouts rather than the yellowing button ones, which may be younger but are not so good, whatever the greengrocer may say. Anyone who has watched the stallholders in a market stripping the outside leaves off wilting cabbages to make them look small and young again will know what we mean.

Peel vegetables thinly if at all; their vitamins are most concentrated just under the skin. So boil potatoes in their skins, do no more than scrub young carrots, turnips and parsnips and leave the skin on young courgettes and aubergines.

The cooking of all green vegetables should be started in boiling salt water and they should never be cooked with a lid, or they will lose their bright colour. If you find the flavour of leeks, onions, celery, Belgian endive or cabbage too strong, blanch them for 5 minutes in boiling salted water before braising or cooking them in some other way.

Salads should be perfectly dry before you put the dressing on, wet salads are reminiscent of school dinners and similar institutional food. The ideal green salad has several different *green* ingredients but no jumble — tomatoes and radishes are much better served separately. Mayonnaise should not be served with green salad, it won't coat the leaves in the glistening way oil and vinegar dressing does, it simply sticks them together in horrid bundles. A salad made with a cold cooked vegetable on the other hand — cold broad beans or cold peas, is very good with a mayonnaise lightened with a bit of top of the milk or cream.

The cooking of dried vegetables or pulses is simple but needs plenty of time. They may need soaking overnight, they get harder and harder as the year goes by. New season's haricot beans, dried peas or lentils, bought in the autumn can probably be cooked straight away or need no more than ½ hour's soaking. But if pulses are more than several months old and don't seem to get tender even after hours of soaking and simmering, throw them away — they will never be tender again. Chick peas bought in this country always need overnight soaking. If you are in a hurry a pressure cooker is invaluable for cooking pulses.

Brussels Sprouts with Chestnuts

1 lb brussels sprouts
2 oz butter
½ lb chestnuts
salt, pinch of sugar
stock (about ½ pint)

Skin and cook the shelled chestnuts in the stock with a little salt and sugar, until they are tender (about ½ hour). Clean and trim the sprouts, cook them in salty boiling water until done (not too soggy) — about 10–15 minutes, according to their size. Drain well and melt half the butter in a pan and sauté the sprouts in it for about 10 minutes. Serve them mixed carefully with the chestnuts and any of their juice which remains. Take care not to crush the chestnuts or sprouts as you mix them. Leave them for 5–10 minutes in a warm place before serving.

☐ *A winter dish, and traditionally served with turkey.*

For 4–6

Hot Baked Beetroot

1 lb raw beetroots
salt, fresh ground pepper
butter
a squeeze of fresh lemon juice
¼ pint cream (optional)

Wash the beetroots but do not break the skin or peel or cut them in any way. Put them in a brown paper bag and bake them in a very low oven, if you are using it for a stew or other slow-cooking dish, for about 3–4 hours at Reg 1/275°. Otherwise boil them in their skins in salted water until tender (2 hours). When they are soft (easily pierced with a skewer) skin them while they are still hot, slice them and lay the slices in a buttered gratin dish. Dot with butter and sprinkle with salt, pepper and lemon juice and heat them gently. Just before serving you can pour on some warmed cream or more melted butter and lemon juice. Sprinkle with parsley and serve as an hors d'œuvre or with hot sausages or game (roast pigeons, hare, etc.).

For 4

Hot Beetroot with Garlic

5–6 small beetroots (the smallest you can buy)
1 clove garlic
olive oil
salt, sugar, chopped parsley

Boil the beetroots with 1″ of stalks and their tails left on. Very small beetroots need about ½ hour's gentle boiling, larger ones need longer — up to 2 hours. Peel them while still hot and heat the slices of garlic in the oil in a flat fireproof dish which you can take to the table.

Slice the beetroot into the oil and sprinkle with a little fine salt, sugar and parsley. Moisten it all with a little more oil, and leave to keep hot. Serve as soon as possible or the beetroot begins to lose its shine. It is also, if kept moist, nice cold this way.

For 6

Hot Cucumber with Herbs

1 large cucumber
1 oz butter
chopped parsley, dill, chives (parsley alone wil' do)
a squeeze of lemon
salt, pepper
top of the milk, or dash of single cream

Peel the cucumber, quarter it lengthwise and chop it into 1½″ lengths. Melt the butter in a shallow heavy saucepan. Put in the cucumber and sprinkle it with salt. Cover the pan and let it sizzle away gently and toss it around from time to time. As it begins to soften, sprinkle on the chopped herbs and squeeze some lemon juice and a grinding of pepper. After about 15 minutes, it should be tender, take off the lid and pour on some top of the milk, or cream, and serve at once.

☐ *This can be served with fish (if you are feeling rich, salmon or trout are especially nice), or roast or boiled chicken.*

For 3–4

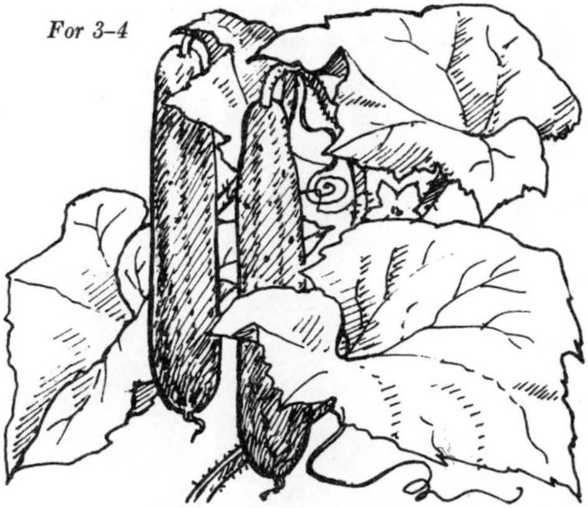

Braised Cucumber

2 cucumbers
2 oz butter
salt, pepper
chopped parsley
tarragon or fresh dill
juice of ½ lemon

Peel the cucumbers and quarter them lengthwise. Scoop out their seeds with a teaspoon, and cut them into 3″ lengths. Bring some salted water to the boil, and cook them for 5 minutes. Drain them well, and return them to the saucepan (which should be a good thick one, with a lid) with the butter and a little salt and pepper. Let them stew, covered, over a very low heat for about ½ hour. Turn them frequently with a wooden spoon to prevent them sticking or burning. Finally, add the chopped parsley and tarragon or dill, and the lemon juice and serve as soon as possible.

☐ *A useful vegetable when you want a hot vegetable to go with delicately flavoured foods like chicken, veal or poached fish. You can use old or misshapen cucumbers for this dish.*

For 4

Chanterelles (Three Ways)

Wash them well and split them up if they are large. Sauté in oil or butter, season with salt and pepper, and then *either* sprinkle with finely chopped parsley and as much cream as you can get them to take, *or* beat two eggs, seasoned with salt and pepper, and scramble them with the chanterelles. Serve in both cases with a squeeze of lemon and toast, fried bread, rice or good fresh bread.

Or prepare as above, chop garlic and parsley finely and cook it in plenty of oil with chanterelles. Season well. Strew thickly with fresh white breadcrumbs to soak up the garlicky oil, cook a little longer and again serve with a squeeze of lemon and toast, fried bread, rice or good fresh bread. Also delicious in a risotto.

☐ *If small, cèpes can be cooked the same way. The stalks are better than the caps, so don't throw them away. They need garlic.*

Cabbage with Sour Cream and Dill

1 cabbage
1 5 oz carton sour cream
1 teaspoon dill seeds
salt
freshly ground pepper

Quarter, core and wash the cabbage. Drop the pieces into boiling salted water and cook until just tender. Drain well and return to the pan with the sour cream, dill, a little salt and plenty of freshly ground pepper. Heat gently and cook, stirring to separate the pieces of cabbage from each other, until the water that drains from the cabbage has evaporated and the still greenish, but no longer bright green, leaves are bathed in a creamy sauce. Serve with pork chops or sausages.

☐ *Very successful with children who don't usually like cabbage.*

For 4

Coleslaw

½ small white cabbage, shredded finely
2 new or 1 old carrot, grated
1 or 2 sticks celery, shredded lengthwise into matchsticks
1 eating apple, grated

For the dressing

½ teacup of vinaigrette dressing
½ teacup of mayonnaise made with lemon
a little top of the milk

Mix the grated and shredded vegetables together in a china bowl. Add the vinaigrette dressing, made with a pinch of sugar, and turn and mix it well. Leave it to become absorbed for a little while. Thin the mayonnaise with the top of the milk and mix this in well too. Taste for seasoning. It should be a soft pale creamy salad, almost sweet, but with a slightly crisp vinegary bite.

☐ *This keeps well overnight, so if you are making it for a party it can be one of the things you can make in advance. You can alter the proportions of cabbage, etc., but don't be tempted to spoil it by adding onions, or herbs, not even parsley. It is very good with hamburgers or frankfurters*

For 6

Cabbage with Noodles

1 medium-size white cabbage
1 onion
2 oz butter
salt, black pepper
½ lb dry noodles

Drop the washed, cored and quartered cabbage into boiling salted water and cook 5 minutes. Drain well. Meanwhile chop the onion finely and soften it in the butter in a large pan or casserole, then add the cabbage and stir well. Cover and cook 30–40 minutes, turning from time to time, until soft and golden. Season with salt and plenty of black pepper while the cabbage is cooking. Drop the noodles into boiling salted water and when they are just tender drain them well. Time it so that they are ready together. Mix into the cabbage and add a little more butter. Serve on its own or with meatballs or pork chops.

For 6–8

Frances's Cabbage

1 medium-size cabbage, any sort
1 oz butter
1 rasher bacon, diced
2 oz sultanas
a pinch each of cinnamon, nutmeg, cayenne
1 dessertspoon brown sugar
1 dessertspoon wine vinegar

Shred the cabbage, chop it up and leave to soak for 1 hour in cold water. Melt the butter in a large pan, throw in the well-drained cabbage, vinegar, bacon, sultanas, brown sugar, cinnamon and nutmeg, pinch of cayenne. Cook slowly, covered, for 1 hour, turning occasionally. It needs little or no salt.

For 4

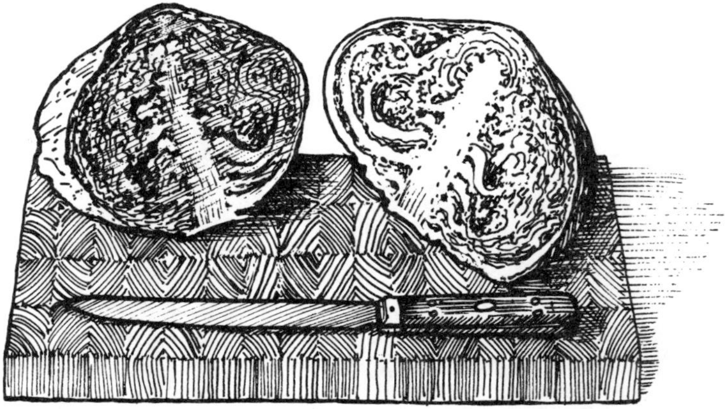

Cabbage Strudel

Pastry as for apple strudel (page 144)
1 firm white cabbage weighing 2 lbs
1 small onion
1 oz butter
salt, black pepper
nutmeg
4 juniper berries

Shred the cabbage. Wash it well and drop it into boiling salted water for 2 minutes. Drain well. Soften the onion in the butter in a sauté pan for several minutes, add the well-drained cabbage and stir it well. Cover and cook 30–40 minutes until soft and golden. Season with crushed juniper berries, salt, plenty of pepper and some nutmeg. Allow to cool. Preheat oven to Reg 8/450°.

Pull out the strudel pastry on a floured cloth. Brush with melted butter. Lay a line of the cabbage along one edge and roll as for apple strudel. Bake at Reg 8/450° for 10 minutes, then at Reg 6/400° for 20 minutes, brushing with more melted butter two or three times during baking.

☐ *Makes 2 strudels.*

For 8–10

Glazed Young Carrots

1 lb young carrots
1–2 oz butter
salt, sugar
chopped parsley

If the carrots are really fresh and young, they need not be peeled. Trim their tops and tails, and wash them.

Put them in a pan with cold water and bring to the boil for 2 minutes, drain and, refresh them under the cold tap. Return them to the pan, just cover them with water again, add 1–2 oz butter, a teaspoon of sugar, a pinch of salt. Cook briskly until the water is all evaporated and only the carrots and butter remain. Toss them about away from the fire. Tip them into a serving dish and sprinkle with parsley. They should be tender and shiny.

For 4

Keftades of Marrow and Cheese

1 lb marrow
1 chopped onion
4 oz soft cheese (feta, ricotta, cottage)
4 oz hard cheese (Parmesan, Gruyère)
2 eggs
4 oz breadcrumbs
salt, pepper
lots of chopped parsley

Peel, deseed and cube the marrow. Cook it in boiling water, for 10–20 minutes until tender. Drain it well and chop it into a mush. Squeeze as much moisture as you can out of it. Brown the onion in a little oil or butter and add it to the marrow with both cheeses, beaten eggs, salt, pepper and parsley, and enough breadcrumbs to make the consistency thick enough to handle with a spoon. Heat some deep fat or oil and drop the mixture in, spoonful by spoonful. Remove when golden and serve hot.

☐ *These are very light and delicate in flavour, so the cheese and parsley are very important. Cheddar cheese would be too strong. Serve by themselves or with casseroles and roasts.*

For 3–4

Leeks and Bacon

1 lb leeks, small rather than large
4 oz bacon, cut into cubes
1 oz butter
salt, pepper

Wash and trim the leeks, and cut them into 1″ pieces. Melt the butter in an earthenware pot or a heavy saucepan and fry the bacon in it. Shake the leeks dry in a cloth, then add them to the bacon, with salt and pepper. Cook gently, uncovered, stirring occasionally, until the leeks are tender (about 30–40 minutes).

☐ *This is an occasion when it might be wise to blanch the leeks first before cutting them up.*

For 4

Mushrooms in Cream and Lemon Juice

4 oz mushrooms
1 oz butter
thin slice of lemon
½ teaspoon flour
2 tablespoons stock
salt, pepper
a dash of cream or top of the milk

Trim the stalks off the mushrooms, cut them in quarters if they are large, but little button mushrooms are best for this dish. Melt the butter in a small fireproof dish and throw in the mushrooms and a slice of lemon, stirring once or twice. When they have absorbed plenty of butter and are becoming tender, remove the slice of lemon, add the flour, and when it thickens stir in the stock. Cook on for a few minutes, stirring, then add the cream, heat through and serve.

☐ *This is a rich dish, you need very little. Serve with steak or on toast.*

For 2

New England Tomatoes

1 lb tomatoes
6 spring onions
6 tablespoons olive oil
thyme, parsley, bay leaf
salt, pepper
3 slices bread, cut in cubes and baked hard in the oven, or very dry bread toasted and then cut in cubes

Skin the tomatoes (it is easier if you first pour boiling water over them) and chop them. Skin and chop the spring onions. Sauté the tomatoes and onions with the chopped herbs for 20–30 minutes, until they are soft. Add salt and pepper and the toasted cubes (these should go in at the last minute as they don't stay crisp for long) and cook on for a few minutes more. The croûtons should still be crisp when served, but it doesn't matter if they aren't.

☐ *Very good with beef or lamb.*

For 4–6

Little Glazed Onions

1 lb little pickling onions
2 tablespoons butter
2 heaped teaspoons sugar

Neatly skin all the onions and boil them in salted water until tender (about 15–20 minutes). Drain them very well. (This part can be done in advance and they will be then very well drained if left standing in a colander.) Melt the butter in a shallow heatproof serving dish, tip in the onions and sprinkle them with sugar. Cook them on a medium heat, turning them from time to time until they are all yellow and shiny. This takes about 20–30 minutes. Serve as they are, in the same dish.

☐ *Very good with roast game or lamb.*

For 4

Rösti

2 lb cold boiled potatoes (kept overnight in refrigerator or cold place to dry them out)
2–3 tablespoons butter
a dash of olive oil
salt, pepper

Grate the potatoes through a coarse grater. Let them stay in a light mass while you melt the oil and butter in a heavy frying pan. Tip the potato heap in to the pan, and press it down gently so that you can get a lid on. Season well and cook over a brisk heat at first and then turn down to medium, for 10–15 minutes, making sure it is not burning, (a) by sound (b) by smell. Remove lid, loosening the cake with a spatula and sliding a little more butter or oil down the side if necessary. Shake the pan until it rustles on the bottom, which is after a few minutes. Serve turned upside down on to a heated dish, and cut in wedges like a cake.

For 4–6

Josephina's Potatoes

2 lbs potatoes
flour, seasoned
2 small eggs
olive oil
¼ lb small pieces of ham (optional)
1 onion
1 carrot
1 stick celery
a small glass of white wine
½ pint water or stock
salt, pepper

Peel the potatoes and cut them into slices almost ½″ thick. Have two saucers, one for flour, one for the beaten eggs. Heat ½″ of oil in a deep-sided frying pan. Cut a potato slice almost in half again, put a little piece of ham in between the two halves like a sandwich, then press them together and dip them first into the flour to coat well and then into the egg. Drop straight into the hot oil and fry gently until brown and soft inside, turning once or twice. Do the same with the rest of the potatoes, putting the browned slices into a dish. When they are all done, keep them warm. Brown the chopped onion, carrot and celery in the remaining oil and then add two tablespoons of flour, left from dunking the potatoes, and stir it round until nicely browned. Gradually add the wine, let it bubble, and then the stock. To make a smooth sauce cook for 5 minutes and then strain over the potatoes.

For 6 or more

Potato Salad

1½ lbs potatoes (new waxy ones if possible)
clove of garlic
salt, pepper
1 tablespoon vinegar
2 tablespoons mayonnaise, thinned with top of the milk to a pouring consistency

Optional
parsley, chives, chopped
a pinch of cayenne, paprika, ground cumin or ground coriander, or pinch curry powder

Boil the potatoes in salted water in their skins to help keep them intact, and do not overcook them. Peel them, and while still warm, slice them. Rub a nice bowl with garlic. Put in the potatoes, add salt and fresh black pepper and sprinkle on the vinegar.

When they are a bit cooler pour on the thinned mayonnaise to which you have added whichever spice you prefer (or a mixture of very small quantities of several spices). Mix well and serve cold, sprinkle with parsley and chives.

☐ *Using twice the amount of thinned mayonnaise you can add shredded cold cooked chicken and hard boiled eggs, which makes a very good Potato, Egg and Chicken Salad.*

For 4

Sorrel Purée

1 lb sorrel
½ oz butter
½ oz flour
a pinch of salt
a pinch of sugar

Optional
1 egg
a dash of cream or top of the milk

Strip the thin red stems from the sorrel leaves, which have been well washed. Shake them fairly dry and put them as they are in a saucepan over a lowish flame, stir occasionally. As you stir they will change colour, soften and turn to a purée. Mash the butter and flour together (beurre manié) and drop little pieces of the mixture on to the sorrel; stir, and it will thicken somewhat. Add the salt and sugar to taste. It is ready to eat at this point but you can further improve its texture and consistency by stirring an egg or two into it, and adding a dash of cream.

☐ *This is very good with fish and can be treated either as a sauce or a vegetable or used as an omelette filling. You don't usually find sorrel in shops but it is one of the easiest vegetables to grow, and as long as you prevent it from flowering you can eat it almost all the year round. Moreover it is a perennial, so once planted (from seed) you have it for ever. Make sure it is French sorrel, not wild English, which is more bitter.*

For 4 (a little goes a long way)

Sweet Corn Fritters

10 oz of corn kernels, cooked and stripped off the cobs (or a 12 oz tin of corn kernels)
2 oz flour
1 egg
¼ pint double cream
walnut of butter
6 rashers of bacon
salt, pepper

Drain the corn kernels. Put the flour in a bowl. Make a well in the centre, break in the egg and stir it into the flour until it is smooth. Then add salt, pepper and cream and the sweetcorn. Heat a nut of butter in a frying pan. Fry the bacon in the butter and then keep it hot while you drop tablespoons of the sweetcorn mixture carefully into the sizzling fat. Fry over a moderate heat — turn it down if the fat starts to smoke or darken. You can do three or four fritters at a time. When the underneath is brown and set turn them over carefully and brown the other side. Eat hot, though they are quite good cold.

☐ *If you are using tinned corn, avoid the sort which includes strips of pimento.*

For 6 or more

Spinach or Swiss Chard Gratiné

1 lb Swiss chard or spinach
2 medium-size onions, sliced
3 tablespoons olive oil
¼ lb mushrooms, dried or equivalent of fresh (optional)
2 cloves garlic
2 eggs
2 tablespoons grated cheese (Parmesan if possible)
salt, pepper, chopped parsley
½ cup breadcrumbs

Remove large stalks for another recipe (see this page) wash and shred leaves, cook with a little salt without shaking the wetness off the leaves in a covered pan for about 10 minutes, stirring occasionally. Turn into a colander and press dry. Brown onions in olive oil in a saucepan. Add mushrooms, drained chard, garlic (crushed) and parsley. Cook for 5 minutes, then allow to cool. Beat eggs with cheese, salt and pepper. Mix with cooled chard, turn into a buttered gratin dish, or shallow casserole, sprinkle with breadcrumbs and bake for 20 minutes at Reg 4/350°.

Can be eaten hot or cold.

For 4

Chard Stalks in Cheese Sauce

1–1½ lbs chard
½ pint Béchamel Sauce (page 183)
1 tablespoon grated cheese
½ oz butter

Trim the leaves from the stalks and use them for Spinach or Swiss Chard Gratiné (this page). The stalks can be up to 3″ wide, cut them into pieces about 3″ long. Bring a large pan of salted water to the boil and cook the stalks for 20 minutes. Drain them very well.

Make half a pint of thickish Béchamel sauce (page 183). Put a layer of hot sauce into a fireproof gratin dish and sprinkle with a tablespoon of grated cheese. Then put a layer of chard stalks, then more sauce, then more cheese, more chard stalks and so on. Finish with a last layer of sauce and cheese and dot with butter. Bake in a fairly hot oven (Reg 7/425°) for 15 minutes until it is golden on top.

☐ *Swiss Chard, also known as sea kale beet or blettes, is very easy to grow. This recipe can also be used with spinach stalks.*

For 4

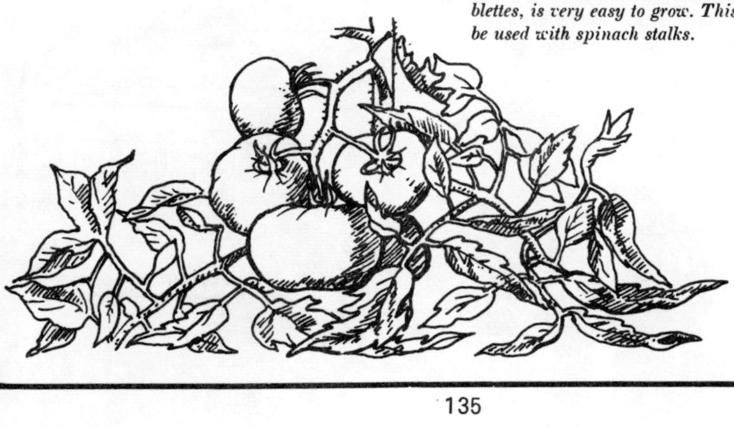

Ratatouille

3 aubergines
3 onions
3 courgettes
2 lbs tomatoes
2 green or red peppers
3 cloves garlic
¼ pint oil
marjoram, salt, pepper

Sprinkle the quartered and sliced aubergines with salt. Allow them to drain in a colander or sieve while you prepare the other vegetables. Slice the peeled onions and the courgettes into thin slices. Skin the tomatoes and chop roughly. Cut the peppers into strips, removing every seed. Peel the cloves of garlic and squash them. Start cooking the onions gently in the oil, without browning them. When they are transparent add the garlic and the aubergine shaken to remove the drops of moisture that form on the slices. After 5–10 more minutes add the peppers and courgettes and a little more oil if necessary. Keep stirring the vegetables gently to prevent them sticking at the bottom. After another 10–15 minutes add the tomatoes, marjoram and pepper. Taste for salt — there was some on the aubergines and you may not need much more. Cook until everything is tender and you have an aromatic stew with the individual vegetables still distinguishable.

For 8–10

Turnip Tops

4 healthy turnip tops (or 1 lb turnip tops)
salt
water
oil
lemon juice

Keep the turnips for another day and look at the leaves. Reject any yellow or tough ones. Strip the stalks off all the others, and wash them well.

Bring a pan of salted water to the boil, fling in the turnip leaves, boil until tender, 15–20 minutes. Tip into a colander, drain and press dry, and chop them up a bit. Put them in a hot china dish and pour oil and lemon juice over them before serving.

Do the same with spring greens and curly kale.

For 4

Turnips in Cream Sauce

6 small young turnips (about 1 lb in all)
2–3 oz butter
salt, pepper
sugar, nutmeg
1 tablespoon flour
½ pint milk
a little chopped parsley

Put the peeled turnips in a pan of cold salted water to cover. Bring it to the boil and after 2 minutes remove the turnips and run cold water over them. Drain them and put them in a pan large enough to allow the turnips to lie in one layer. Add about ½″ of warm water, 1 tablespoon butter, a pinch of salt, and a sprinkling of sugar. Cook fairly briskly, turning them about from time to time, until all the water has evaporated, and you are left with just the butter. Keep the turnips warm while you make a sauce with the rest of the butter, flour and milk. Season it with salt, pepper and nutmeg and cook until thick and smooth. Tip the turnips into it, with all their buttery juice. Serve sprinkled with parsley.

☐ *Very good with roast lamb or duck.*

For 4

Lentil Purée

1 lb lentils
1 onion
1 carrot
2 cloves garlic
a little salt
parsley

Wash the lentils and leave them to soak for an hour. Put them in a pan and cover with fresh water by about 1″. Bring to the boil with the onion, carrot and garlic and salt, and simmer for about 1–2 hours until they are done. If the water is gone before they are tender add a little more. They should finish soft, with all the water absorbed. Sieve, onion and all, and if you are roasting or stewing some meat at the same time, add a little of its liquid, or if the purée is very dry some good stock. Chop some parsley and stir it in check the seasoning and serve with a little butter.

☐ *Very good with rabbit, hare or other game.*

For 6

Benahavis Lentils

1 lb brown or green lentils (soaked overnight)
1 onion
1 large carrot
thyme, bay leaf
salt, pepper
1 whole head of garlic
olive oil
2–3 rashers bacon or 2–3 ozs salt pork
¾ lb black pudding
¾ lb spiced continental sausage

Wash the lentils and start cooking them in plain water, to cover them by about 1–1½″. Peel and chop the onion and carrot and add the herbs, tied in a bunch.

Keeping it intact, fry the entire head of garlic in olive oil in a small frying pan, until it is almost black all over. Put it in with the lentils, chop up the bacon or salt pork and fry them in the same oil for a minute or two. Add them and the oil to the lentils, cover and simmer until the lentils are tender; they should absorb most of the liquid. Remove the lid if there is too much liquid when they are nearly cooked, and let them simmer on until of a thick porridgy consistency. Cut the black pudding and sausage into 1″ lengths and fry them lightly, then add them to the lentils. Season with salt and pepper and serve, giving those who like it a clove of garlic, which is soft and fragrant but not pungent by this time.

For 6–8

Three Bean Salad

4 oz dried red kidney beans
4 oz dried haricot beans
4 oz flageolets or chick peas
6 chopped spring onions
8 tablespoons olive oil
1–2 tablespoons red wine vinegar
salt, chilli pepper (about as much as you would use of ordinary pepper)

Soak the beans overnight in separate bowls and cook them separately as some take longer than others. Add salt towards the end of cooking time. Drain, allow to cool and then mix all together with a dressing made of the olive oil, vinegar, salt and chilli pepper. Allow to stand for an hour or so to absorb the dressing, stir in the chopped onion, which should not be chopped until the last minute, and sprinkle with freshly chopped parsley.

☐ *This salad is very pretty but extremely filling. Serve it with lamb or as a starter to an otherwise light meal.*

For 6

Purée of Split Peas

1 lb green or yellow split peas
1–2 oz butter
1 bay leaf and sprig of thyme tied together
salt
water or stock
1 small onion, finely chopped

Wash the peas and soak them overnight, especially if you don't know how old they are (although if you are in a hurry you can cook them straight away). Put them in a pan with enough cold water or stock to cover them by 1″. Add a walnut of butter and the herbs. Let them simmer, covered, over a low heat, adding more hot water or stock if necessary. Don't let them dry out too much or they will burn. Add salt when they are half-cooked. When they are completely cooked (after about 1½ hours) remove the herbs, sieve the peas, and stir in the finely chopped onion, which has been softened in the remaining butter. Reheat it very gently, with a little more stock if necessary.

☐ *This is very good with sausages instead of the usual mashed potato. It is also delicious on its own with croûtons fried in butter as a filling first course.*

For 6

Traditional Pease Pudding

½ lb split peas, soaked overnight
1 large potato
2–3 pints bacon stock

Cut the potato in cubes and put it with the peas in a bag, or tied in a cloth, and stew it in the bacon stock. When soft, after about 1½ hours, mash or sieve the peas and potato and eat hot or cold. Keep the liquid in which they were cooked, and if there is any pease pudding left mix it in a bowl with a few tablespoons of the stock. Then return it to a saucepan with the remaining stock and you have some nice soup.

☐ *If you are having salt pork or boiled bacon you can cook this in the same pot. Up North it is eaten with fish and chips.*

For 3–4

Pilau Rice

½ lb patna rice, 2 oz butter
1 onion peeled and sliced into rings
½ teaspoon turmeric or 1 packet saffron (large pinch)
6 cloves, 6 cardamoms
1–2″ cinnamon stick
1 teaspoon coriander seeds
½ teaspoon caraway seeds
1 teaspoon cumin seeds
2 teaspoons pistachio nuts browned in butter
1–2 oz blanched almonds browned in butter
2–4 oz raisins browned in butter

Soak the well-washed rice in water for 1–2 hours or longer, even overnight. Drain it well and shake it as dry as possible in a cloth. Soak the saffron in a tablespoon of water.

Fry the onion in the butter in a heavy sauté pan with a lid. Add all the spices except the saffron. Then add the rice and stir it until the grains are well-coated with butter. Then add salt, soaked saffron and enough cold water to cover. Stir and cover. Cook, adding more water when necessary, until the rice is tender and dry. Finish by adding the fried almonds, raisins and the pistachio nuts.

☐ *This is a marvellous accompaniment to curry, especially curried meat dishes.*

For 4

Risi Bisi (Risotto with Peas)

2 shallots or small onions chopped
1 oz butter
2–3 rashers, green bacon or 2 slices ham, cut small
1 lb of peas
1½ pints chicken stock
6 oz rice (Italian or long grained)
Parmesan cheese grated
salt and pepper

Melt the butter in a saucepan or earthenware dish. Soften the chopped onion in it without browning. Add the ham or bacon, and when they are cooked add the peas, stir them until they are coated with the butter and then add ⅓ of the heated stock. When it comes to the boil add the rice, and as it absorbs the stock add more liquid and continue to do this until the rice is cooked and the mixture of a creamy consistency. Season if necessary, depending on the strength of the stock, and stir in half the grated Parmesan cheese. Serve it with more grated Parmesan.

☐ *If you like you can stir in a few spoons of cream and allow it to heat through, just before serving. This form of risotto is supposed to be served 'rippling' which means it is much moister and creamier than usual. Italian rice absorbs more liquid than long grain rice, and takes a little longer to cook.*

For 4

Puddings

Puddings

The sort of puddings you make depends very much on whether you are trying to fill people up or just to please them. Since most filling puddings contain large quantities of fattening things they are becoming less and less pleasing to more and more people, including the mothers who make them and see their hungry children beginning to bulge and remember menacing words about forming life-long over-eating patterns.

So our recipes are mainly for puddings that use fruit, with perhaps beaten eggs or a light pastry crust, ice-cream and mousses where the emphasis is on quality rather than quantity, pancakes which make a small amount of flour go a long way and the occasional luxurious pudding made with cream.

For a glimpse into the British heritage of puddings look at any run-of-the-mill cookery book of about 1890 and you will find recipe after rib-sticking recipe for steamed and boiled puddings, baked puddings, cabinet puddings, diplomat puddings. They are probably all very good, but because almost every family has at least one member who should be thinner we have mainly, out of kindness, left them out.

Apple Flan

2 lbs cooking apples
4 oz sugar
2 egg yolks
½ teaspoon crushed coriander
1 tablespoon butter
peel of 1 lemon
¾ lb rich sweet pastry (page 185)

Peel the apples and, keeping one back for the top of the pie, simmer the rest, cut in pieces, with the sugar and a couple of tablespoons of water to get them started. Mash them with a potato masher, and away from the heat add the two egg yolks, the coriander and a tablespoon of butter. Cut the zest off the lemon and chop it finely, put it in a sieve and blanch it by dipping it for 1 minute into boiling water and then repeating with fresh boiling water. This is very important as it makes the peel less bitter. Stir the peel into the apple mixture and allow to cool. Preheat the oven to Reg 5½/385°. Line a 9″ flan tin with the rich pastry, fill with the apple mixture and finish with a prettily arranged layer of apple slices. Sprinkle with sugar and bake 25–30 minutes.

Eat cold with cream.

For 6–8

Apple Charlotte

2 lbs cooking apples
8 oz breadcrumbs (brown or white)
4 oz sugar (brown or white)
a sprinkling of grated nutmeg
2 oz butter
2 slices lemon peel

Preheat the oven to Reg 4/350°. Peel and slice the apples. Mix half the sugar with the breadcrumbs in the bottom of a buttered pie dish and sprinkle with nutmeg. Pack in the apples with the remaining sugar, most of the butter and the lemon peel. Cover the top with the rest of the crumbs, dot the top liberally with butter and bake covered for 20 minutes to ½ hour. Then cook on uncovered for 20–30 minutes.

☐ *This pudding is very light.*

For 6–8

Apple Strudel

For the pastry
12 oz flour
1 egg
½ teaspoon oil
a large pinch of salt
¼ pint lukewarm water
½ teaspoon white vinegar
½–1 oz melted butter for brushing

For the filling
2 lbs cooking apples
4 oz currants or sultanas
½ teaspoon cinnamon
3 oz caster sugar
2 oz ground almonds and 2 oz walnuts *or* 6 oz breadcrumbs and 3 oz butter
a teaspoon of grated lemon peel
1–2 oz butter for brushing

Sieve the flour into a bowl, make a well in the centre and add the egg, oil, salt, vinegar and enough lukewarm water to make a pliable, silky dough. Pummel, knead and beat the dough for 5–10 minutes. Allow to rest in a warm place, well covered with a damp cloth and a lid, for 30 minutes.

Peel, quarter and core the apples. Cut the quarters in half then slice them thinly, like cucumber. Mix the slices with the sugar, currants, cinnamon and roughly chopped walnuts. If you are using breadcrumbs fry them in butter.

Remove your rings and put half the warm strudel pastry on a well-floured tablecloth and roll it as thin as you can with a rolling pin. Then gradually pull it into an oblong shape, putting one floured hand right underneath with the fingers spread out, to ease the pastry evenly towards the edges (see diagram). Gradually pull and work the whole thing very gently into a thin sheet (you should be able to see your hand through it). When it is 2 to 3 feet by 18 inches to 2 feet and without too many holes, stop pulling. Cut off the thick edges and let it harden for about 15 minutes. Brush with butter, sprinkle with breadcrumbs or almonds and lay half the apple mixture over ⅔ of the pastry (the part with the fewest holes). Roll by lifting the cloth evenly at one side so the pastry wraps itself round the filling, and roll to the end (see diagram). Pinch the ends of the roll and cut off any extra pastry.

Make the second strudel in the same way.

Preheat the oven to Reg 8/450°. Lay the strudel in a crescent on a buttered baking tin and brush with the remaining butter. Bake at Reg 8/450° for 10 minutes and Reg 6/400° for 20 minutes. Brush with butter two or three times during baking. When it is cooked, dust with icing sugar and allow to cool or serve hot with cream.

☐ *Practice makes perfect. This is also good with cabbage (page 129) or stoned cherries, stoned plums and cream cheese.*

For 16 (2 strudels)

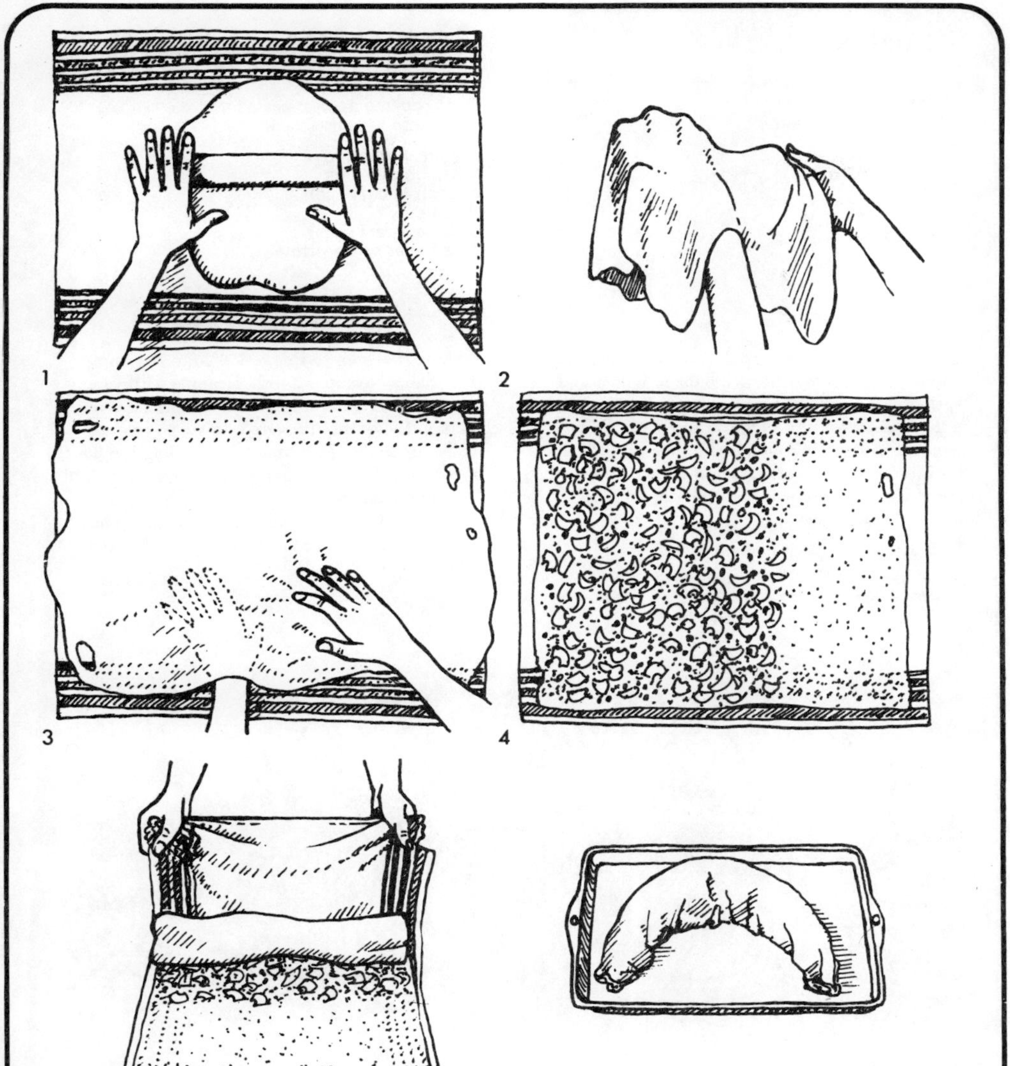
1
2
3
4
5
6

Baked Apple Slices

1½ lbs cooking apples
1–1½ oz unsalted butter
2 oz sugar

Peel, core and slice the apples. Arrange them in an open ovenproof dish with dabs of butter and sprinklings of sugar between layers. Finish with a layer of butter and sugar on top. Cook them uncovered in a low to moderate oven (Reg 2/300°) until browned and soft (about ¾ hour). You need add no water, they will be swimming in butter and their own juice.

Best eaten warm, with cream.

☐ *Very delicious.*

For 4–6

Crisp Apple Crumble

2 lbs cooking apples, peeled and sliced
A squeeze of lemon juice

For the crumble
1 oz porridge oats
a pinch of cinnamon
3 oz flour
6 oz demerara sugar
4 oz butter or margarine

Preheat the oven to Reg 4/350°. Put the apples in a shallow ovenproof dish, sprinkle with lemon juice and 1–2 oz of the demerara sugar, and put them in the oven, uncovered, to start cooking, while you make the crumble by rubbing the flour, oats, sugar, butter or margarine all together. Add the cinnamon, sprinkle over the apples, which have started to cook, and bake at the same heat for 30–40 minutes, or until the top is crisp and coloured.

For 4–6

Buttered Baked Apples

4 nice firm eating apples
4 thin slices bread
2 oz butter
3–4 oz sugar

Preheat oven to Reg 3/325°. Peel the apples very carefully and remove the cores. Butter a square gratin dish. Cut the crusts off the bread and lay the slices in the gratin dish. Stand an apple on each one. Fill the hole with sugar then put in a nob of butter. Bake the apples slowly, adding more sugar and butter two or three times, taking care the bread does not catch or burn. If it appears to be doing so, turn down the oven.

After 1 hour the apples should be soft (big ones may take longer).

Serve them in their dish, basted with their juice and sprinkled with sugar. They are baked a light brown, and the bread is crusted and golden.

For 4

Spiced Apple Pudding

1 lb apples (windfalls)
1 oz soft brown sugar (pale,
¼ teaspoon ground cinnamon
¼ teaspoon ground cloves
a pinch of nutmeg
8 oz self-raising flour
2 oz butter
4–6 oz caster sugar
grated rind and juice of 1 lemon
2 eggs
4 tablespoons milk

Preheat the oven to Reg 4/350°. Line a square 7″ cake tin with buttered greaseproof. Peel, core and slice the apples. Mix the brown sugar and spice. Rub the butter into the flour, add the caster sugar (judging the quantity according to the sourness of the apples), lemon rind and juice and eggs beaten together with the milk, beat well until the mixture is a soft dropping consistency. Spoon half the mixture into the cake tin. Arrange ⅓ of the apples over this. Cover with the remaining mixture, arrange the rest of the apple slices prettily on top, sprinkle with the spiced sugar. Bake for 1½ hours until cooked through. Cover the top with greaseproof paper if it is browning too quickly. Take it out of the tin and serve hot with cream or cold in slices like cake.

For 6 or more

Snow Ice

1 pint milk
2 whites of egg
5 oz granulated sugar
1 piece cinnamon about ½″ long
1 strip lemon peel
ground cinnamon

Bring the milk to the boil together with the lemon peel, cinnamon stick and 4 oz sugar. Let it simmer for 5 minutes without boiling over (put a small saucer in the bottom of the pan to prevent this). Let it cool. Beat the whites of egg till very stiff and add the remaining sugar gradually, beat until stiff again and then graaually add the strained cold milk very slowly. Freeze in ice tray forking once or twice. Serve the ice scooped into glasses and sprinkle with ground cinnamon.

☐ *A delicious and refreshing pudding and a very good way of using egg whites.*

For 6

Blackberry or Blackcurrant Kissel

1½–2 lbs blackberries or blackcurrants
4 oz sugar
2 tablespoons cornflour
1 tablespoon brandy (optional)

Simmer the fruit with a little water and the sugar, until soft enough to sieve. You should then obtain about a pint of juice-purée (make it up with a little water if there is not enough). Allow to cool a bit.

Mix the cornflour with a little water, add the brandy if you have any, add a little of the fruit juice and mix very well. Add the cornflour mixture to the rest of the fruit juice. Bring to the boil, stirring well, and simmer 2–3 minutes. Allow to cool a bit, stirring occasionally before pouring it into glass dishes. Serve very cold with cream. It should set, not hard, but as thick soft jelly.

For 4–6

Plain Cooked Rhubarb

1 lb rhubarb
½ lemon
2 oz sugar
a little water

Wash the rhubarb and cut it into square chunks. Cut the lemon in half lengthways and then into thick semi-circles, or long crescents, whichever you think looks prettier. Put them, with the rhubarb and sugar and a little water, into the top half of a double saucepan. Cook them over gently boiling water for 20 minutes to half an hour, until the rhubarb pieces are soft but not falling to pieces. Allow to cool and serve with the bright yellow lemon pieces still there. It makes quite a lot of juice. You can also cook it, covered, in a moderate oven, if you are baking something else.

For 4

Rhubarb Fool

1 lb rhubarb (cooked as for Plain Cooked Rhubarb)
½ pint egg custard

Sieve or liquidise the rhubarb when it is cold (first removing the lemon slices it was cooked with). Fold the custard in gently when it too is set and cool. (If you do it when hot it will curdle.)

If you are not feeling frugal you can add instead of the custard, ½ pint double cream whipped lightly but not too stiffly or it won't mix with the fruit.

Taste for sweetening. Serve cold.

For 4–6

Lemon Mousse

1 large lemon, rind and juice
½ lb cottage cheese
¼ pint single cream
2 oz caster sugar
½ oz powdered gelatine
¼ pint milk

Grate the lemon rind then squeeze the lemon. Whisk the cream and cheese together well, or liquidise. Stir in the rind and juice and add the sugar. Heat the milk and dissolve the gelatine in it. Leave it to cool but not to set, so that it mixes homogeneously, otherwise the solids go to the bottom and liquids to the top. Just before it sets mix in quickly the cream and cheese and leave to set. This needs something to eat with it, like a compôte of fruit, or puréed apricots, plums, blackberries, or biscuits.

For 4–5

Fruit Soufflé

6 oz any soft fruit, such as strawberries, raspberries, blackberries, peaches, apricots
3 large dessertspoons caster sugar
3 egg whites
a little butter

Try to use a white china or glass 6″ soufflé dish. Butter it well. Preheat the oven to Reg 6/400°. Make a purée of the fruit by sieving it, and add the sugar.

Beat the egg whites very stiffly (an old fashioned test is to see if a penny will stay on top without sinking in — these days, use 2p). Mix gently but well with the purée and turn it into the soufflé dish. Flatten the top smooth and level so that there are no peaks or ridges to go brown and spoil its appearance. Bake in the centre of the oven for exactly 13½ minutes, after which it should be perfectly cooked. (All ovens vary slightly so watch the result carefully the first time you cook this dish in order that you can time it accurately in future). It is good with cream.

☐ *This is very useful for using up egg whites and squashy fruit.*

For 3–4

Mont Blanc

1 lb chestnuts
½ lb caster sugar
½ pint of double cream

Shell the chestnuts and boil them in water, or ½ milk and ½ water, until they are soft. This takes about ½ hour. Make sure they don't boil dry and burn; while they are cooking they absorb a lot of the liquid. Drain them and put them, with most of the sugar, through a mouli-légumes or sieve them letting them fall as lightly as possible into the dish from which they will be served and ending up with a little mountain of sweet, airy chestnut. Whip the cream with a little more caster sugar, until it thickens a little, but not too stiffly, then spoon it over the chestnuts. It should look like a softly enveloping snow cap, hence the name of the dish. Decorate the peak with angelica and a cherry if you feel frivolous.

☐ *Suitable when chestnuts are cheap.*

For 6–8

Oeufs au Lait

4 small eggs
1 pint milk
2 strips lemon peel and 1–1½ oz sugar
or 1 oz vanilla sugar

Put the milk, the lemon peel and the sugar or the vanilla sugar in a saucepan and bring to the boil. When it boils pour it into a bowl on to the well-beaten eggs, and mix well. Strain the mixture into a gratin dish and bake, covered with foil, in a slow oven Reg 3/325° for 30 minutes. When the eggs are creamy allow them to cool. Chill the custard, and just before serving sprinkle the top with caster sugar to a depth of ⅛″–¼″ and push the dish under a very hot grill. When the sugar melts and caramelises, serve the pudding. The caramel will start to melt if you leave this standing for more than a few hours.

☐ *Luxurious but cheap. Like crême brulée but not so rich. The custard can be made well in advance if necessary.*

For 6

Cold Orange Soufflé

2 oranges, their grated rinds and their juice
juice of ½ lemon
3 eggs
3 oz caster sugar
½ oz gelatine
2 tablespoons water
¼ pint double cream, lightly whipped (optional)
crystallised orange slices for decoration

Using a soufflé dish of about 1½ pints capacity, extend its height by tying a band of oiled greaseproof paper round the outside. Make it about 3″ higher. Put the rind, orange and lemon juice into the top of a double boiler, with the yolks of the eggs and the sugar. Whisk and whisk (very easy if you have an electric hand-beater). As the mixture heats up it thickens, and as you whisk it becomes like fluffy custard. This takes a long time, but aim at a thickish foaming mixture. Dissolve gelatine in water (don't let it boil) until it is totally melted, add it to the whisked mixture, and let it cool so that it is almost setting. Fold in the cream, beat the egg whites stiffly and fold them in. Pour it into the soufflé dish and leave in a cold place to set. Before serving, remove the paper and decorate with slices of crystallised orange. It looks more spectacular if it rises above the soufflé dish.

For 8

Orange Sorbet

1 pint water
8 oz sugar
½ pint orange juice (about 4 juicy oranges)
juice of ½ lemon

Put the sugar and water in a heavy pan and stir, heating gently, until the sugar has dissolved. Bring to the boil and boil 5 minutes. Allow to cool, stir in the freshly-squeezed orange and lemon juice, and freeze, stirring once or twice while it is setting. Makes 1½ pints of sorbet.

For 6

Rich Rice Pudding

2 oz rice (pudding rice, round, not long)
1 pint water
2 oz sugar
1 oz butter
1 pint milk
grating of nutmeg
a pinch of salt
1 bay leaf (or a little slice of lemon peel)
1–2 eggs, yolks and whites separated

Preheat the oven to Reg 3/325°. Cook the rice in the water until it is amost tender (about 10–13 minutes). Drain it well and put it, with the sugar, butter, heated milk, nutmeg, salt, bay leaf, in an ovenproof dish. Cover it with foil and bake in the oven for 2 hours. Stir once or twice to prevent a skin forming. Take it out, remove bay leaf or lemon peel, and beat in the egg yolks. Before serving whip the egg whites stiffly with a little sugar and fold into the pudding. Serve hot or cold, with strawberry or raspberry jam on each helping.

☐ *If you don't want to use the oven it can be cooked in a double saucepan, but watch the water level in the bottom half.*

For 4

Prune Pudding

½ lb prunes
4 egg whites
6 oz caster sugar
¼ teaspoon cream of tartar

Soak the prunes for 12 hours in cold water then stew them until tender (about 15 minutes). Remove the stones. Preheat the oven to Reg 6/400°. Strain, and stir the fruit for 5 minutes over a low heat until it is a purée, adding a little of their cooking liquid. Beat the egg whites till stiff. Stir in the sugar and the cream of tartar. Fold in the prunes, turn into a pudding dish and stand it in a tin of water. Bake for 15–20 minutes. Serve at once with whipped cream.

☐ *Very good if you like prunes and have a lot of egg whites. It is a sort of soufflé.*

For 4–6

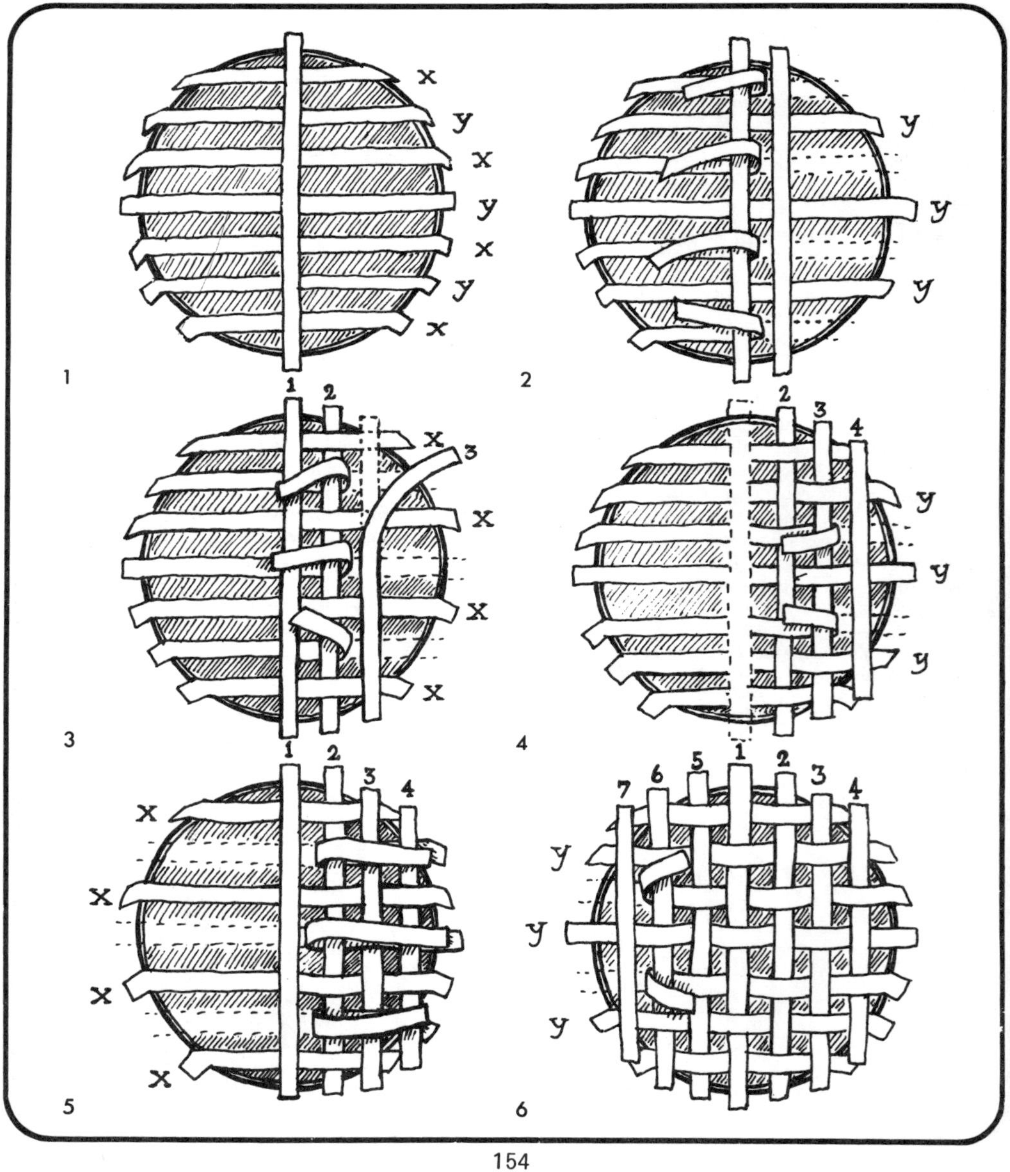
1
2
3
4
5
6

Marmalade Tart

10 oz rich sweet flan pastry (page 185)
½ lb–¾ lb marmalade
2 egg yolks

Preheat oven to Reg 7/425°. Use ⅔ of your pastry, thinly rolled, to line a 7″ flan tin.

Warm the marmalade gently and mix it thoroughly with the beaten egg yolks. Let the mixture cool, then put it into the flan case. Cover with a basketwork pattern of pastry, cut into ½″ strips (see diagram). Bake at Reg 7/425° for 10–15 minutes and then a further 15–20 minutes at Reg 4/350°.

Serve hot or cold with cream.

☐ *If you want to make a closer basketwork pattern you should use narrower (¼″) strips and a less rich pastry.*

For 6

7

Strawberry Omelette

2 eggs
2 teaspoons sugar
a pinch of salt
1 tablespoon cream or top of the milk
a handful of strawberries
or 2 tablespoons of strawberry jam
Caster sugar to glaze
Butter

If you are using fresh strawberries, cut up large ones and, if possible soak the fruit in any white liqueur, for instance kirsch. Mix eggs, sugar, salt and cream and make omelette in usual way, folding in the fruit or jam quickly as it starts to set. Flip it in half and slide on to a heatproof dish or plate. Have the grill very very hot, sprinkle the omelette with caster sugar and leave it under the grill until the sugar forms a crisp pale brown glaze, or use a salamander. This is just to caramelise the sugar, and not to cook the omelette any more. Eat at once.

☐ *The sugar glaze contrasts beautifully with the creamy omelette, and its surprising chunks of fruit.*

For 1

Little Chocolate Creams

4 oz bitter or cooking chocolate
2 egg yolks
½ pint creamy milk or ¼ pint milk and ¼ pint single cream

Preheat the oven to Reg 3/325°. Put the chocolate in a mixing bowl and stand this bowl in a saucepan of hot water — be sure the water will not come over the top of the bowl. Put over a medium heat and while the chocolate is melting beat the egg yolks and milk together to a froth, then beat them into the chocolate — still over the hot, but not boiling water. When they are very frothy and the chocolate is dissolved pour the mixture into little pots or ramequins standing in a tin of hot water. (Use a jug for doing this as pouring neatly from a bowl is almost impossible.) Put the pots in their tin of water into the oven and bake 35–40 minutes.

Allow to cool, chill and serve with cream.

☐ *If you are making this for children, they may prefer it sweeter.*

For 4

Mrs Sylvester's Christmas Pudding with Beer (1910)

¾ lb sultanas, 1 lb raisins
2 oz Valencia almonds
1 lb currants
6 oz mixed peel
1 lb suet, 1 lb breadcrumbs
1 lemon and its grated peel
1 lb dark raw brown sugar
1 small nutmeg, grated
5 eggs, a little brandy
about ½ pint stout

Mix all the dry ingredients together. Beat the eggs and lemon juice and add to the mixture. Stand overnight. Add enough stout and brandy to make a good mixture. Fill four 1½ pint pudding basins and cover them with paper and cloth. Secure with string or rubber bands. Steam or boil for 7 hours. Change the papers or cloth and store in a cool dry place. Steam a further 3–4 hours on Christmas Day.

☐ *It is a light but rich dark pudding. This fills 4 1½ pint pudding basins making 4 × 2 lb puddings.*

Each pudding for 6–8

Cakes Buns & Bread

Cakes, Buns and Bread

Cake-making is one of the more precise parts of cooking — you have to take care with weighing ingredients and follow certain rules, otherwise your cakes are going to be amazingly home-made looking. There are a few rules that help to get the right texture, which is the most important factor in making a nice cake — it doesn't matter nearly so much if it is cracked or crinkled or a bad shape but dry cakes are just not worth making.

The chief reasons for cakes being too dry are that the oven is too hot or the mixture is the wrong consistency — if it doesn't go nicely into the corners of the tin then it is too dry. You can always add a little lemon juice, brandy, water or even milk, but do not overdo it, because too much liquid makes the cake less rich.

Another reason for dry or open-textured cakes is that the butter and sugar are not properly creamed. If you don't have an electric beater do it over a bowl of hot water; it takes much less time to get to the point where the sugar has really melted into the butter. When folding in, you are trying to mix the cake without losing the air you have put into it; always stir a few spoonfuls of the light mixture into the heavy mixture first, to lighten it. Then fold the rest in lightly but thoroughly. Always scrape down the sides of the bowl at least twice while you are mixing a cake, otherwise it may be uneven.

It is very important to have the right tin — too large a tin will mean that the cake will be cooked too fast and won't rise properly. Too small means it won't have room to rise, ideally the mixture should fill the tin to within half an inch of the rim.

Ovens vary a great deal, one may be hotter at the back than the front in which case the cakes must be turned half-way through cooking, another may overheat at the top. So get to know your oven, and if every cake comes out burned use a lower temperature than the recipes say.

Cakes that take a long time to cook can be prevented from burning on the sides and bottom by lining the tin with foil or greaseproof paper. The top can be covered with two layers of greaseproof paper towards the end of cooking. If you are making a fruit cake it really works to shake the fruit in a little flour from the amount in the recipe. It won't sink to the bottom so readily, and will stay separate.

Fruit cakes should be allowed to cool in their tins to prevent them falling apart when you turn them out.

If you love making cakes you will find these recipes interesting but hardly a complete guide to cake-making, and we can recommend as a really fine book on the subject *The Wine and Food Society's Guide to Bakery, Cakes and Simple Confectionery* by Madame Floris.

Angels' Food

4 eggs
½ teaspoon cream of tartar
3 tablespoons cold water
12 oz caster sugar
scant ¼ pint boiling water
¾ teaspoon baking powder, pinch of salt
8 oz plain flour
a few drops of vanilla
grated rind ½ lemon

Preheat oven to Reg 2/300°. Butter and flour a cake tin 8″ across by 4″ deep. Beat the egg whites with the cream of tartar until they are stiff. In a separate bowl beat the egg yolks and cold water in the mixer for 3 minutes at least or by hand for 5 minutes. Gradually add the sugar, beating away, now gradually add the boiling water. The yolks should be going paler and paler. If you are using a mixer let it go on beating the mixture while you sieve flour, baking powder and salt. Add them gradually to the egg yolk mixture, add the vanilla and lemon rind, then gently fold in the beaten egg whites by hand. Turn the mixture into the cake-tin and bake for 1½ hours.

It rises like a soufflé, so do make sure the tin is large enough.

☐ *A light white fluffy cake. Ice it with Chocolate Icing (page 162).*

Dundee Cake

8 oz brown sugar (soft, dark)
8 oz butter, 4 eggs
4 oz each of sultanas, currants, raisins and candied peel
3 oz blanched almonds
4 oz cherries, halved
grated rind of 1 lemon and 1 orange
10 oz plain flour
a pinch of bicarbonate of soda
1 tablespoon whisky

Grease an 8″ cake tin and line with well-buttered greaseproof paper. Cream the sugar and butter together really well until fluffy and creamy (the sugar should melt completely). Add the eggs, beating each one in thoroughly before you add the next. Mix the currants, raisins, sultanas, peel chopped small, ¾ of the almonds coarsely chopped or broken, and the halved cherries in a bowl with 1 oz of flour and the grated orange and lemon rind. Preheat the oven to Reg 3½/335°. Fold in the flour, sieved with the bicarbonate of soda, then fold in the fruit. Stir in the whisky and turn the mixture into the tin. Smooth the top and decorate with the whole almonds. Bake for 2½ hours, turning the tin and covering the top when well-browned with dampened double greaseproof paper.

Makes an 8″ cake

Mace Cake

2½ oz margarine
7 oz caster sugar (vanilla sugar if possible)
¼ pint sour cream
2 eggs
8 oz plain flour
1 teaspoon baking powder
1 teaspoon bicarbonate of soda
¼ teaspoon salt, 1 teaspoon mace
For the topping
3 oz chopped nuts
1 oz sugar

Preheat the oven to Reg 4/350°. Cream the margarine and sugar thoroughly, then add the sour cream. Add the eggs and beat them in, then gradually add the flour, sieved with the rest of the dry ingredients. Turn the mixture into a buttered and floured 7″ square or round tin. Mix the topping into the top of the cake a bit and bake for ¾–1 hour.

Flap Jacks

8 oz rolled oats
7 oz butter
6 oz soft brown sugar
a pinch of salt
1 teaspoon ground ginger

Preheat the oven to Reg 4/350°. Warm the butter and beat it to a cream. Put the oats, salt, ground ginger and sugar in a bowl and stir well. Turn them into the bowl with the butter in it and mix thoroughly.

Butter a flat baking sheet, turn the mixture on to it and flatten it out to a cake ¼″ thick. Bake for 25 minutes. When cooked leave it in the tin for a few minutes, then turn it out and cut it into squares. They are dryer and more crumbly than flap-jacks made with golden syrup, but taste much better.

Makes plenty (about 12–18)

Chocolate Icing

8 oz icing sugar
2 tablespoons hot water
2 ozs bitter chocolate
1 tablespoon butter

Sieve the icing sugar into a bowl. Soften the chocolate in the top of a double boiler, add the hot water and stir into the icing sugar in its bowl. While you stir, melt the butter, also in the (unwashed) top of the double boiler, collecting the rest of the chocolate. Stir the melted butter into the icing sugar for a minute or two — do this by hand or it will get too thick. Pour the icing over the top of the cake in bands, backwards and forwards, and smooth it over the sides with a spatula.

Enough for a large cake.

Lardy Cake

1 lb bread dough (page 167)
3 oz lard, very cold from the fridge
3 oz sugar
4 oz mixed dried fruit mixed with 1–2 teaspoons mixed spice
For the glaze
1 oz sugar
1 tablespoon water

When the dough has had its first rising (after mixing and kneading, it is left in a warm place to rise and double in size), roll it out flat again into an oblong about ½″ thick. Cut the lard into small pieces and dot the dough with ⅓ of it, also ⅓ of the sugar, and ⅓ of the fruit and spice. Roll it up, turn it round and roll it out again. Repeat this procedure twice more, and finish by rolling it flat. Score it across with a sharp knife, and lay it in a shallow greased baking tin. Cover with a cloth. Allow it to rise again while you preheat the oven to Reg 9/475°. Bake 15 minutes then lower the heat to Reg 4/350° and bake a further 25–30 minutes.
Melt the sugar in the water and glaze the cake as soon as you take it out of the oven, but leave it in the tin until it is cool to reabsorb the lard which has run out of it during cooking. Sprinkle with granulated sugar while it cools.

Hot Cross Buns

½ oz fresh yeast (or ¼ oz dried yeast)
2 oz sugar
½ pint tepid milk and water
1 lb plain flour
1 teaspoon salt
½ teaspoon nutmeg
½ teaspoon cinnamon
4 oz currants
1 oz candied peel
1 egg, beaten
2 oz melted butter

For the crosses
1 oz fat
2 oz flour
water
For the glaze
2 tablespoons sugar
2 tablespoons water
2 tablespoons milk

Cream the yeast in a small bowl with a teaspoon of the sugar, stir in half the milk and water (tepid), sprinkle a little of the flour over the surface and leave in a warm place for about 20 minutes, when it should be covered in little bubbles as the yeast begins to grow. Sift into a large warm bowl the flour, salt, spices and sugar. Make a well in the centre and mix in the yeast liquid. Add the currants and peel, the beaten egg and melted butter. Mix with your hand adding enough tepid milk and water to make a dough. It will be very sticky at first, and softer than bread dough or pastry but firm enough to handle. Mix until it is smooth and leaves your hands and the bowl clean. If you *have* added too much liquid add more flour.

Leave in a warm place in the bowl, covered with a damp cloth, to rise until double in size. Knock it down and measure it off in about 1½ oz pieces, form into bun shapes and place on greased and floured baking sheets, with enough space round them for their increase in size during baking. Mix the fat, flour and water into pastry, roll it out and cut it into thin strips, brush with milk underneath each strip and lay in crosses on the buns (or if you have a steady hand, make the pastry runny by adding a bit more water and pour the crosses on, using a little jug). Other methods of making crosses are simply to cut the cross on the bun with a sharp knife, or lay it with strips of wet rice paper. But the runny pastry method looks the most professional. Heat the oven to Reg 7/425°, while the buns prove again in a warm place, when they will rise, and become smooth and puffy. This takes about 20 minutes. Make the oven steamy-hot, which buns like, by putting a tray of water in the bottom. Make the glaze by boiling the milk, water and sugar together for 1–2 minutes and keep it warm, with a pastry brush ready. Bake the buns for 15-20 minutes. Five minutes before the end brush with the glaze and return to oven.

Eat split in half, toasted, with butter,

☐ *These buns are traditionally eaten at Easter but are delicious sticky buns for any time of year.*

Makes 12–16 buns

Marble Cake

15 oz self-raising flour
or 15 oz plain flour and 3 teaspoons baking powder
6 oz butter or margarine
15 oz caster sugar
4 eggs
¼ pint milk
4 oz bitter or cooking chocolate, grated
½ teaspoon cinnamon

Preheat the oven to Reg 5½/385°. Butter and flour a cake tin 8″ across by 4″ deep. Sieve the flour into a large bowl. In another bowl cream the sugar and butter together really well. When they are pale and creamy and the sugar has dissolved (and is no longer gritty) add the eggs, beating them in one at a time. Now add the milk and flour alternately, beating them in.

When you have a smooth light mixture, put a quarter of it back into the flour bowl and mix in the grated chocolate and cinnamon.

Put a layer of white mixture in the tin, then a layer of chocolate then more white, more chocolate and finish with white — don't try to get it even. Bake in the centre of the oven for 1 hour or more until cooked through.

Spicy Fruit Cake

about 2–3 cooking apples
4 oz butter
8 oz caster sugar
8 oz plain flour
1 teaspoon mixed powdered cloves and cinnamon
1 teaspoon bicarbonate of soda
6 oz mixed raisins and currants
a sprinkling of demerara sugar

Begin by making a purée, without sugar, of the apples. Peel and core them and cook them with a little water to soften and disintegrate. Leave the purée to get completely cold before using it. There should be about ⅓ pint.

Preheat the oven to Reg 4/350°. Cream the butter and sugar until pale and fluffy. Fold in the cold apple purée, sift in the flour, spices and bicarbonate of soda, add the currants and raisins. Butter a 7″ cake tin and bake for 1½ hours. Ten minutes before the end sprinkle with brown sugar on top.

☐ *This is also very good if you undercook it by mistake. It should be fruity, spicy and crumbly.*

Grandmother's Special Sponge Cake

For the cake
2 large eggs, 4 oz caster sugar
4 oz plain flour, 1 teaspoon baking powder
1 teaspoon lemon juice and a little grated lemon peel
For the filling
6 oz caster sugar, 3 oz unsalted butter
1 oz grated bitter chocolate

For the icing
6 oz icing sugar, 3 oz unsalted butter
1 good teaspoon rum
chocolate vermicelli

First make the cake. Grease and flour two 8″ sandwich tins. Preheat the oven to Reg 6/400°. Separate the egg yolks from the whites. Cream the sugar and yolks until the sugar has totally dissolved and the mixture is a paler yellow than before. When you lift the spoon the mixture should form 'ribbons'. Add the lemon juice and peel. Whip the whites very well, but not as stiff as for meringues. Fold them into the egg yolks. Sieve the flour and baking powder into the egg mixture. Fold all together with a metal spoon or spatula, keeping the air in, but incorporating all the flour. Do this very delicately *by hand*. Put equal quantities into each tin and bake at the centre of the oven for 20 minutes (if the tins are on different racks the top one will be ready first). Leave them to cool a little in the tins before turning out and allowing to cool completely.

While the cake is cooking make the filling and the icing. Make the filling by creaming together the butter and sugar until light and fluffy, then adding the chocolate.

Make the icing by creaming together the icing sugar and butter, and then adding the rum (using more or less according to your taste). Spread the filling thickly between the two halves. Stick them together and cover the top roughly with the icing. You can make ridges with a knife or ripples with a fork: it isn't meant to be smooth. Sprinkle chocolate vermicelli over the top before it loses its softness. When you cut the cake the icing and filling should be the same thickness as the cake, which should be very airy, and crisp on the edges.

☐ *The main point of this cake is the contrast between the cream-coloured slightly stiff rum-flavoured icing, and the delicious soft chocolate-flavoured brown filling. The cake is just to keep them apart.*

Treacle Buns

4 oz butter
4 oz sugar
4 tablespoons golden syrup
10 oz self-raising flour
1 teaspoon ground ginger (optional)
2 teaspoons bicarbonate of soda and a little water

Preheat the oven to Reg 7/425°. Slightly warm the butter, sugar and syrup in a large basin over hot water. Beat to a cream, add the flour and ginger, and the bicarbonate of soda dissolved in a little cold water. Mix and work into a stiff dough, adding more flour if necessary. Pull off pieces the size of a small walnut. Roll into balls and bake on a well greased flat tin, keeping well apart, in the centre of the oven for 15 minutes.

The result will be flattish biscuity buns, crisp on the outside and soft inside, like Cornish fairings.

Makes 24–30 buns

Bread

FLOUR FOR BREAD MAKING

The flour used in white bread making should be strong flour that is made from especially hard-grained wheat. You can also make a good loaf with unbleached flour.

Plain flour of the sort that is used for making cakes and pastries, produces a perfectly good but rather soft and bland loaf.

THE CONDITIONS FOR BREAD MAKING

A warm kitchen is ideal for bread making. Yeast grows best in a warm but not hot atmosphere. Heat kills yeast and cold inhibits its growth.

Rising can be done almost anywhere warm — in the days before central heating, people used to take it to bed with them, but nowadays setting it down by a radiator or in a warmed airing cupboard is just as effective.

White Bread

2½ lbs flour
½ oz butter
1 oz yeast
2 dessertspoons coarse salt or 1 dessertspoon fine salt
1–1¼ pints tepid water

Making bread, like so many things, is easy when you know how. The more often you bake the better your bread will be. Once you are confident, this recipe can be altered according to how you like your bread — if you like it richer, add more butter, if you like it soft, add some milk to the water. You can sprinkle the top with sesame or poppy seeds, or glaze it with a strong salt and water solution (but don't drench it). If you are making a tin loaf add a little more liquid than you would for a round loaf so that you can press the dough well into the corners of the tin. For plaits, knots and twists, make a stiffer dough with less liquid or they will lose their shape. This recipe is for very plain everyday bread.

Warm the flour in its bowl. Make a well in the centre and if using fine salt, sprinkle it round the edge of the well. If using coarse salt, dissolve it in the water.

Cream the yeast with 2–3 tablespoons of tepid unsalted water and pour in the warm melted butter. Allow to stand for 5 or 10 minutes, Pour it into the middle of the flour, flick a little flour over it and then gradually add the liquid, mixing it thoroughly with your left hand as you pour with your right, until the dough is even and pliable.

Knead for 10 minutes. Cover the bowl with a damp cloth, a folded towel and a lid and allow to rise for 2 hours.

Shape into loaves on two floured baking sheets, sprinkle the tops with a little flour and rub it over, then slash them and put to rise again (prove) for ½–¾ hour. Preheat the oven to Reg 9/475°.

Bake the loaves at Reg 9/475° for ½ hour, move the tins so that all the bread has time on the top shelf and bake a further 30 minutes at Reg 5/375°. Tap the bottom crust of the loaf with your knuckles — if it sounds hollow and feels hard but springy, it is done. Allow to cool on racks. A pan of hot water set in the bottom of the oven during cooking makes a steamy atmosphere. which suits the bread.

Makes 4 loaves

Brown Bread

Add 1 oz more butter. Mix wholewheat flour and white flour in a proportion that suits you. Two-thirds wholewheat to one-third white is delicious, but if you want really healthy bread, use all wholewheat flour. It takes more liquid than plain flour, say about 1½ to 2 pints to 2½ lbs flour.

Barm Brack

1 lb plain flour
½ teaspoon powdered cinnamon
¼ teaspoon grated nutmeg
½ teaspoon salt
2 oz butter, 1 oz yeast
3 oz caster sugar
½ pint tepid milk
1 egg
8 oz sultanas
4 oz currants
2 oz mixed chopped candied peel

Sieve the flour, spices and salt into a warm bowl. Rub in the butter. Warm the milk; it should only be tepid. Mix the yeast with a teaspoon of the weighed amount of sugar and a teaspoon of the milk. Mix the rest of the sugar into the flour then pour in the yeast and the milk into which you have beaten the egg. Make a stiff batter and beat it very well. The best method for this is to sit down with the bowl between your knees and the wooden spoon held firmly in both hands, or use an electric mixer with a dough hook. The mixture should become very springy and stretchy.

Add the washed and dried fruit and the peel, mix it in well. Cover the bowl with a floured cloth and a towel and lid and put it in a warm place to rise for about 1½ hours until it is puffy and has doubled in size. Divide the dough and put it into two 7″ greased cake tins or 1 lb loaf tins. Allow to prove a further 30 minutes, and meanwhile preheat the oven to Reg 6/400°. Bake the loaves 40 minutes, turn them round, cover lightly with damp double greaseproof paper and bake 20 minutes more at Reg 4½/360°. Cool on a rack and eat fresh with butter.

☐ *This Irish yeast cake is a sort of superior currant loaf, and is eaten in slices spread with butter. When stale it is good toasted.*

Makes 2 loaves

Malt Bread

8 oz self raising flour
1 level teaspoon salt
1 level teaspoon bicarbonate of soda
3 oz sultanas
2 oz caster sugar
2 tablespoons (4 oz) golden syrup
2 tablespoons (4 oz) malt extract
¼ pint milk
1 egg, beaten

Preheat oven to Reg 5/375°. Sift the flour, bicarbonate and salt into a bowl. Stir in the sultanas and sugar. Melt the syrup and malt over gentle heat in a saucepan, then gradually blend in the milk. Make a well in the centre of the flour, pour in the syrup mixture and egg and mix well. It is a fairly wet mixture. Pour into a greased and floured 1 lb loaf tin. Bake for about 50 minutes or till golden and springy to touch. Cool on a wire rack. Keep in airtight tin for 2 days before using.

For 6–8

Sauces preserves sweets

Avgolemono Sauce

2 egg yolks
½ juicy lemon
½ pint water, stock, or water in which fish, vegetables or chicken have been cooked
salt, pepper

Beat the egg yolks, add the juice of the lemon, pour on the hot (not boiling) stock or water. Thicken very carefully in a small pan over the lowest flame, or in a double boiler. Stir all the time and watch that it doesn't boil (this is a slow job) or it will curdle. Add salt and pepper to taste.

☐ *For meat balls, broad beans, poached fish.*

Barbecue Sauce

1 onion, peeled and chopped
1 oz butter
1 small tin tomatoes (or 4 fresh, chopped peeled ones — or purée)
3 tablespoons wine vinegar
2 tablespoons Worcestershire sauce
2 teaspoons brown or demerara sugar
1 teaspoon made mustard
1 teaspoon paprika
1 teaspoon salt

Lightly fry the onion until transparent, add chopped tomatoes and all other ingredients. If using for spare ribs, bring to the boil before pouring sauce on to ribs and roasting (page 94). If using on already fried, grilled or barbecued meat, simmer a little while, for the sauce to amalgamate, before using.

☐ *Also good with epigrams, chops, kebabs*

For other sauces see Basic Recipe Section, pages 183–4.

Chilli Mayonnaise

2 egg yolks
⅓ teaspoon or more chilli powder
salt, pepper
¼ pint olive oil or a little more
white wine vinegar

Mix the egg yolks with the chilli powder, salt and pepper. Gradually add oil as you would if you were making plain mayonnaise. When the mixture becomes too thick, thin it with a little wine vinegar.

☐ *This is a beautiful golden colour. Very good with cold poached halibut, cod or other fish. Sprinkle the flaked fish with a little lemon juice or vinegar and oil, and serve the mayonnaise separately.*

Breton Sauce

2 egg yolks
2 dessertspoons Dijon mustard
1 scant dessertspoon wine vinegar
2 oz very soft butter
2 tablespoons chopped fresh herbs (parsley, chives, chervil, tarragon)
salt, pepper

Mix the egg yolks with the mustard and vinegar. Add the softened butter gradually (it must not be runny but it must be soft enough to mix in easily). The resultant sauce will be thick but not quite as smooth as mayonnaise. Add the herbs, and taste for salt and pepper, which you add if needed. This sauce can curdle, and if it does, let it get quite cold, then beat it.

☐ *For cold fish (especially mackerel) or cold meat.*

For 4

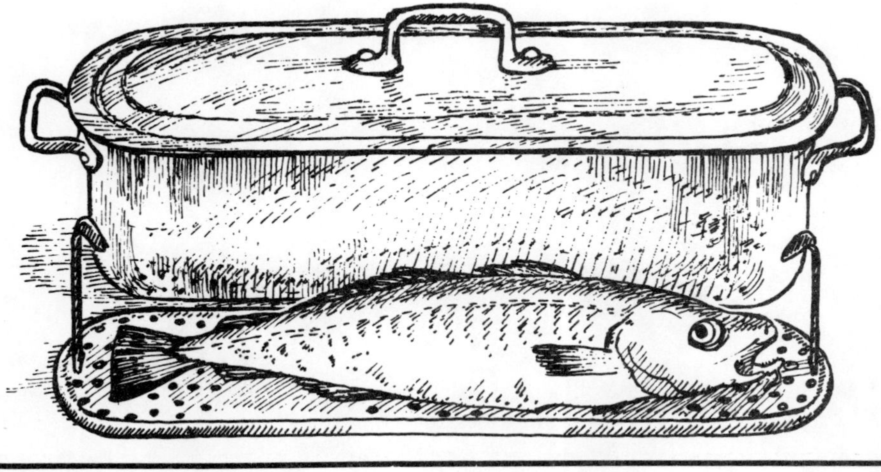

Cheese Sauce (Mornay Sauce)

1 oz butter
1 oz flour
½ pint hot milk
salt, pepper
1 teaspoon of made mustard or dusting of Cayenne pepper
1 oz or more grated cheese (Parmesan, Cheddar or Gruyère)

Make a white roux with the flour and butter (just melt the butter stir in the flour and let it bubble a minute or two, but do not let it start to sizzle or change colour). Stirring carefully with a small wooden spoon gradually incorporate the hot milk. Let it return to the boil after each addition of milk and stir it well to absorb the flour before you add more. When all the milk is combined smoothly with the roux add salt, pepper and, if you like a sharp sauce, the mustard or Cayenne. Let it simmer at least 5 minutes, to cook the flour, before you add the cheese. When all the cheese is melted the sauce is ready.

Black Butter

2 oz butter
1 tablespoon chopped parsley or chopped capers
1 teaspoon vinegar

Using a very small pan fry the parsley in the butter; when the butter is dark nut brown, but not black, stir in the vinegar and pour the sizzling sauce immediately over whatever you are serving it with.

If you prefer to use capers, omit the parsley and put the capers in with the vinegar.

☐ *This is for brains, poached eggs, skate or liver.*

Sauce Gribiche

1 hard-boiled egg
a little chopped lemon peel
a tablespoon of chopped gherkin
oil
vinegar
salt, pepper

Mash the yolk of the egg, season and gradually add as much vinegar as you would use for making a vinaigrette, then gradually stir in the oil. Add the finely chopped egg white, lemon peel and gherkins.

☐ *This sauce is good with cold meat, brawns, cold cooked leeks and fish salad.*

Walnut Sauce

2 oz shelled walnuts
juice of 1 lemon
2 tablespoons olive oil
2 tablespoons chopped parsley
½ teaspoon salt

Pound the walnuts in a pestle and mortar until they go creamy, add lemon juice and keep pounding. Add salt, gradually add oil until well mixed, and finally the parsley.

☐ *For use on hot ham, boiled bacon, or pasta.*

For 4

Curry Sauce

1 small onion, chopped finely
thyme, bay leaf, mace
1½ oz butter
1 or more teaspoons curry powder
¼ pint of fish or chicken stock
¼ pint of milk
½ oz of flour
salt, pepper

In a saucepan make a Béchamel using 1 oz of the butter, flour, stock, milk, salt and pepper.

Meanwhile cook the onion and herbs in the rest of the butter without browning, then add the curry powder. One teaspoon is not too strong, but add more if you want a very definite flavour. Let it sizzle a minute then stir the onion, etc., into the sauce. Cook a further 10 minutes. Strain and serve. This sauce should be fairly thin.

☐ *For fish or egg croquettes.*

For 4

Salsa Verde

1 clove garlic
1 hard-boiled egg
2–3 anchovies
1 tablespoon capers
bunch parsley (preferably the flat kind)
2 teaspoons fresh white breadcrumbs
1 tablespoon wine vinegar
3–4 tablespoons olive oil

Cut a clove of garlic in half and score the cut side with a knife. Rub a bowl with the cut clove of garlic so that it is well-coated with the juice — you must press quite hard. Chop the hard-boiled egg, anchovies, capers and parsley quite finely and put them into the bowl. Soak the crumbs in the vinegar, drain them and stir them into the other ingredients. Now add olive oil, gradually stirring, until you have a smooth, soft sauce.

☐ *For boiled meat and fish. This sauce keeps well; if you leave out the egg it will keep indefinitely in a cool place.*

For 4

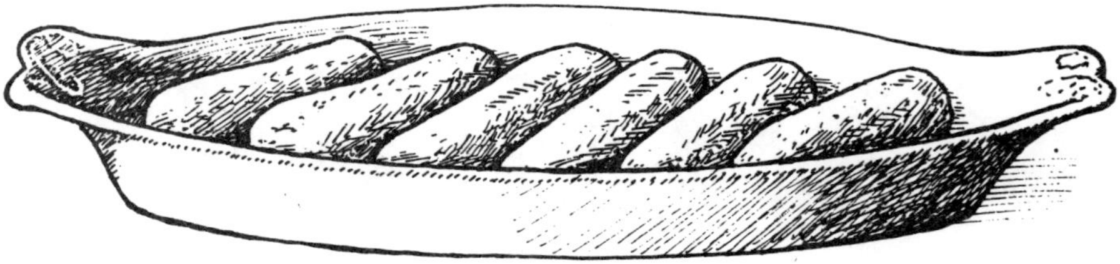

Hot Chocolate Sauce

4 ozs cooking chocolate
4 tablespoons single cream or top of the milk
2 tablespoons good strong black coffee

Melt the chocolate in the top of a double boiler, stir in the hot coffee and cream and keep stirring over hot water until you have a smooth sauce.

☐ *For vanilla ice-cream.*

Chestnut and Apple Stuffing for Pork or Goose

½ lb chestnuts
2 shallots, or 1 small onion
1 small cooking apple
salt, pepper, sugar
parsley, thyme, or sage (whichever you like but only use one besides parsley)
single cream
1–2 oz butter

Slit the chestnuts with a knife, then cook them either by baking in a little oil for 10 minutes in a hot oven, or by boiling in water for 10 minutes. Shell them and remove the skin beneath the shell by boiling them in fresh water for another 20 minutes when the chestnuts should also be tender and pink inside instead of hard and yellow. Mash them with a little single cream and season with salt, pepper and a little sugar, so that you have a purée.

Meanwhile, peel and chop the onion very finely and soften in a small pan with some of the butter for 15–20 minutes. Peel and grate the apple and add it to the onion with more butter. Cook until both are soft. Add them to the chestnut purée with the chopped parsley and thyme leaves, or a very few sage leaves. Mix well and taste for seasoning, balancing sharpness and sweetness to your liking. The consistency must be fairly thick, or it will drip out in the cooking of the meat.

☐ *Use it to stuff a boned hand of pork or a goose.*

Oven Method of Bottling Blackberries and Apples

apples, windfalls, peeled, cored and cut into sugar-lump sized chunks
blackberries, ripe and dry (no stalks)
2 cloves in each jar, if liked
the cores and peelings of apples
water, sugar
Kilner jars and tops (sold specially for bottling)

Make a light syrup from the apple peelings and cores (don't include any bruised or bad pieces), adding some blackberries. Do this as follows: Put the berries and peelings in to a pan and cover with water. Simmer for 1 hour. Strain through a jelly bag or fine sieve. Measure the resulting juice, add 8 oz sugar to every pint of juice and heat, stirring until the sugar dissolves.

As a rough guide, 1½ pints of syrup should be enough to bottle 7 lbs of fruit. But this depends on how tightly you pack the fruit and how much the fruit shrinks, etc. This has to be borne in mind when packing the fruit. The proportion of apples to blackberries is a question of taste, about ½ and ½ is nice. Pack the jars as tightly as you can without squashing the fruit. Bang the jar on the table (put a cloth or newspaper under it first) to settle the fruit down and fill up to the top. Fill a spare jar with fruit for topping up. The fruit will shrink by ⅔ or ¼ in the oven, so put one spare bottle for every 2 or 3. Place all the jars with lids on but not done up in the oven, preheated to Reg 1/275° and leave for 1 hour. Sterilize the rubber rings if you are using this method, by boiling them in water for 15 minutes. Bring the syrup to the boil (and keep it simmering) just before the hour is up. Have everything ready, for speed is essential, and everything is very hot. Put a thick layer of cloth on the table (or several layers of newspaper) for standing the jars on. Have the rings near and ready, the lids and the screw rings. Make sure they are the right sizes, and there are enough. Make sure the pan with the boiling syrup is easy to pour from. Put a kettle of water on to boil in case there isn't enough syrup. Have a good oven cloth for holding hot jars and have a spoon for filling up gaps. Take out a spare jar of fruit, and the first jar. Give it a bang to settle the fruit again and top it up from the spare bottle. Pour the boiling syrup up to the top of the jar. Put on the ring, making sure the surfaces are clear of fruit and juice or the seal won't work. Put on the lid, and screw up tight. Leave until the next day to test for success (the Kilner jars with tin lids and rubber seal joined on are much easier to use but must only be used once). Continue filling one jar at a time. This method depends on sealing by vacuum, which in this case is caused by the heated contents of the jars cooling and shrinking, which sucks the lids down tight on to the rubber seals. Therefore the hotter it is done, the greater the chance of success. Test the next day. You should be able to pick up the jar by the lid alone (unscrew the ring first). If it drops off — it is no good!

Pickled Cherries

Boil ½ pint distilled vinegar together with a teaspoon of salt and 2 teaspoons of sugar for 15 minutes. Let it cool. Wash and dry 1 lb of firm sound cherries and remove the stalks. Pack them loosely in a jar with white peppercorns and sprigs of tarragon, pour on the cold pickle and cover. After 48 hours pour out the vinegar without moving the cherries, boil it up and let it cool. Refill the jars. Cover and store 2 weeks before eating with cold meats (especially game).

To make 1 lb

Potted Blackberries (or Raspberries)

2 lbs blackberries
2 lbs sugar
1 oz butter

Pick over the fruit carefully, removing all hard bits of stalk, etc. Bruised berries are all right but not mouldy ones. Warm the sugar in a bowl in the oven. Rub the butter round a preserving pan, and cook the fruit in it over a low heat. The juice will run. When it begins to simmer pour in the sugar and go on cooking for half an hour, or until set, stirring with a wooden spoon. Put into pots and cover like jam.

Sloe Gin

1 bottle of gin (about 1½ pints)
1 lb clean dry sloes, picked in October
3 oz sugar

Prick the sloes all over (it is rather nice to use one of their own thorns for this, otherwise use stainless steel or silver). Put them with the sugar into a large Kilner jar with a screw top, pour over the gin. Screw lid on tight. Shake the jar every day at first, then less often, for 3 months. It will be dark red, and ready for Christmas and New Year, strained and bottled and nicely labelled.

☐ *A very welcome gift for old ladies. The sad truth is the better the gin (i.e. more expensive) the better the gift — still, the sloes cost nothing.*

Bramble Jelly and Bramble Cheese

blackberries
water
sugar
Optional additions
1–2 cooking apples
or a handful of raisins
or 2 sweet geranium leaves

Stew the blackberries, plus the optional additions, with a very little water (enough to cover the bottom of the pan). Press them from time to time with a wooden spoon to extract all the juice. Stop when they have completely softened and changed colour from black to purple.

For Jelly: Strain overnight through a cloth. You will use only the juice.

For Cheese: Press through a sieve. You will use the resulting purée, but leave out the pips.

For Jelly and Cheese: Measure the juice, or purée, and for each pint of liquid take 1 lb sugar. Bring liquid to the boil in a large pan, add the sugar, stirring well to dissolve it. Continue cooking fast, until setting point, about 20–30 minutes. Pour into warm jars, allow to cool, cover and seal.

3 lbs blackberries makes 4–5 little pots.

Tomato Purée

2–3 lbs tomatoes
1 onion
3 whole cloves garlic
1 teaspoon dried basil
sugar
a little salt, several black peppercorns
1 tablespoon olive oil
1 oz butter

Soften the sliced onion in olive oil without browning. Cut the tomatoes in quarters and add them to the pan, mashing with a wooden spoon, then add the whole cloves of garlic, basil, salt and peppercorns. Simmer until you have a nice sauce (about 25–30 minutes). Pick out the cloves of garlic and peppercorns if you happen to see them, and sieve the rest. Return it to the pan and reduce it, stirring all the time to prevent it from sticking and burning, to a thick purée. (This will take some time.) Taste for seasoning and turn out into small sterilised jars (see note on sterilisation). Pour on a thin coating of oil and cover. If covered properly and stored in a cool dry place this should keep well and is very good used diluted with a bit of melted butter and water as a sauce for pasta or meat, or neat as an addition to Bolognese sauces or stews.

Sterilising Tomato Purée

Have ready a large pan of almost boiling water, and enough *hot* clean preserving jars (with rubber bands, glass discs and screwbands, or metal discs or screwbands) for your quantity of purée.

Bring the purée to the boil and pour it boiling into the jars, closing each one at once with lids and screwbands, and immersing them in hot water. Keep them from touching with a cloth pad. When all are done bring it to the boil and boil for 10 minutes. Remove jars, tighten bands if necessary, leave to cool and test for vacuum sealing after 12 hours.

Fresh Mint Chutney

large bunch mint
1 teaspoon finely minced onion
1 teaspoon chopped green chilli
1 teaspoon chopped green ginger
a sliver of pounded garlic
a squeeze of lemon juice
Cayenne pepper
salt
3–4 tablespoons yoghurt

Scald the mint leaves, pound them, and mix with the remaining ingredients except the yoghurt. Stir it in and serve in a small pot.

☐ *Very good with curry, mutton or chicken especially.*

Fresh Brinjal Chutney

2 aubergines
½ teaspoon chopped green chilli
1 teaspoon chopped green ginger
1 teaspoon vinegar
1 clove garlic
salt, black pepper
green onion tops, chopped

Cook the whole aubergines in boiling salted water until they are completely soft. Drain them, squeeze out some of the water and let them cool. Skin them, chop the flesh and pound it with the other ingredients except the onion tops. Pack the mixture into a little pot, sprinkle with finely slivered or chopped onion tops and serve cold.

☐ ***Very good with curry, dhal, chicken, etc.***

For 3–4

Dripping for Toast

1 teaspoon Bovril, or an Oxo cube
a little hot water
dripping, from beef preferably

Dissolve the Bovril in a little hot water, just enough to make it runny. Slightly melt the dripping and mix the Bovril well in. Allow to set.

Use as a thick spread on thick hot toast.

☐ *This is slightly cheating, but in families where dripping toast is popular, the brown jelly at the bottom of the dripping bowl gets very quickly snatched up, while the plain pure dull dripping is left behind. This trick makes all the dripping taste delicious, and is very nourishing and warming as well.*

Toffee Apples

½ lb sugar (lump is good, other kinds will do)
a coffee-cup of water
a few drops of lemon juice
9 nice hard eating apples
9 ice-lolly or other sticks (or ask butcher for wooden skewers)

Wash and dry the apples, remove the stalks and trim away the flower centres. Impale each one through the core with an ice-lolly stick.

Over a very low heat melt the sugar in the water to which you have added the lemon juice. As soon as the sugar has melted, turn the heat right up and, without stirring, allow to boil fast until the caramel colours. Tip the pan gently from side to side to colour the caramel evenly.

When it is a nice golden brown, turn the heat right down, tip the pan and quickly turn each apple in the caramel until it is evenly coated. Turn it round a few times over the pan until it starts to solidify and then stand on lightly oiled foil to set. The whole process must be done quickly as the caramel must not be allowed to set or burn in the pan. Toffee apples only keep a day or two.

Devilled Salted Almonds

8 oz almonds
1 tablespoon olive oil
1 dessertspoon salt
a good sprinkling of cayenne

Blanch the almonds by pouring boiling water over and then skinning. Dry them, then toss in the oil. Sprinkle on the salt and Cayenne and spread them on a baking tray. Bake in a very low oven, Reg $\frac{3}{4}$–$\frac{1}{2}$/250–60° for about 2 hours until golden brown.

Makes ½ lb

Golden Honeycomb

4 oz sugar
2 tablespoons golden syrup or honey
1 tablespoon butter
1 teaspoon bicarbonate of soda

Put sugar, golden syrup and butter into a heavy pan, stir over a low heat until melted, and then cook until the mixture starts to brown, stirring as little as possible. Remove from the heat, stir in bicarbonate of soda; it will foam up amazingly, which makes it good fun for children to cook. Pour it into a buttered tin. Break it into pieces when set.

☐*Rather like the inside of a Crunchie bar but not quite so professional.*

Makes ¼ lb

Turkish Coffee

Fill pot to the brim with water, and sugar it to taste. Bring to the boil, remove one little cup of water and put in one cup of finely ground coffee. Let it boil again, once to the top. Wait a few seconds, tap it to settle grounds, replace the removed cup of water. Serve.

Basic Recipes

Hollandaise Sauce

2 tablespoons white wine vinegar
1 tablespoon water
2–3 peppercorns
½ bay leaf
1 blade mace
1 large egg yolk
4–5 oz slightly salted butter

Cut the butter into small cubes and if it is very hard let it soften a bit. Put the vinegar, water, peppercorns, bayleaf and mace into a small saucepan and reduce to half their quantity. Allow to cool and remove peppercorns, bayleaf and mace. Take a double saucepan, or a pan into which a suitable bowl or basin will fit, and heat some water in it to just below boiling point. In order to lessen the risk of the sauce curdling keep the water below the boil, and make sure it doesn't actually touch the base of the bowl or pan in which the sauce is cooking. Using the bowl or pan which is to go over the water, mix the reduced vinegar and water with the egg yolk and a cube of the soft butter. Place it over the hot water and stirring all the time with a wooden spoon, add the cubes of butter one at a time, letting each one melt before you add another. If the sauce shows signs of thickening too fast, or curdling, remove it at once from the water. If it is too thick add a few drops of water or the top of the milk. Taste for salt. If it is too sharp add some unsalted butter. It should be smooth and fairly thick, and is served lukewarm.

☐ *For serving with Oeufs Bénédict, poached fish and asparagus.*

Béchamel (White) Sauce

1 oz butter
1 oz flour
½ pint milk
salt, pepper

Heat the milk to just below boiling point (see note below on infusion). Melt the butter in a small saucepan over a moderate heat without browning. Tip in the flour and stir to amalgamate it with the butter. This mixture is called a white roux and should not be allowed to brown. When it starts to honeycomb, i.e. when small bubbles start to break all over the surface of the mixture, pour in one third of the milk, stirring vigorously until you have a smooth mixture. When it has thickened into a smooth paste add one third more milk. Stir again and when it has thickened gradually add the rest of the milk until you have a smooth sauce of the consistency you require. Season and cook very gently, stirring from time to time, for five minutes to cook the flour.

The best sauce is made with milk which you have previously infused with various flavourings to make it tastier. Simply put a small sliced onion, a bayleaf, a small bunch of parsley and a few peppercorns into the cold milk, bring it to boiling point, turn the heat right down and let the milk stand just not boiling over a very low flame for up to half an hour. Strain the milk before you make the sauce.

☐ *This makes ½ pint, medium thick sauce.*

Tomato Sauce

2 onions
2 cloves garlic
2 tablespoons olive oil
1½ lbs tomatoes
½ glass red wine
sprigs of thyme and rosemary and a bay leaf
salt and freshly ground pepper

Chop the onions and garlic finely and soften them in the oil in a saucepan for about ten minutes without browning. Add the skinned roughly chopped tomatoes, seasoning, red wine and bundle of herbs. Simmer 45 minutes, uncovered.

□ *For pasta, fried fish, etc.*

For 6

Plain Sponge Cake

4 oz caster sugar
4 oz unsalted butter
4 oz self-raising flour, or 4 oz plain flour plus 1½ teaspoons baking powder
2 eggs

Preheat the oven to Reg 5/375°. Butter and flour two eight-inch sandwich tins. Cream the sugar and butter together and when white and fluffy add the well-beaten eggs, a little at a time. Fold in the sifted flour thoroughly.

Spread half the mixture in each tin as lightly as you can, spreading it to the sides with a palette knife so that the finished cake will be flat rather than domed.

Bake in the top half of the oven for 15–20 minutes. Do not open the oven while the cakes are cooking or they may go sad. When they are cooked take them out and cool on a wire rack. Spread one half with whipped cream and the other with jam. Press the halves together so jam and cream are both in the middle.

Vinaigrette

4–5 tablespoons oil
½ teaspoon sea salt
several pinches freshly ground black pepper
1 teaspoon white sugar (optional)
2 teaspoons wine vingear

Take a small bowl, mix the salt, pepper and sugar and add the oil. Then stir in the vinegar with a teaspoon; it should become thick and cloudy.
If you like garlic add a clove, first thoroughly pulverised with the salt, using the point of a stainless kitchen knife. If you only quite like it, put a few cubes of dried bread or rusk, thoroughly rubbed with cut cloves of garlic, into the bottom of the salad bowl. If you like a thick mustardy dressing, mix the vinegar with half a teaspoon of Dijon mustard and season this, leaving out the sugar, before you gradually add the oil.

□ *For salads and cold vegetables.*

To Clarify Stock

Have the stock gently boiling, drop in the white of an egg beaten to a soft peak, and whisk. Boil it up until the froth rises in the pan, remove it from the heat and whisk again. Repeat the boiling and whisking twice more to make sure the egg white is cooked. Put a cloth wrung out in hot water over a colander with a large wire strainer on top. Pour the stock through. The sediment will be caught in the egg white, leaving the stock crystal clear.

To Make and Bake a Fruit Flan

Preheat the oven to Reg 5½/390°. Press the pastry into an 8″ loose flan ring, previously buttered, on a baking sheet, also buttered. It is too crumbly and sticky to roll out. Arrange the fruit (sliced apples or halved stoned apricots or plums) prettily in the flan. Sprinkle with sugar and bake 10 minutes. Then lower heat and bake another 20 minutes at Reg 4½/360°. Allow to shrink and cool before sliding away the ring and lifting the tart with excruciating care on to a plate or dish. Glaze the top with syrup from in between the fruit, or with melted apricot jam.

Plain Biscuit Mixture

4 oz unsalted butter
4 oz caster sugar
8 oz plain flour
1 small egg

Cream the sugar and butter together, add the beaten egg, stir in the sifted flour, mix to a firm dough. Ideally leave it to rest in the refrigerator, but if in a hurry carry on. Set the oven to Reg 5/375°. Roll the dough thinly and cut into shapes. At places like Fortnum & Mason they cut them into stars and moons, oakleaves and acorns. Place the shapes in a buttered and floured tin, brushing some with beaten egg, if liked. Put the tin near the top of the oven for ten minutes or until done. Leave to cool and crisp on the tin and then on a wire rack.

Variations: dip half of each biscuit (especially for acorns and oak leaves) into melted chocolate; or cover with white icing, flavoured with vanilla or almond essence.

You can add ginger or vanilla or chopped nuts to the mixture before baking.

☐ *This is so easy that children can make it by themselves.*

Rich Sweet Flan Pastry

6 oz plain flour
2 oz slightly salted butter
2 oz cooking fat
1 oz granulated sugar
1 egg yolk
a few drops of cold water
a pinch of salt

Sieve the flour and salt into a mixing bowl. Chop the butter and fat into small pieces in the flour. Add the sugar and rub it all together very lightly with your finger tips until it is integrated. Blend in the egg yolk, using a knife, and then add just a few drops of water to make it the consistency of soft, light marzipan. Leave it in a cool place wrapped in greaseproof paper, cloth, or polythene for at least ¾ hour.

Basic Savoury Pancakes

4 oz plain flour
1 egg
½ pint milk
salt

Beat the egg thoroughly into the milk. Season the flour and stir in the milk and egg mixture gradually, to make a smooth lump-free batter.

Beat for several minutes with a wooden spoon with the bowl of the spoon turned over, so that the air in the hollow of the spoon gets into the batter, or beat with a balloon whisk or an electric beater. Allow to stand for two hours before using.

☐ *This mixture makes 6–8 pancakes; make it 2 hours before it is needed.*

Simple Fritter Batter

4 oz flour
1 egg
salt
1 tablespoon oil
¼ pint milk, or less

Sieve the flour with a pinch of salt into a bowl, and make a well in the centre. Separate the egg and keep the white aside. Mix the yolk carefully with the flour, blending well with a wooden spoon. Add the oil and then the milk, a little at a time, drawing in the flour gradually. When you have a thick, smooth, creamy batter stop adding milk and beat the mixture well. Allow it to stand as long as possible in a cool place; about 2 hours is ideal. Just before you need it, beat the white of the egg stiffly and fold it into the batter.

This is for fritters to be fried in deep oil. If using it for sweet things you can add a spoonful of liqueur to replace some of the milk.

☐ *This is good for sweet fritters, or fairly solid things like corned-beef fritters.*

Enough for fritters for 4–6 people

Low Fat Pastry for Pies

½ lb self-raising flour
2 oz Nutter or butter
2 oz margarine (kosher is best)
a pinch of salt
ice-cold water

Sieve the flour and salt into a bowl.
Rub or grate the fat into the flour. Add just enough water to hold it together. It should be fairly crumbly and dry, and hard to handle. Roll out straight away. Bake at Reg 9/500° for 10 minutes, then at 4/350° for 20 minutes.

☐ *This recipe was invented for somebody on a diet that had to be completely free of animal fats. It turns out to be wonderful pastry.*

Eliza Acton's Fritter Batter

1 oz butter
½ pint cold water, or a little more
6 oz flour, plain
a pinch of salt
white of an egg

Put about 4 tablespoons of the water and the butter in a small pan and bring to the boil. When the butter has melted add the rest of the cold water. Put the flour into a larger basin, and mixing well all the time, pour in the tepid buttery water. Stir well to get rid of all lumps, add the salt, and leave to stand 1–2 hours. Just before you want to make the fritters, whisk the egg white very stiff and fold it into the batter.

This makes a very light delicate batter for fritters.

For 6–8

Cooking Haricot and Other Dried Beans

Soak the beans for about 5–6 hours. Put them in a pan and cover well with cold water, put in a peeled onion and a clove of garlic. Bring slowly to the boil, skim and simmer for about ¾ hour. Add salt and simmer on for ¼ hour or so. When tender but not mushy, drain and cool.

Chick Peas

You cannot skimp the soaking of chick peas — they must be soaked overnight. Wash them first, then put them in a bowl large enough for them almost to double in size. Cover well with water and after their soaking cook them gently in the same water. A pinch of bicarbonate of soda softens the water and shortens the cooking time (rain water is, in fact, the best thing to cook all pulses in). Add no salt until the peas are almost tender. Cooking time depends on the age of the peas: new, they can take as little as half an hour, old, up to 2 hours.

Index

Note Carving instructions occur between pages 67 and 109 and are also indexed under individual cuts of meat and birds. Diagrams are listed on page 5.

Poor Cook

by Susan Campbell and Caroline Conran

Poor Cook published in 1973 by Sphere, contains over 300 recipes for deliciously simple food. The recipes are arranged under the following headings:

Soups
Eggs and Cheese
Pasta, Pancakes, Gnocchi, Dumplings and Fritters
Fish
Pâtés, Terrines, Pies and Brawns
Meat
Poultry and Game
Vegetables
Stuffings and Sauce
Puddings
Cakes, Biscuits and Bread

Plus a section of unclassifiable recipes and tips ranging from a miraculously economical marmalade to how to peel chestnuts. Diagrams similar to those in *Family Cook* show you how to: Fillet a fish; Dress a crab; Make a pork pie; Make Cornish pasties; Bone a breast of lamb or veal; Recognise cuts of beef, pork, veal, and lamb; Stuff a pork fillet; Bone a shoulder of lamb or veal; Truss a bird; Bone a chicken or a duck; Make apple dumplings; Boil puddings; Steam puddings.